PIMLICO

429

THE RISE OF DESIGN

Charles Saumarez Smith is Director of the
National Portrait Gallery.

THE RISE OF DESIGN

Design and the Domestic Interior
in Eighteenth-Century England

———

CHARLES SAUMAREZ SMITH

PIMLICO

Published by Pimlico 2000

2 4 6 8 10 9 7 5 3 1

First published in Great Britain as
Eighteenth-Century Decoration:
Design and the Domestic Interior in England by
Weidenfeld & Nicolson 1993
Pimlico edition 2000

Pimlico

Random House, 20 Vauxhall Bridge Road,
London SW1V 2SA

Random House Australia (Pty) Limited
20 Alfred Street, Milsons Point, Sydney,
New South Wales 2061, Australia

Random House New Zealand Limited
18 Poland Road, Glenfield,
Auckland 10, New Zealand

Random House (Pty) Limited
Endulini, 5A Jubilee Road, Parktown 2193, South Africa

The Random House Group Limited Reg. No. 954009
www.randomhouse.co.uk

A CIP catalogue record for this book
is available from the British Library

ISBN 0-7126-6476-9

Papers used by Random House are natural,
recyclable products made from wood grown in sustainable forests;
the manufacturing processes conform to the environmental
regulations of the country of origin

Typeset by Deltatype Ltd, Birkenhead, Wirral
Printed and bound in Great Britain by
Mackays of Chatham PLC

For Otto
and in memory of
Philip Core
1951–1989

Contents

List of Illustrations

The family of John Bacon, by Arthur Devis, *c.* 1742–3. (*Yale Center for British Art, Paul Mellon Collection, New Haven, Connecticut*)

Children in an interior, by Arthur Devis, *c.* 1742–3. (*Yale Center for British Art, Paul Mellon Collection, New Haven, Connecticut*)

The dining room at Kirtlington Park, by John Sanderson, 1747. (*The Metropolitan Museum of Art, Rogers Fund, 1970.674.1, New York*)

A chinoiserie saloon, by Timothy Lightoler, 1757. (*British Architectural Library, Royal Institute of British Architects, Early Works Collection, London*)

The Dining Room at Kedleston, by Robert Adam, 1762. (*Kedleston Hall, Derbyshire; National Trust Photographic Library*)

Perspective view of the gallery at Syon, by Robert Adam, *c.* 1764. (*Courtesy of the Board of Trustees of the Victorian and Albert Museum, London*)

Queen Charlotte with her two eldest sons, by Johann Zoffany, 1764. (*Royal Collection, © Her Majesty the Queen*)

Sir Lawrence Dundas with his grandson, by Johann Zoffany, 1769. (*The Marquess of Zetland; E.T. Archive*)

The Library at Strawberry Hill, by John Carter, 1788. (*Courtesy of the Board of Trustees of the Victoria and Albert Museum, London*)

This is a sorry sight! by James Gillray, 1786. (*The British Museum, Department of Prints and Drawings, London*)

The Miser's Feast, by James Gillray, 1786. (*The British Museum, Department of Prints and Drawings, London*)

The Holbein Chamber at Strawberry Hill, by John Carter, 1788. (*Courtesy of the Print Collection, Lewis Walpole Library, Yale University, Farmington, Connecticut*)

The staircase at Buckingham House, by Sir John Soane, *c.* 1792–5. (*Courtesy of the Trustees of Sir John Soane's Museum, London*)

The Breakfast Room at 12 Lincoln's Inn Fields, by Joseph Michael Gandy, *c.* 1798. (*Courtesy of the Trustees of Sir John Soane's Museum, London*)

Preface

This book was first published in 1993 under the title *Eighteenth-Century Decoration: Design and the Domestic Interior in England*. As such, it was one of a series of illustrated books published by Weidenfeld and Nicolson, which concentrated on the publication of contemporary visual source material for the study of interior decoration, following on from the success of Peter Thornton's *Authentic Decor: the Domestic Interior 1620–1920*. In this form, I hope the book served its purpose by making available a much wider range of contemporary illustrations of eighteenth-century interiors than had previously been available for purposes of visual reference.

However, I always regretted the fact that the form of its original publication meant that, buried within a surfeit of contemporary illustrated source material, was a text which aimed to provide an account of changing attitudes to eighteenth-century interiors. During the years which led up to the publication of the book, I had been involved in postgraduate teaching at the Victoria and Albert Museum and had become interested in new approaches to the study of eighteenth-century architecture, furniture and design. Instead of an account of changing attitudes to interiors informed only by the history of style, I wanted to write a history of interiors which made reference to new ways of thinking about eighteenth-century society, including, for example, the secondary literature on attitudes to luxury and the research which was being undertaken at that time – and since – on the origins of consumerism. In this way the book was written as a text for the study of eighteenth-century design history.

Now that the book is being published as a paperback, I have been delighted that its publisher, Will Sulkin, has reversed the relationship between text and illustration. Instead of an illustrated book, which has explanatory text secondary to it, the book now stands (or falls) as a book about attitudes to interiors and their decoration, a history which will, I hope, be read not only by people who want to know what eighteenth-century interiors looked like, but also by those who want to understand the aspects of social, economic and cultural experience that shaped them.

In preparing the book for paperback publication, I have not made changes to the text, other than to add a section to the bibliography on recent research in order to indicate the wealth of new work which has been undertaken since 1993. Also, I have not reproduced the full acknowledgements and introduction which were specific to the original book. I would merely wish to place on record my indebtedness to the innumerable people who helped me in writing it, especially: Helen Clifford for assistance with the original picture research; the H. F. du Pont Winterthur Museum for the award of a Benno Forman Fellowship and the Royal College of Art for a South Square Fellowship; John Styles for his invaluable advice and long-standing friendship; Julia Brown for her magnificent work on the illustrations; Michael Dover who commissioned the book; and my brother John and the Duke of Devonshire who made its publication possible.

Charles Saumarez Smith
National Portrait Gallery

Pre–1700

Architectural Drawings

During the greater part of the seventeenth century it was rare for British architects (in so far as the term itself has any validity to cover the multitude of working practices in the conception of buildings) to concern themselves at all systematically with the physical layout and appearance of the interiors of houses. The design of the house was the responsibility of the patron and the master builder. The master builder might provide a plan in advance of construction, but it was unlikely to consist of anything much more than an indication of the layout of the rooms and perhaps an elevation of the principal façade. The appearance of the interior was more the product of the craft practices of the various specialist trades involved in building construction than the execution of a preconceived design by an architect.[1] However, as the seventeenth century progressed, it became more common to have a rudimentary drawing in advance of building. In May 1617, Fulke Greville wrote to the Master of Jesus College, Cambridge:

> Let me entreat you farther, that a Platt may be drawne to shewe the contrivinge of the lights, stayre-cases, chimneyes and studies, with the severall charges of them, to the intent, that by

I

conference with some workmen here, I may see if anie thinge may be altered for the better.[2]

Working drawings in advance of construction were used to clarify the methods of work of the various trades involved, including masons, carpenters and joiners. In 1660 the gentleman architect Sir Roger Pratt drew up a series of recommendations for anyone who was considering building a country house:

> First resolve with yourself what house will be answerable to your purse and estate, and after you have pitched upon the number of rooms and the dimensions of each, and desire in some measure to make use of whatsoever you have either observed, or heard to be excellent elsewhere, then if you be not able to handsomely contrive it yourself, get some ingenious gentleman who has seen much of that kind abroad and been somewhat versed in the best authors of Architecture: viz. Palladio, Scamozzi, Serlio etc. to do it for you, and to give you a design of it in paper, though but roughly drawn, (which will generally fall out better than one which shall be given you by a home-bred Architect for want of his better experience, as is daily seen) . . .[3]

By the end of the century it was normal for anyone involved in building to have some idea of at least the dimensions of the various rooms before work began. In May 1681 Sir Christopher Wren wrote to the Dean of Christ Church, Dr John Fell, 'It is not a picture I send you or an imperfect Essay but a designe well studied as to all the Bearing'[4]; and Joseph Moxon in the second edition of his invaluable handbook of the working practices of craftsmen defined a draft as 'The Picture of an intended Building discribed on Paper, whereon is laid down the devised Divisions and Partitions of every Room in its due proportion to the whole Building'.[5]

Yet although drawings might define the various dimensions of the rooms, there is little evidence of their physical appearance being conceived three-dimensionally. Once the layout had been decided, the detailing was left to individual craftsmen.

One of the first English architects to design a complete room was John Smythson, who was the son of the major Elizabethan architect Robert Smythson, and who produced a complete working drawing of one of the rooms inside the so-called 'Little Castle' (that is, the keep) at Bolsover Castle in Derbyshire. It is a perspective view of the interior, like a small stage set, showing the marble vaults, a balcony, described on the drawing as the 'pergulae', and a stove in the corner.[6]

At more or less the time this room was designed in its precise, perspectival idiom, the conventions of architectural drawing were dramatically changed by Inigo Jones's contact with the drawing style of Italy and, especially, of Palladio. Jones was able to convey the depth and three-dimensionality of a building through the fluency of a drawn line; and instead of being interested in how an interior was laid out, he concentrated much more on the individual components of a room, especially the design of chimneypieces. In the 1630s, when his drawing style became freer as a result of his endless copying of Italian figure drawings, he produced some wonderfully inventive designs for chimneypieces in the Queen's House, Greenwich.[7] Yet, while his drawings include designs for specific features and ground plans showing the layout of rooms, he seems never to have thought of attempting to integrate the two, in order to suggest the physical appearance of a complete interior.

Jones's pupil John Webb, on the other hand, did provide drawings of complete rooms. On 4 July 1651, Dr Prujean asked the council of the Royal College of Physicians, of which he was president:

If I can procure one, that will build us a Library, and a

3

Repository for Simples and Rarities, such a one shall be suitable and honorable to the College; will ye assent to have it done or no, and give me leave and such others as I shall desire to be the designers and overlookers of the worke, both for conveniency and ornament?[8]

In the event the commission was given to John Webb; and the drawings he prepared for the building (which was destroyed in the Fire of London) show him thinking about the layout of the interior 'for conveniency and ornament'.

After the Restoration, although Webb was not, as he had hoped, appointed Surveyor of His Majesty's Works, he was responsible for the design of the King Charles block at Greenwich. In January 1665 a payment was made to Richard Gammon 'for bringing two Boxes out of Sommersetshire with books prints and drawings of Mr Webbs for his Majesties use';[9] and, during that year, he made thirteen drawings for the design of the King's Bedchamber, producing an image which was to become an important icon in the eighteenth century, when his drawings were acquired by the Earl of Burlington. These drawings reveal Webb's precise and highly fastidious draughtsmanship. They show in detail the physical appearance of the cornice, and how the alcove of the bedchamber was to have been supported by huge, overarching palm fronds, which were probably emblems.[10]

After Webb, one of the most significant seventeenth-century drawings of a complete room survives in the collection of Roger North's manuscripts in the British Library.[11] Roger North was a well educated Norfolk gentleman lawyer who, following a fire in the Middle Temple in 1678, was involved in the negotiations between the gentlemen of the Middle Chamber and the speculative builder, Nicholas Barbon. He himself describes how it was that 'drawing the model of my little chamber, and making patterns for the wainscot' showed him for the first time 'the joys of designing and executing known only to such as practise or have practised it'.[12] Following this introduction to architectural practice he bought the works of Palladio and Scamozzi, and John Evelyn's translation of Fréart de Chambray, *Parallel of the Antient Architecture with the Modern*. North devoted more hours than he felt he should have done to architectural drawing. His drawings, although slightly crude, show him exploring the layout of houses; and in the 'Treatise on Building' which he wrote following his retirement from legal practice in 1691, he described how:

> It is a want of applycation of thought, not to perceive from draught, as well as model, any designe of building, and erect it in your mind sufficiently clear and distinct for your judgment and use. And being continually at your work to observe and direct, the artificers wil not run into errors, as when left to themselves. In which case it is almost necessary you should have a specie-image to guide them. It is wonderful what a vivid representation of building may be made *in plano*. I have made the erection, of the uprights; and by the help of perspective, delined a flying prospect of each story, representing the view one hath, that looks into a model, to my intire content, and if farther exactness had bin required I could have as well done it, as sometimes for exercise and tryall, I have drawne the image of a line of rooms as they would appear, if the walls were taken downe and floors onely standing.[13]

This passage suggests the main reason for the desire to have a fully developed representation of an interior: so that the patron could envisage the interrelationship of the different rooms and how they would look in advance of construction. It would then be possible to ensure that the work was satisfactorily completed.

When the interiors of Hampton Court Palace were designed in the last decade of the seventeenth century, large numbers of drawings were prepared for the interior, which survive in an exceptionally handsome bound volume in Sir John Soane's

Museum. These have traditionally been attributed to Grinling Gibbons.[14] They show the patterns for the wood carving round the doorcases and chimneypieces, and designs for decorating the Queen's closet.

In 1699 William Talman, Comptroller of Works to William III, was commissioned to design a Trianon for Hampton Court, on the model of Louis XIV's Grand Trianon at Versailles. His drawings include a complete cutaway section through the building, which indicates both the position and the physical appearance of the state beds, the most important feature of the interior furnishings, and the design of the chimneypieces and the decoration in the cornices.[15] It is clear from this drawing that Talman saw his responsibilities as extending beyond the physical appearance of the exterior façades into the layout and decoration of the interior.

During the course of the seventeenth century, therefore, it is evident that architects began to think systematically about the relationship between the exterior of buildings and their interior organisation: how and where the various rooms would be located, and what they would look like. But it was the exception not the rule, an aspiration of architectural theory which was seldom observed in practice.

Pattern Books

In the absence of direct recommendations by architects, the craftsmen involved in the layout and decoration of an interior relied primarily on inherited experience and training and, to a lesser extent, on various prints and pattern books. Yet, during the course of the seventeenth century, in the same way that there was an increasing amount of planning on the part of architects, so too there was more substantial knowledge of Continental design sources and greater interest in their application.

There are quite a few extant late sixteenth-century examples of architectural details derived from pattern books.[16] Fireplaces in the grandest Elizabethan houses, such as Wollaton Hall, Hardwick Hall and Burghley House, can be seen to derive from Sebastiano Serlio's *Regole generali di architettura*, published in six parts between 1537 and 1575, which provided a practical manual of how to use the classical orders.[17] In 1611 the first five books were published in an English edition by the London printseller Robert Peake, with a dedication to Henry Prince of Wales and the hope that the work might

> benefite the Publicke; and convey unto my Countrymen (especially Architects and Artificers of all sorts) these Necessary, Certaine, and most ready Helps of Geometrie: The ignorance and want whereof, in times past (in most parts of this Kingdome) hath left us many lame Workes, with shame of many workemen.[18]

Mannerist ornament in interiors was copied from the prolific publications of the Antwerp engraver Hans Vredeman de Vries.

Descriptions of private libraries in the seventeenth century suggest that they were likely to contain a number of architectural publications. These were used both as a source of inspiration for the patrons involved in building and, sometimes, as more practical manuals for the masons. For example, in 1621, Sir Roger Townshend ordered six books to be sent to him at Raynham in Norfolk, where he was engaged in supervising a new house, and a subsequent letter of Sir Roger Pratt says that Townshend owned 'many Italian and French books of Architecture'.[19]

During the seventeenth century, the standard Continental source books, such as Palladio, Serlio, Scamozzi and Vredeman de Vries, were supplemented by manuals which were intended to assist specialist craftsmen.[20] An early example of such a work is Walter Gedde's *A Book of Sundry Draughtes, Principaly Serving for*

Glasiers. And not Impertinent for Plasterers, and Gardiners, besides sundry other professions, published in 1615. This was specifically intended to help the practice of working craftsmen, 'knowing the expert maister is not unfurnished of these usuall draughts, though each workman have not all of them'.[21] This was followed by an ever increasing flood of source books and specialist manuals to assist the process of design. For example, in 1635 Robert Peake's son, who continued his father's business as a printseller, published an English translation of the *Booke of Five Collumnes of Architecture* by the German artist Hans Blum, which was explicitly intended 'for the benefit of Free-Masons, Carpenters, Goldsmiths, Painters, Carvers, In-layers, Anticke-cutters, and all others that delight to practise with the Compasse and Square'. Both the work of Blum and the earlier translation of Serlio were reissued by Thomas Jenner during the 1650s.

This demand for a specialist architectural literature, including manuals for master builders and masons, intensified in the years after the Restoration, as a result of the interest in the reconstruction of London which both preceded and followed the Fire. In 1662 Balthazar Gerbier, a royalist courtier who had been Keeper of the Duke of Buckingham's collection of paintings in the 1620s and had opened an academy of drawing for the sons of gentlemen at his house in Bethnal Green in 1649, published *A Brief Discourse concerning the Three chief Principles of Magnificent Building*. In 1663 this was followed by his *Counsel and Advice to all Builders*. In 1664 John Evelyn, another courtier who had spent the early years of the Civil War and Commonwealth travelling on the Continent (he was in the Low Countries in the summer of 1639, in France, Switzerland and Italy between 1643 and 1646, and in Paris between 1649 and 1652),[22] published his translation of Roland Fréart, Sieur de Chambray under the title of *A Parallel of the Antient Architecture with the Modern*. This was apparently read and admired by the King, who complimented Evelyn especially on the engravings.[23] In 1667 Stephen Primatt, a lawyer, published his *The*

City & Country Purchaser & Builder and, in 1668, William Leybourn, a printer, bookseller and surveyor, produced his *Platform for Purchasers, Guide for Builders, Mate for Measurers*, one of the most influential and widely distributed manuals of housebuilding.[24] These publications exhibit a desire to provide specialized information which would assist architects and craftsmen in the task of composition, so that both architecture and town planning could be considered theoretical disciplines, worthy of consideration by the Royal Society.

These books were stocked by booksellers, especially in the area round St Paul's Cathedral, and by the more specialist print dealers. Robert Walton, a print dealer, had a shop at the sign of the Globe and Compass at the west end of St Paul's, which in 1666 advertised its stock-in-trade as including

> Maps, Pictures, Coppy-Books, Books of Beasts, Birds, Flowers, Fish, Fruites, Flies, neatly cut in Copper and worth buying; being very pleasant Ornaments for Houses, Studies and Closets; and also extraordinary useful for Goldsmiths, Jewellers, Chasers, Gravers, Painters, Carvers, Embroiderers, Drawers, Needle-women, and all Handicrafts.[25]

The most important of the printsellers who specialized in the supply of architectural books and prints was Robert Pricke, who in 1669 was established in a shop in White Cross Street near Cripplegate, where he sold 'a choice of Mapps, Copy Books, chimney pieces and ceiling pieces'. In 1675 he moved to larger premises. He sold pencils to the scientist and architect Robert Hooke, as well as 'Books of Birds, Beasts, Flowers and Fruits and Italian, French and Dutch Prints, Books of Geometry, Perspective and Architecture'.[26]

The increasing availability of specialist pattern books as an aid to the design of interiors is likely to have influenced the visual consciousness of their form, of how they might be laid out, and their detailing. It suggests a degree of design consciousness on the part of specialist craftsmen, long before the era of so-called designers. At the same time, it is important to recognize the limitations of this type of source material. It never showed full interiors, only patterns for specific details. The engravings were purely schematic, demonstrating forms in outline, not their physical shape. The accompanying text consisted of tips for the craftsmen, or hints on drawing in perspective, without any information about different types and styles of interior fitting. Although there was an awareness that it was possible to turn to books in the design of the interior, this happened in a piecemeal fashion; nor is there any information on how furniture might be arranged.

Topographical Art

In the absence of either architectural drawings or pattern books showing the layout and furnishings of seventeenth-century interiors, it might be hoped that topographical artists would have recorded their appearance; but it is remarkable how far late seventeenth-century topographical artists concentrate on exterior views of buildings and not on their interiors. For example, the artist and engraver Wenceslaus Hollar, who arrived in England in 1636, provided an extensive and minute image of aspects of the English countryside, bird's-eye views of towns, and sometimes excellent illustrations of individual buildings; but not of the rooms inside.[27] During the latter part of the seventeenth century, there were a number of artists who depicted the English landscape and country houses but, again, they did not think it necessary or desirable to illustrate the interiors of houses; nor did their owners ask them to.[28]

The two drawings of the interior of Samuel Pepys's library, which are thought to have been drawn in 1687, are a striking exception to this rule. The fact that one of the first topographic illustrations of an interior should be of Pepys's library is not surprising. Pepys, as any reader of his diary will know, was a passionate and enthusiastic collector of books, not merely for their content, but also for their bindings, repeatedly making resolutions to curb his appetite, but soon afterwards succumbing to recurrent temptation.[29] Like all true bibliomaniacs, he attempted to justify his lust on the grounds that he was making a solid investment, necessary for self-improvement and useful for his career, but in reality it was an almost physical desire that impelled him so often to the booksellers in St Paul's Churchyard, to savour the terrifying choice as to which volumes he could afford, and to describe the guilty pleasure with which he handled them after the purchase. On 13 October 1660 he spent a whole afternoon 'setting up shelfes in my study'.[30] A characteristic entry for 10 December 1663 runs:

> To St. Paul's churchyard, to my bookseller's; and having gained this day in the office by my stationer's bill to the King about 40s. or 3l., I did here sit two or three hours, calling for twenty books to lay this money out upon, and found myself at a great loss where to choose, and do see how my nature would gladly returne to the laying out of money in this trade.[31]

By the begining of 1665 Pepys's constant acquisition of books both new and old was beginning to cause a certain amount of disarray, which was offensive to his systematic mind. Just as he was trying to regularize the practices of the navy, so he decided to standardize the binding of his books. On 18 January 1665 he set off 'To my bookseller's, and there did give thorough direction for the new binding of a great many of my old books, to make my whole study of the same binding, within very few'.[32] It cost him £3, but he was pleased with the result, strutting 'Up and down to my chamber among my new books, which is now a pleasant sight to me, to see my whole study almost of one binding'.[33]

Rebinding was, however, only one step towards the proper arrangement and organization of Pepys's library. He needed some more permanent and practical method of housing each new volume, so that they did not constantly clutter the vacant chair of his office. He therefore decided in July 1666 to consult with Thomas Simpson, a master joiner in the Deptford dockyard, who had done some odd joinery jobs for him in the past, to see if between them they could devise a piece of furniture in which Pepys's books could be stored, out of reach of thieving hands, yet easily accessible and presenting a most impressive and rich display of Pepys's wealth and learning to any visitor. On 23 July 1666 Pepys wrote in his diary:

Up and to my chamber, doing several things there of moment. And then comes Simpson the Joyner, and he and I with great pains contriving presses to put my books up in; they now growing numerous, and lying one upon another on my chairs, I lose the use, to avoid the trouble of removing them when I would open a book.[34]

Between them Pepys and Thomas Simpson invented the glass-fronted bookcase.[35]

Given the importance which Pepys attached to the display of his books, it is not therefore surprising that he should have wanted an artistic record of the room in which they were displayed. The views have been attributed to Sutton Nicholls, an engraver and topographical draughtsman, who lived in Aldersgate Street. They are dated to 1687 on the grounds that only seven bookcases are shown, whereas by the 1690s there were twelve.[36] The drawings of the library are completely straightforward descriptive images of the physical appearance of the room, showing without any trace of idealization how the room would have looked in Pepys's lifetime.[37]

A second important seventeenth-century topographical view of an interior is a well known scene of a coffee house drawn by an unknown artist in a simple, rather naive style.[38] As with Pepys's library, it was probably the novelty of coffee houses which stimulated the desire to record their appearance.

Coffee had been first recorded by a European in a letter of 1603 in which a traveller in Syria described how

> Their most common drink is coffa, which is a blacke kind of drinke made of a kind of pulse like pease, called coaua; which being ground in the mill, and boiled in water, they drinke it as hot as they can suffer it; which they find to agree very well with them against their crudities and feeding on hearbs and rawe meates.[39]

By the Restoration a number of coffee houses had opened in both London and Oxford, and they had become an important place of rendezvous for gossip, political discussion and, at least in their early days, financial dealings. Normally the floor space of a coffee house was divided off into high-backed boxes which permitted a degree of privacy; but in this illustration everyone is shown assembled at long tables. The serving boy is pouring out coffee from coffee pots with conical tops, while more pots are being kept warm in front of the fireplace; at the table one man is smoking a pipe and another is drinking from a handleless cup. The illustration suggests the benefits of coffee houses, which were described by Henri Misson in the 1690s:

> These Houses, which are very numerous in London, are extreamly convenient. You have all Manner of News there: You have a good Fire, which you may sit by as long as you please: You have a Dish of Coffee; you meet your Friends for

the Transaction of Business, and all for a Penny, if you don't care to spend more.[40]

Instructive as these topographical illustrations of interiors are, much of their interest comes from their extreme rarity. For the most part the appearance of interiors, what they looked like, and how people used them, was not thought worthy of record.

The Influence of France

Considering the paucity of surviving images of seventeenth-century English interiors and domestic life, it is important to examine the influences which in the eighteenth century led to a different conception of the significance of private space. What made people aware by the end of the seventeenth century that the domestic interior could be used as an instrument for the expression of taste? There can be no doubt that the most powerful influence on the late seventeenth-century English idea of the interior was the tendency of the French in the seventeenth century to invest private space with public meaning. It was from France that England derived the ideals of personal luxury and domestic grandeur.

The origins of the French interest in the physical comfort of their surroundings has been traced by Peter Thornton, following Harold Nicolson (who was in turn unexpectedly indebted to the writings of Norbert Elias), to the ideas of Catherine de Vivonne, Marquise de Rambouillet, refurbishing her father's house in Paris in 1619, and her subsequent promotion of ideas of civility through her fashionable *salon*.[41] As Harold Nicolson wrote, 'At a time when Louis XIV was but a boy, shrinking under the hand and darting eyes of Mazarin, Mme de Rambouillet, in her boudoir of blue velvet and silver, was imprinting on French manners the feminine pattern of elegance from which they have never quite recovered.'[42] Contemporaries admired the layout of the Marquise de Rambouillet's interiors, in which she had taken a personal interest; indeed the myth grew up that she had actually planned her house herself. She is also credited with the innovation whereby, instead of sleeping in the principal *chambre de parade*, she slept in the adjacent *garde-robe*, which she converted into a *chambre à alcove*; and the last room in her private apartments was her so-called 'loge de Ziephir', where she received her *salon* of literary friends, who became known as *précieux*. According to her inventories, her chairs were covered in *point de Hongrie* and *tapisserie à l'aiguille*; her bedhangings were of black satin with floral embroidery in multi-coloured silks; and her rooms were filled with flowers festooned in huge bunches.[43] Certainly, she does seem to have been the sort of person who was able to stamp an individuality on her surroundings, a characteristic which was acknowledged and duly admired by contemporaries.[44]

Yet this pedigree for the origin of the idea of comfort needs to be treated with a degree of scepticism. First, the idea of *civilité* in French society can be traced far beyond the Marquise de Rambouillet. The belief that the moral character of an individual could be judged by the forms of behaviour in society, by education and upbringing, stretches back at least to Erasmus's work on the tutelage of children *De civilitate morum puerilium libellus*, first published in 1530 and issued in numerous translations throughout Europe during the sixteenth century. The Marquise de Rambouillet merely gave these ideas a more aristocratic and restrictive inflection.[45] Second, Anthony Blunt has pointed out that many of the innovations in internal planning with which Madame de Rambouillet has been credited were already present in the sixteenth century.[46] The importance of what Madame de Rambouillet was doing was not so much in providing an environment of personal comfort, in which few French aristocrats had any interest, as in the way her surroundings were treated as a projection of her personality.

Whatever the precise role of the Marquise de Rambouillet in stimulating an interest in the layout and appearance of interiors in the first half of the seventeenth century, there is no doubt that it was a period of substantial new building in Paris and that there was as much interest in the layout of the rooms inside the *hôtels* as there was in their exterior façades.[47] During the reign of Henri IV Paris became the centre for the court, and the King himself showed an interest in urban design with the construction of the Place Royale, now the Place des Vosges. In the next half-century large numbers of important *hôtels* were built for members of the nobility, who lived in Paris on the rents from their estates. Where the nobility set an example of conspicuous expenditure, so the *haute bourgeoisie* followed, building fine houses by the Seine and along the quays of the Ile Saint-Louis, which they filled with luxury goods – mirrors, glassware and porcelain. [48]

In 1623 Pierre Le Muet published his *Manière de bien battir pour toutes sortes de personnes*, providing a set of models for the layout of houses and advocating equally close attention to the *distribution* – the formal plan of the public and private areas – thereby concentrating the minds of his readers as much on how to move through these houses as on the more conventional virtues of beauty and solidity. In 1624 Louis Savot's *Architecture françoise* described the various considerations in building a house, including its basic form, the different types of room required, their size, and where the doors and fireplaces should be positioned. These publications enabled foreigners to appreciate French innovations in planning without necessarily visiting Paris. In 1647 Le Muet's work was published in an enlarged edition, showing work which had actually been built, instead of only hypothetical recommendations.

By the middle of the seventeenth century the French were enjoying a high standard of luxury in their domestic surroundings; well made, fashionable goods were easily available; and Parisian society was, if anything, exaggeratedly conscious of the way that physical surroundings reflected an individual's status in society. It was during the 1630s that the engravings of Abraham Bosse depicted the life of the well-to-do Parisian *haute bourgeoisie* in surroundings of considerable opulence. There are tapestries on the walls, carpets draped over tables, and chairs lined against the walls.[49]

By the time Colbert came to reorganize the luxury trades in the 1660s, many of the innovations with which he has traditionally been credited had already been attempted, including enticing specialist craftsmen into France, the establishment of state workshops for the production of luxury goods, and an attempt to regulate the quality of domestic production through government legislation.[50] Colbert merely pursued government policies which had been established under Richelieu, with renewed vigour and the advantages of a decade of peace and the support of the King. He recruited skilled craftsmen from all over Europe, including tapestry makers from the Netherlands; silk workers, glassblowers, embroiderers and lacemakers from Italy; and leatherworkers from Spain. In 1667 he established a royal factory for the furnishings of the Crown at the Gobelins. A series of government edicts regulated the quality of manufactures, 'to render uniform all those products of the same type, name and quality, in whatever place they may be made, both to increase their sale inside and outside our kingdom, and to prevent the public from being cheated'.

Closely associated with Colbert's attempts to reorganize the luxury trades was Louis XIV's determination to regulate and control every aspect of court behaviour and ceremonial. It was in the two decades following Louis XIV's resumption of power in 1661 that the ruthless organization of French court life, which determined all forms of behaviour in and around Versailles, became most asphyxiating.[51] In this carefully organized and orchestrated court society, the importance of gesture, of how and where to stand in a room, became paramount. It was a small step from the control of physical forms of behaviour to the desire to provide an equally elaborate sense of the arrangement of the physical surroundings of royal interiors. And indeed Charles Lebrun had under his control, as *Directeur de la Manufacture royale des Meubles de la Couronne*, a whole army of 250 specialist weavers, dyers, embroiderers, goldsmiths, cabinetmakers, and woodcarvers, all of whom were required to supply appropriate furnishings to Versailles so that the palace could be a showpiece for his artistic policy.

At the same time, engravers were employed to make the patterns of French decoration which became known throughout Europe. Paul Androuet du Cerceau published designs for textiles, such as his *Bouquets propres pour les étoffes de Tours* and his *Dessins nouveaux pour étoffes de brocart à fond d'or ou d'argent*. The houses of the period were published by Jean Marot in his *Recueil*, known as the 'Petit Marot', and in his *L'Architecture*, the so-called 'Grand Marot'. Jean Le Pautre published a massive number of engravings of ornament, including designs for panelling and ceilings, as in his *Lambris à la françoise, Plafonds à la romaine*, published in 1665, and for chimneypieces and doors, as in his *Nouveaux desseins de Chemineés à l'italienne, Chemineés à la romaine, Chemineés à la moderne, Nouveaux desseins de Chemineés à peu de frais, Chemineés et Lambris, Grandes Alcoves à la romaine*, published in 1667. Through these engravings France established a pattern of interior decoration which was imitated throughout Europe.

The grandeur and luxury of mid-seventeenth-century Parisian interiors, and especially those at Versailles, clearly made a great impression on English visitors.[52] In his book *The State of France*, published in 1652, John Evelyn described how

the Gentlemen are generally given to those laudable Magnificencies of Building, and furnishing their Palaces with the most precious Moveables, much of the luxe and excesse of Italy, being now far entred among them, as may well serve to exemplifie, when in the Duchess of Chaulnes her Palace neer the Place Royal in Paris, the pernaches, or tufts of plumes belonging to one of her beds onely, is estimated worth fourteen thousand livers, which amounts to neer a thousand pounds sterling of our money.[53]

In 1665 Wren visited Paris specifically to study current French modes of building. According to Edward Browne in a letter to his father, he was particularly impressed by the château at Raincy, which he thought was 'small but extremely neat, and the modell pleased Dr Wren very much: the chambers are excellently well painted, and one room with a handsome cupola in it is one of the best I have seen'.[54] William Hunter, one of Samuel Pepys's correspondents, was likewise impressed by French modes of interior decoration when he visited Paris in August 1675:

> wee have as yet seen only the Kings house and garden at the Versaile, the place called the Goblings where the King employs the yeare round severall Artificers to worke for him, as Painters, Stone Cutters, makers of hangings, Silver Smiths and a hundred more sort of artificers . . . I shall not take upp your time in troubling you with the perticulers of what wee have seen, which is all soe fine and magnificent, that as I never in my life saw the like, soe I doe beleave there cannot in the whole world be any thing that is finer, but more perticulerly the Kings house and garden at the Versaile.[55]

It was, of course, possible to know about the appearance of French interiors without actually visiting Paris, through the medium of engravings, which were brought back by visitors and could also be obtained from specialist dealers in London. For example, the highly entrepreneurial London printseller Peter Stent sold moralizing versions of the engravings of Abraham Bosse from his shop in Newgate in the 1640s.[56] But the most important way in which knowledge of French interiors came to London was through French Huguenot craftsmen, exiled by Louis xiv's persecution in the 1680s.

Throughout the seventeenth century there had been a steady trickle of French refugees from the restrictive conditions imposed on Protestant worship. During the 1680s this trickle became a flood as Louis xiv embarked on a policy of systematic persecution, culminating in the revocation of the Edict of Nantes in 1685. Many of the Huguenots who came to England had lived in towns and were used to mercantile activity. They were forced to make a new living in England and, not surprisingly, many of them decided to specialize in those trades for which France was well known, especially the production of silks and high-quality metalwork and paper.[57]

During the 1690s these Huguenot craftsmen made many of the luxury furnishings which transformed the physical appearance of grand London interiors. Francis Lapierre, an upholsterer with a shop in Pall Mall, was able to rent out the accoutrements of an apartment, including a bed of crimson Genoese velvet, to the Duke of Schomberg, and supplied expensive furnishings both to the Royal Household and to the nobility.[58] Likewise, Philip Guibert, whose shop was in Jermyn Street, St James's, was able to supply furnishings to the court, including 'a fine black soffa in the new fashion'.[59] Many of the most important silversmiths of the 1690s were also Huguenots, including Pierre Harache, who was described as 'lately come from France to avoid persecution and live quietly' when he was admitted to the Goldsmiths' Company in 1682; and David Willaume, the son of a goldsmith in Metz, who settled in England in 1687 and in 1690 was married in the French church of La Patente in Spitalfields. These two Huguenots revolutionized the appearance of silver by introducing a number of French types of buffet plate, such as the helmet-shaped ewer; and a different style of workmanship, which tended to favour large, monumental forms and flat surface engraving, very different from the heavy embossed ornament that had previously been popular.[60]

These craftsmen must have brought to the design of domestic interiors not only a knowledge of French ornament, but also some idea of the way a complete room could be set out in order to enhance a sense of visual display. Many of the goods which were supplied by the Huguenots were intended not for use, but as items of ornament: magnificent state beds covered in cascades of expensive silk, grand plate which could be set out on the sideboard, fine materials which enhanced the sense of lavishness in the interior. Thus they stimulated a consciousness of the room as an arena for display.

The most important single influence in bringing French styles of interior decoration to England was the Huguenot architect and designer Daniel Marot.[61] His father Jean Marot was active as an architect and engraver at the court of Louis xiv, so Daniel Marot must have been inculcated in his youth with a knowledge of the working practices of the most skilled artisans at the Gobelins. He would have developed a consciousness of the way interior furnishings could be used to enhance the grandeur of a domestic environment. In 1684 Marot's name appears in a list of Protestant refugees in Holland, where he created the staircase and other interiors of the Castle of Zeist, near Utrecht. Soon afterwards he entered the service of William of Orange and, during the 1690s, held the title of 'Architecte de Guillaume III Roi de la Grande Bretagne'. He is known to have been in England on several occasions around this time, producing a drawing for the parterre at Hampton Court in 1689, getting married at the Huguenot church in Leicester Fields in 1694, and being paid for work on the gardens at Hampton Court in 1698.

Although it is certain that Marot spent some time in England during the 1690s, the exact nature of his influence on styles of interior decoration is less clear, because this is not at all well documented. He would have brought with him an understanding of the ways an interior space could be furnished and decorated as an ensemble. It is this idea of the interior as a total environment which is recorded in the suites of engravings which he published. For example, he illustrates the complete furnishings of a library, with globes and busts along the tops of the bookcases, and a single-backed chair in front of a rather austere reading desk; and he demonstrates the way that a state bedchamber could be arranged, with long rows of chairs lined against the wall. Through these engravings Marot may have conveyed to English architects of the time how a room could be much more than its constituent parts. So, if one is looking for an origin of the concept of interior decoration in England, it is logical to trace it back to Marot, who introduced ideas of comfort and luxury which were, by the end of the seventeenth century, already familiar in France.

Interiors of the 1690s

Although the appearance of interiors at the end of the seventeenth century does not survive either in architects' drawings or in contemporary topographical illustrations, it is possible to conjure up an idea of what they looked like by close attention to the descriptions of contemporary travellers. Travellers, especially Celia Fiennes, were attentive to the way interiors were arranged, and to particular features, both for their own sake and as a way of providing an indication of the tastes of their owners. It is clear from literary descriptions that, by the end of the seventeenth century, there was an awareness of the way interiors might be laid out, and an interest in their decoration. Indeed, one way of thinking about critical attitudes to the layout and furnishings of interiors is not so much through the way they were recorded visually as through the language in which they were described.[62]

The most important and influential interiors of the 1690s were those of the royal palaces, on which a great deal of money was spent, to the disgust of the general populace. Soon after their accession William and Mary began to make substantial additions to the royal palace at Hampton Court, which included redecoration of the interiors.[63] While construction work was taking place it was decided that a small freestanding building by the river, known as the Water Gallery, should be made into a set of luxurious private apartments for the Queen. Here she was able to demonstrate her Francophile tastes in furniture and decoration. The Water Gallery was demolished in the autumn of 1700, but its appearance is recorded in the description of Celia Fiennes, who has left a detailed record of all the places she visited on her indefatigable travels on horseback round England:

> There was the Water Gallery that opened into a ballcony to the water and was decked with China and fine pictures of the Court Ladyes drawn by Nellor [Kneller]; beyond this came severall roomes and one was pretty large, at the four corners were little roomes, like closets or drawing roomes one pannell'd all with Jappan another with Looking Glass and two with fine work under pannells of Glass; there was the Queens Bath and a place to take boat in the house.[64]

Our conception of the Water Gallery can be made yet more vivid by the account of Daniel Defoe, in his *Tour through the Whole Island of Great Britain*. According to Defoe,

> Her majesty had here a fine apartment, with a sett of lodgings, for her private retreat only, but most exquisitely furnish'd; particularly a fine chints bed, then a great curiosity; another of her own work, while in Holland, very magnificent, and several others; and here was also her majesty's fine collection of Delft ware, which indeed was very large and fine; and here was also a vast stock of fine china ware, the like whereof was not then to be seen in England; the long gallery, as above, was fill'd with

this china, and every other place, where it could be plac'd, with advantage.[65]

These two descriptions give us important clues to the nature of fashionable decoration in the last decade of the seventeenth century. Everything here was made of the most expensive and ornate materials. Mirrors were used to extend the sense of space, and japanned wood lent an air of exoticism. In particular, Queen Mary was responsible for introducing the idea of filling an interior with imported porcelain.[66]

The death of Queen Mary in December 1694 interrupted fitting out of the interiors of the new royal apartments at Hampton Court. The designs for wood carvings and chimneypieces, thought to have been made by Grinling Gibbons, were not executed. Work on the completion of the palace was resumed in April 1699, when Wren presented an estimate for 'fitting the Inside of the Roomes of State at Hampton Court, from the entrance out of the Portico to the roomes already finished above staires, Containing the Great staires, the Guard-Chamber, the Presence-Chamber, Drawing roome, Anteroome, Great Bed-chamber Lobby & Gallery for the pictures'.[67] A detailed estimate submitted by the Duke of Montagu, who was Master of the Great Wardrobe, documents the cost and appearance of the furniture which was supplied by specialist cabinetmakers and upholsterers, including 'the Crimson Velvet Bed sold to his Majesty by the Earl of Jersey'.[68]

By the time Celia Fiennes visited Hampton Court once more, these rooms had been furnished with an opulence comparable to that of the Water Gallery. As she wrote:

Thence you go into an anty-room hung with tapestry, thence into the Common Audience roome where was a throne and cannopy crimson damaske with gold fringe the form the same round the roome; here was King Charles the Firsts picture on horse back over the mantelpiece; all the rooffes of the roomes are curiously painted wth different storyes, out of this you enter the grand State Roome which has King Williams picture at length on the mantelpiece, fine pictures over all doors, and carvings in wood, the throne and cannopy here was scarlet velvet with rich gold orrice [arras] and window curtains; thence into the dineing roome where hangs in the middle a chrystall branch for candles, its hung with tapistry, I think its here the Queen of Bohemias picture is over the chimney piece, Sophia's mother; the window curtaines flower'd crimson damaske with gold fringe; thence the drawing roome which has a silver branch in the middle and sconces and Queen Marys picture, here is crimson velvet . . . [69]

Again, this description provides a slightly overwhelming impression of the physical appearance of a royal palace around the year 1700: the succession of rooms each one more magnificent than the last; the way the walls were hung with rich tapestries and damask hangings; the carved doorcases, the candelabra, and the gold-fringed curtains.

William and Mary were also responsible for substantial internal changes to Kensington House, which they bought from the Earl of Nottingham for use when they were in London.[70] On 3 January 1690 Constantijn Huygens visited the King at Kensington and wrote that there was much work needing to be done in fitting it up. On 17 March 1690 he recorded the setting up of a new bed. On 26 July 1690 Queen Mary wrote to her husband:

I have bin this morning at Kensington, for tho I did believe you would not be willing to stay at Whitehall yet I confesse what you write me would make me a milion of fears specially since I must needs confess my faults. I have not bin pressing enough till it was too late, the outside of ye house is ye fideling work wch takes up more time than one can imagin and while ye schafolds are up the windows must be boarded up but as soon as yt is done your own apartment may be furnisht and tho mine can not possible be ready yet awhile, I have found out a way if you please, wch is yt I may make use Lord Portland's & hee ly in som of ye other roomes, we may ly in your chamber & I go throw [through] ye councel roome down or els dresse there.[71]

There is ample evidence in the documents concerning the furnishing of Kensington Palace of Queen Mary's personal interest in the selection of particular fabrics and, especially, of her passion for things oriental. Every room in the Queen's apartments was stuffed full of porcelain: her Gallery contained 154 pieces over the doors, over the chimneypieces, on cabinets, under the cabinets, and under tables. She also liked lacquerware, which was present in abundance including, in the Gallery, twelve 'India-Jappan' chairs with India silk cushions.[72]

The 1690s were also a decade in which the upper echelons of the nobility spent huge sums of money on interior decoration. Just as William and Mary imitated the court of Louis XIV in making their arrangements for court ceremonial, so the nobility followed the example of the monarchy in spending vast amounts on the furnishings and decoration of their country houses. Although these interiors do not seem to have been consciously designed in the sense of being conceived prior to execution by a single individual, they certainly have an effect of complete control, with matching curtains and chair covers and rooms dominated by overwhelming state beds; and it is possible that the upholsterer may have provided some advice about the interior fittings.

The most remarkable example of opulent interior furnishings in the reign of William and Mary was at Chatsworth, the great house built by the first Duke of Devonshire on his estate in Derbyshire.[73] The Duke of Devonshire was able to employ the best possible craftsmen locally and from London. The first evidence of the supply of interior furnishings was on 17 July 1688, when the well known cabinetmaker Gerrit Jensen received £50 'in part of payment for Glasse for the Hall at Chatsworth', and thereafter the progress of work is documented in detailed accounts.[74] In July 1689, Henry Lobb and his partner Robert Owen were paid for 'oake boards for ye floor of ye upper story', and on 9 September 1692 Joel Lobb, William Davis and Samuel Watson were employed to 'carve ye ornaments of lime tree worke for the great chamber to the designe aprooved by his Lordsp'. In 1697 'Mr. Lapiere' (that is, Francis Lapierre, the upholsterer) was paid £470 in regular instalments for the supply of a state bed, and in March 1699 and 1700 Gerrit Jensen received further payments for the supply of damask. In June 1702 a large consignment of furniture was purchased from Thomas Roberts in London, including '12 large walnuttree Armed Chaires', '2 large Saffaws carved' and '6 Banketts of Walnut-tree'; it was delivered in nine large packing cases. The final payment was in 1706 'to Mr. Tompson for the brass worke for close stools'; in other words, the flushing mechanism for the fine alabaster and cedarwood water closets which survive in the house.

The original appearance of the Chatsworth interiors and the impression they made can be reconstructed from the many contemporary descriptions. In 1700 the house was described by Charles Leigh:

> It is the Seat of his Grace, *William*, Duke of *Devonshire*; the Passage to it is of an easie Ascent; the Gate itself is very remarkable, adorn'd with several Trophies; the Hill composes a stately Square, from which through a gallery upon Stone-Stairs, so artfully contriv'd, that they seem to hang in the Air, you have the Prospect of a most beautiful Chappel, as likewise of the Hall, in both which are choice and curious Paintings, perform'd by Seignior Vario, Master of that Art; in the Hall is the History of *Caesar*, stabb'd in the Senate; and in the Chappel an admirable and lively Draught of the Resurrection: Hence we

were conducted into the Chambers, which are Noble and Great, and most richly Inlaid, with the choicest Woods, and Compose a very stately Gallery. At the upper end of it is his Grace's Closet, richly beautify'd with Indian Paint, where there are various Figures of Birds, as Drawn by the Native *Indians*: Here stands a stately Looking-Glas, which, when you approach it, reflects the whole Gallery back again, and so deceive the Sight, that the Walk seems to continue to the Eye, though you have reach'd the Bounds of the Gallery.[75]

Here we find the same constituent elements of the great interior as have already been observed at Hampton Court: elaborate ceiling paintings; inlaid woods to provide a complexity of ornamental surface; japanning; looking-glasses which extended the appearance of interiors and reinforced the sense of the interior as a spectacle.

Chatsworth was not alone in the magnificence of its interiors. Other houses newly constructed or refurbished during the 1690s were Petworth House, built for the sixth Duke of Somerset; Lowther Castle in Westmorland, for Sir John Lowther, Viscount Lonsdale; Burley-on-the-Hill in Rutland, for Daniel Finch, first Earl of Nottingham; and Chippenham Park in Cambridgeshire, for Edward Russell, first Earl of Orford.

At Lowther Castle the progress of furnishing and decorating the interiors can be followed in the building accounts.[76] The carpenter was James Swingler, responsible for wainscoting and laying the floors. There were two carvers, Mackadams and Livermore; and two joiners, Clarkson and Shelton. Swingler apparently agreed to floor the whole house for £30, including the provision of the nails. They used cedar, walnut and oak for the wainscot, deal and Norway oak for the floorboards. By August 1693 the house was ready to be painted and Sir John Lowther wrote to his steward, William Atkinson, informing him that he had sent 'a quantity of oils and colours for Mr. Verrio's painting the Great Room'.

Sir John Lowther kept in constant touch with his steward

concerning the progress of the interior fittings: in January 1694 he was concerned that the wainscot would spoil owing to the greenness of the walls; in February he was worried about the cost of transporting twelve little statues from Kendal to Lowther and that the workmen were behind their schedule; in March the rooms were being painted Spanish white and he was beginning to be thankful that the labour and the expense were nearly over; in April he was making preparations for a visit. The upholsterer was sent for to re-erect old hangings; a local lady was ordered to air the beds; the larder was furnished with hooks, shelves and a bread bin; Lady Lowther's chamber was decorated with red mohair; the buttery was given a press for table linen. On 28 April 1694 Lowther wrote that he hoped to reach the house in a fortnight's time and that several great looking-glasses had been sent on ahead.

The finished appearance of these interiors is recorded by Celia Fiennes. She entered the house through the porch, which had pillars of limestone:

> Below-staires, you enter a space that leads severall wayes to all the offices and on one side is a large parlour which lookes out on these green plotts with images; the staircase very well wanscoated and carv'd at the top; you are landed into a noble hall very lofty, the top and sides are exquisitely painted by the best hand in England which did the painting at Windsor [Verrio].[77]

It is evident that Celia Fiennes was aware of planning and the organization of interior space; also that she appreciated craftsmanship. She continued

> thence into a dining room and drawing-roome well wanscoated of oake large pannells plaine no frettworks nor carvings or glass work only in chimney pieces; 3 handsome chambers, one scarlet cloth strip'd and very fashionably made up the hangings

the same, another flower'd damaske lined with fine Indian embroidery, the third roome had a blew satten bed embroider'd.[78]

She reveals her fascination with the character and quality of textiles, her ability to recognize different types of cloth, and she comments on their fashionability and probable provenance. She was particularly impressed by some 'very fine orris hangings in which was much silk and gold and silver', which had apparently been made for the Duke of Lauderdale at Ham, but which Sir John Lowther had managed to buy, in spite of the fact that they were covered with the Lauderdale arms.

At Chippenham Park in Cambridgeshire, the interiors can be reconstructed, as at Lowther, from the descriptions provided by Celia Fiennes. She began in the entrance hall, paved with freestone and with squares of black marble in the corners. She goes on:

there are two fine white marble tables veined with blew, its wanscoated with Wallnut tree the pannells and rims round with Mulberry tree that is a lemon collour and the moldings beyond it round are of a sweete outlandish wood not much differing from Cedar but of a finer graine, the chaires are all the same.[79]

Here, as at Lowther, one can observe her sensitivity to the nature and properties of materials, her ability to differentiate quite precisely between woods, and her appreciation of the skill with which they were employed in the wainscot.

Turning again to textiles, she remarks:

the whole house is finely furnish'd with differing coulloured damask and velvets some figured and others plaine, at least 6 or 7 in all richly made up after a new mode; in the best drawing roome was a very rich hanging gold and silver and a little scarlet, mostly tissue and brocade of gold and silver and border of green damaske round it.[80]

Once again, one finds the extreme richness of texture, and the very ornate physical properties of the late seventeenth-century interior – characteristics which she obviously appreciated. The damask and velvet were probably silk, the best of which came from Genoa, but which could also be obtained from subsidiary centres such as Lyons and was beginning to be manufactured in England. The window and door curtains were of the same green damask as the wall hangings, producing a completely coherent effect.

Celia Fiennes goes on to comment on the extensive use of mirror glass. In the best drawing room

> there was no looking-glass but on the chimney-piece and just opposite in the place a looking glass used to be was 4 pannells of glass in length and 3 in breadth set together in the wanscoate; the same was in another drawing roome which was for my Lord; the dineing roome had this looking glass on the two peers between the three windows it was from the top to the bottom 2 pannells in breadth and 7 in length, so it shews from top to toe.[81]

Instead of being free-hanging and framed, like a picture, mirror glass was inset into the wainscot. Like damask, it was an expensive indulgence. At this time the best plates were imported from Venice. Celia Fiennes continues her tour:

> the roomes were all well wanscoated and hung and there was the finest carv'd wood in fruitages herbages gemms beasts fowles, etc., very thinn and fine all in white wood without paint or varnish, the severall sorts of things thus carv'd were exceeding naturall all round.[82]

Although she does not attribute the carving, these are exactly the epithets she uses elsewhere to describe the carved work of Grinling Gibbons; at Windsor, she speaks of 'the most exactest workmanship in the wood carving, which is (as the painting) the pattern and masterpiece of all such work both in figures fruitages beasts birds flowers all sorts, so thin the wood and all white natural wood without varnish'. It is clear that the woodwork at Chippenham, if not by Gibbons himself, was at least by one of his followers and manifested the qualities and excellence that he had introduced: the vivid, naturalistic detail; the virtuoso manipulation of material; the delicacy and refinement.

Thereafter Celia Fiennes's description of the Chippenham interiors tails off and she concludes with a rapid inventory of all the items she has so far omitted. There was apparently very fine china. There was much silver: 'andirons and jarrs and perfume pots of silver'. And the common rooms were said to be 'all new, convenient and neat with double doors lined to prevent noises'.

These descriptions of the grandest houses in England during the 1690s reveal that, by the end of the seventeenth century, there was a detailed interest in the way interiors were furnished. Even though contemporary illustrations do not survive, the journeys of Celia Fiennes on horseback round England have left us with a vivid commentary by an intelligent and perceptive observer of fashions in interior decoration.

1700–1720

Architectural Drawings

One of the first eighteenth-century drawings of a complete interior was made by William Talman's son John, who was dispatched by his father to the Continent to assemble a collection of prints and drawings. On his return they planned a room which was intended to contain the collection, marking the position of the proposed shelves and where the folios were to be kept.[1] As with the drawings of Pepys's library, the mentality of the collector bred a desire to plan and record the surroundings of the collection.

Once the idea of thinking about how a room should be furnished in advance of construction had been established, the practice inevitably became more common. Sir John Vanbrugh, the leading country house architect during this period, was certainly interested in how the ground plan of a house worked. At Castle Howard he produced a much more complex arrangement of interior spaces than had been common in the standard plan of a Restoration double-pile house; and, in a drawing in the Victoria and Albert Museum, there is evidence of him commissioning a detailed design of the so-called 'Eating Room' from his assistant Nicholas Hawksmoor.

At Blenheim Vanbrugh drew a cross section of the whole

house, which shows an early proposal for the inside of the hall and saloon.[2] He and Hawksmoor subsequently provided detailed drawings of both rooms, including a drawing for the hall which shows the nature of the arcading and the overall details of the structure.[3] For the saloon Vanbrugh produced a design showing the arrangement of statuary in niches. This drawing was submitted by the Duke of Marlborough to the French artist Louis Silvestre for his approval. On 20 September 1707 Silvestre sent an alternative design, which unfortunately does not survive, together with critical comments on the fact that Vanbrugh and Hawksmoor had so obviously derived their design from an engraving of the Farnese Gallery: 'Il est souvent dangereux de vouloir imiter qu'on n'a pas vu; et en Matière d'Architecture sur tout cette Maxime est très vraye que ce qui est beau et régulier dans sa place etre choquant et très défectueux dans une autre disposition.'[4] In spite of this criticism Vanbrugh seems to have persevered with the original design, and on 14 July 1709 he wrote to the Duchess of Marlborough describing how the saloon was to be decorated:

> Your Grace will receive by my Lord Herveys Servant to morrow the Designe you desired to See of the Manner intended for finishing the Salon, The Pannells at the bottom are to be of Wainscote, and run even without any breaks so that there will be room for above Twenty Chairs besides Tables. The Pillasters and [Door] Moldings are to be of Marble, with the Moldings About the Niches where the Figures Stand.[5]

Vanbrugh's comments show a strong desire to articulate the different elements of the interior into a satisfactory whole.

At the same time as the interiors of Blenheim were being planned, Lord Raby, the Ambassador to Prussia, was making grandiose plans for alterations to the house he had bought in 1708 at Stainborough in Yorkshire. He commissioned designs from Johann von Bodt, who had been a military engineer in William

III's army before becoming Chief Architect to the Elector of Brandenburg in 1700. Von Bodt's proposals include two different sections of the gallery: one shows the complete arrangement of the room and the other the details of the decoration and, interestingly, the chimney flue.[6] On 15 March 1709 Peter Wentworth reported to Lord Raby how he had shown the plans for the house to his mother and how 'She stood amazed at it, and said that the least such a building cou'd cost inside and out wou'd be ten thousand pounds.'[7]

Beside Talman, Vanbrugh and Johann von Bodt much the most important designer of interiors in the first two decades of the eighteenth century was the artist-cum-architect Sir James Thornhill. Because he was extensively employed by members of the nobility to provide wall paintings for their halls and staircases, Thornhill also became interested in the surrounding visual context in which his paintings would appear. In a sense he acted as a decorator, stipulating the appropriate form of the doorcases and the pilasters, as well as providing huge decorative paintings.

Thornhill was born into an old established Dorset family, which had fallen on hard times, so that his father had had to work as a grocer in the county town of Dorchester.[8] He was apprenticed to a distant kinsman, Thomas Highmore, the King's Sergeant Painter. Under Highmore's tutelage Thornhill learned to draw with great facility, completing his apprenticeship in 1696. In 1699 he started to record his drawings in a magnificent large folio sketchbook, which survives in the British Museum.[9] It shows him thinking not only about the composition of individual works of mural decoration, but also how they would fit into the room as a whole; it was a short step from this to the concept of a painter supervising the whole scheme of interior decoration.

In 1706 Thornhill was at work at Chatsworth; two of his surviving drawings of rooms are thought to be proposals for the decoration of the so-called Sabine Room.[10] They demonstrate how Thornhill thought of decorative painting in terms of the whole wall space, with curtains hanging over the cornice and plump cherubs propping up an arrangement of flowers: it was a very different idea of painting from easel portraits. Indeed, it was much closer to his work as a scene painter for the theatre. The room, instead of being a confined space boxed in by wainscoting, suddenly expanded in scale, with vistas through to temples and the gods falling down from the ceiling. It was space to be enjoyed as a sophisticated form of visual entertainment, not just as a grand setting for the reception of visitors.

In 1708 Thornhill was called in to work at Blenheim. In December of that year he was paid £35 by Hawksmoor 'for painting the Two Great modells both with and without and several historical sketches in the ceiling'.[11] Six years later, in November 1714, he submitted an estimate for painting the Hall, Saloon and Gallery. His estimates may have been appended to the detailed designs for the Saloon, which survive, and a drawing for a corridor, which shows not only the painted decoration, but also the walls and ceiling. Again, Thornhill's verve is evident, as are his vivacity and his great skill as a draughtsman; also apparent is the extent to which his talent was at least as much architectural as it was pictorial, equal to providing a successful accompaniment to the bold architectural forms of Vanbrugh and Hawksmoor.

By 30 June 1716 Vanbrugh was able to write to the Duchess of Marlborough: 'Mr Thornhill goes on a pace in the Hall; and has begun with a better Spirit in his paintings than anything I have seen of his doing before. I hope he'll continue it. I know he piques himself upon appearing well at Blenheim.'[12] But, like Vanbrugh, Thornhill fell from the Duchess's favour and she commissioned Laguerre to paint the saloon for half the price.

Thornhill's last major commission which involved both the design of a house and its mural decoration was at Moor Park in Hertfordshire for Benjamin Styles, a Director of the South Sea Company.[13] Styles had purchased Moor Park in 1720, and by 1725 the Great Hall was ready for decoration. Thornhill signed a contract that he would paint it 'in the best Manner that [he] was Capable of . . . According to his best Skill and Judgement . . . at the best times and when the Weather was best for Doeing Such Work and with the best and Most Proper Colours and Materialls.'[14] However, they quarrelled about the quality of the work and Thornhill's scale of charges, so that Thornhill was forced to go to court to seek payment for his work.

Thornhill's artistic practice, which included designs for the theatre and highly inventive mural decoration, is a substantial step on the road to considering the whole interior as an artistic unity. He was concerned with the appearance of a room as a whole, not of paintings in isolation. Later in his life he turned to the design of complete buildings. It is perfectly possible to imagine him dictating the appearance of a state bed in the same way that he showed the door surrounds and cornices in his proposals for wall decoration. Thornhill, at least as much as Marot, should be seen as a forerunner of the fully fledged interior decorator.

The Print Trade

In the absence of many images of interiors at the design stage, it might be hoped that it would be possible to find satisfactory images of completed interiors among the surviving popular prints of the early eighteenth century. Yet here, too, one finds a singular dearth of portrayals of rooms.

Such prints tend to be artistically crude and the names of famous artists or engravers are not attached to them, so they have been relatively neglected by historians of prints. Yet there was clearly a substantial market for woodcuts and cheap engravings which could be pinned or pasted to the wall. Lorna Weatherill, in her statistical study of inventories, has demonstrated that between 1701 and 1715 86 per cent of the inventories from the London Orphans' Court list some form of picture among the household possessions.[15] This popular market for prints was sustained by the chapmen who travelled the country hawking miscellaneous wares. For example, an early catalogue of prints issued by the dealer John Bowles advertised his shop at Mercer's Hall in Cheapside, 'where merchants, gentlemen, city shopkeepers, and country chapmen may be furnished with them at the best hand, and lowest price'.[16]

Examination of the collection of political prints in the British Museum reveals very few worthwhile depictions of domestic interiors. In any case, the vast bulk of cheap popular prints has simply not survived. Most of those that remain are crude emblematic prints, which were prompted by specific historical events – most notably, in the first two decades of the eighteenth century, the trial of the political preacher Henry Sacheverell. Many of the other prints of the period are straightforward adaptations of Dutch ones, or simple woodcuts attached to broadsides and ballads. The figures are usually drawn in two dimensions and there is no attempt to depict their background in any detail.

I have only been able to find two significant exceptions to this general rule. The first is the frontispiece to Crispin the Cobler's *Confutation of Ben H[oadley]*, a broadside published in 1709.[17] This print is a satire on the consequences of a tradesman becoming involved in politics. The cobbler has read too much of Benjamin Hoadley's writings on the right of subjects to resist their ruler, especially his *The Original and Institution of Civil Government*, which was published in 1710 and, in the same year, ordered to be publicly burnt. He is being attacked by his son with a poker, as a result of which he decides to consign Hoadley's book to the flames. What is interesting about the engraving is that it demonstrates the close proximity in a single room of the workman's bench and of his bed: there is no separation whatever between the worlds of work and of domestic life.

The second print of this period which is used to illustrate almost every book about the nature of early eighteenth-century interiors is *The Tea-Table*, an engraving dated around 1710.[18] This shows a group of fashionable ladies seated at a table, while, according to the verses underneath, 'we see Thick Scandal circulate with right Bohea'. There are a number of interesting features in the engraving. It is striking that one of the ladies sits at an upholstered chair, while the others are sitting on a set of high-backed caned chairs, which are normally regarded as being characteristic of the reign of William and Mary. In spite of the fact that it was unusual to have a carpet on the floor at this date, there is one under the table. Over the fireplace a picture hangs with its top almost at the height of the ceiling. In the background to the left of the fireplace is a buffet containing, among other items, a coffee pot, and to the right is a mirror. But, in general, the very uniqueness of this print demonstrates the limitations of the medium of popular engraving at the beginning of the eighteenth century as a means of conveying how ordinary interiors were furnished. Very often the prints use old-fashioned stereotypes to convey their message. They are not concerned with providing an exact representation of interiors, just as they do not try to provide a precise likeness of individual politicians.

These conventions begin to change only around 1720, partly precipitated by the flood of images engendered by the crisis of the South Sea Bubble. One artist who was instrumental in changing popular imagery was Elisha Kirkall. Kirkall was a Yorkshireman, born in Sheffield in about 1692, the son of a locksmith who taught him the art of engraving.[19] He migrated to London in about 1718, where he specialized in small engravings on metal, such as coats of arms, and plates for book illustrations. According to George Vertue, the antiquarian whose notebooks provide the most ample documentation of the artists and printmakers of this period, Kirkall learned to draw in the Academy of Painting in Great Queen Street and devoted himself to the engraving of ornaments in hard metal for books.[20]

That Kirkall was responsible for an innovation whereby

engraving on metal replaced engraving on wood is corroborated by *An Enquiry into the Origins of Printing in Europe*, published in 1752:

> In the beginning of this Century a remarkable Blow was given to all Cutters on Wood, by an invention of engraving on the same sort of Metal which types are cast with. The celebrated Mr. *Kirkhal*, an able Engraver on Copper, is said to be the first who performed a Relievo Work to answer the use of Cutting on Wood. This could be dispatched much sooner, and consequently answered the purpose of Book sellers and Printers, who purchased these sort of Works at a much ch[e]aper Rate than could be expected from an Engraver on Wood.[21]

Once engraving on metal was possible, then the range of graphic imagery could expand.

Kirkall himself provides two of the best popular images of domestic interiors of this period. These appear as illustrations to the fifth edition of *The Works of Thomas Brown (commonly called 'Tom Brown'), Serious and Comical, &c.*, published in 1719.[22] The so-called 'Declamation of Advarbs' shows Tom Brown sitting in the kitchen of a farmhouse. Kirkall illustrates the characteristic features of an ordinary domestic interior with a low table with crude legs, and a straight backed, presumably oak, chair, which would have been decidedly old fashioned by this date. There is a mullioned window in the background and open rafters. One of the interesting features of the engraving is that, despite the rusticity of the scene, there is a certain amount of pottery displayed over the open fire, as well as a jug, a tankard, and a lantern. A second plate from this work represents the astrologer Dr Silvester Partridge sitting at a table, which is acting as his desk. In the background are his books on shelves covered by a hanging curtain, and his chemical apparatus. From the ceiling hangs a stuffed crocodile, a satire on the surroundings of a virtuoso who had interests in a whole range of natural and technical phenomena.

But, as with the other images of interiors in the first two decades of the eighteenth century, it is their very rarity which makes them precious. Popular printmakers had not yet learnt the ways in which an interior could reinforce the characterization of a scene.

Economic Change

Although the first two decades of the eighteenth century were not a period of substantial change in the visual iconography of interiors, it was at this time that attitudes towards them changed importantly. As in any change in the history of manners and social behaviour, it is difficult to trace these changes in attitude with any degree of historical precision: they are elusive aspects of the *mentalité* of the society, not susceptible of precise definition. None the less, it is possible to detect in the first two decades an increasing interest in the concept of a polite society, whose boundaries extended well beyond the court into the gentry, the higher levels of London merchants, and the professions.

There were several reasons for the formation of this concept of a polite society: first, a general increase in income, which meant that more money was available for the purchase of consumer goods; second, an uneasy feeling that social mores might be undermined by an increase in luxury; and third, a change in the moral constraints governing social behaviour. These social changes produced a determination that commercial prosperity should be reflected in improved standards of living and behaviour. Individuals were increasingly judged by the way they spent their money, on how they presented themselves in public, and what they owned.

The background to this change was the tremendous increase in

British commercial wealth. Growth in the economy was combined with a relatively static population and declining prices. An increase in incomes combined with low food prices inevitably meant that more money was available in household budgets to be spent on new consumer goods and a more luxurious standard of living. Thus economic developments fuelled changing attitudes to the appearance of the interior.

The most powerful engine of growth in the economy was overseas trade.[23] In the first part of the seventeenth century trade had been dependent on the export of woollen cloths known as the 'old draperies' to Hamburg and the ports of the Low Countries. Following a slump in trade in the middle of the century, there was a boom in exports during the three decades after the Restoration. Under the protective framework of the Navigation Acts, new markets were opened up not only in the Americas and the Far East, but also in the Baltic, the Mediterranean and the Levant. Cloth exports are thought to have nearly doubled in value between 1660 and 1700 as a result of diversification into the so-called 'new draperies', which were lighter, less durable and more fashionable textiles. Non-textile exports, including metal goods, pottery and glassware, increased even more substantially. According to Henri Misson, 'The principal Merchandizes which *England* sends to other Countries, are all Sorts of Draperies and Woollen Stuffs, Shaggs [pile fabrics], Flannels, Cotton, Tallow, Skins, Hides, Butter, Cheese, Dry'd Fish, Tin, Lead, Iron, Allum, Sea-Coal, Hops, Liquorice, Saffron, Fuller's Earth.'[24]

Alongside the growth in exports there was a corresponding increase in both imports and re-exports. Softwoods, fir, spruce and pine, were imported from Norway for use by the building trades. Silk and cotton were imported by the Levant Company, fine linens came from France and Flanders, and coarse linens from Germany and Holland. Most important of all in changing attitudes to fashion were the imports of the East India Company, which shipped large quantities of exotic cotton goods and porcelain.

Moreover, enormous amounts of sugar, tobacco, dyestuffs and East India silk and calico textiles were re-exported from England to the ports of Europe. It has been calculated that in the 1660s exports were worth £4.1 million, while imports stood at £4.4 million. By the end of the century these figures had been reversed: exports amounted to £6.4 million and imports £5.8 million.

During the last decade of the seventeenth century there were severe problems in the development of the export trade as a result of the Nine Years' War with France. Shipping was requisitioned to assist with the transport of troops abroad. The engagement of the navy in warfare meant that it was not able to provide protection to merchant ships. There was a trade embargo on the import of French goods, and shipping was hindered by the activities of French privateers. Above all, the immense cost of sustaining troops abroad produced a succession of problems in the economy, including a high level of taxation and the clipping of the coinage.

While in the short term the great expense of sustaining military troops on the Continent caused strains in the economy, in the long term the Nine Years' War produced beneficial changes in the organization of finance. The prohibition on the import of French goods compelled British manufacturers to provide substitutes. The Board of Trade was established in 1696 to protect England's trading interests overseas. And a number of financial institutions were established in order to provide the government with credit, of which the most notable was the Bank of England, first established in 1694.[25]

By the first decade of the eighteenth century England's economy was able to sustain the long and complex military operations required by the War of the Spanish Succession. Although the war prolonged the problems with imports, exports rose steeply. There was a substantial increase in the export of woollen textiles and grain to Portugal, of textiles to Russia (especially in the provision of military uniforms to Peter the

Great's armies), of butter, leather and woollens to the Low Countries, and of cloth to Germany.[26] England's naval supremacy allowed her to compete successfully in the new markets which were opening up during this decade; and England's commercial competitors were hit more severely by the ruinous costs of war. The trade figures suggest that in 1700 £6 million of imports were more than balanced by £6.5 million of exports. By 1710, the figure for exports had dropped slightly to £6.3 million, while the figure for imports had dropped substantially to £4 million. In other words, the first decade of the eighteenth century saw a healthy balance of payments, which lubricated the rest of the economy.

Alongside the growth in exports, there was a substantial inland trade which, although it was not as important as overseas trade as an agent of change and did not occupy as much of the attention of contemporary commentators, was at least as important a part of the overall national economy.[27] It has been calculated that in the 1690s the home market, leaving out agricultural products, accounted for £10.5 million out of a total national income of approximately £50 million, or 21 per cent, while exports only accounted for 10 per cent.[28] The staple goods of the inland trade were wheat, barley and malt; coal was shipped down the coast to London from Newcastle; corn was transported down the river Ouse to King's Lynn; Portland stone for use in London building was shipped along the south coast from Poole; and already in 1700 bottles of Nottingham ale were available for sale in London. It was by the networks of inland trade that both imported goods and the products of English manufacture were sold to the home market.

Related to improvements in overseas and internal trade was the increasing specialization and productivity of agriculture. The conditions which Defoe found in the 1720s in the towns were matched by changes in agriculture, of new techniques being employed to increase crop yield, and of experiments with the fertilization of the soil. Defoe observed the market gardens around the cities of London, Norwich and Bristol. In Wiltshire and East Anglia grassland was converted to arable, while in the Weald of Kent and in the Midlands fields were given over to cattle. The profits which were to be made from supplying London enforced a degree of agricultural specialization: Gloucestershire, Warwickshire, Wiltshire and Cheshire supplied London's cheese; Suffolk, Yorkshire and Essex its butter. Long before the much trumpeted agricultural innovations of the great eighteenth-century landlords, there had been substantial changes in agricultural practice. Clovers, new grasses and root crops had been introduced; turnips were cultivated on a large scale.[29]

It is important to appreciate the changes in the national economy in order to understand and interpret what was happening in the domestic interior. For it was the wealth engendered through economic activity that enabled the purchase of new goods to decorate the home. A higher crop yield meant that curtains could be bought at the local market; a good day in the shop meant that money could be laid by for investment in some pewter plates; the trading activity in London produced the circulation of porcelain; changes in manufacture meant that cheaper silks began to be available.

As wealth and spending increased, there was increasing unease about what would now be called conspicuous consumption, and a feeling that luxury and ostentation were sapping the morals of society.

New Commodities

The most visible sign of new wealth, and an obvious target for social criticism, was the import of luxury goods from the Far East. Of course, this was not a new trade. Throughout the seventeenth century, items of Asian manufacture, including porcelain and japanned furniture, had been imported by the East India

Company; but it was not until the first two decades of the eighteenth century that such goods, instead of being treated as rarities, began to be considered relatively commonplace.

The most decorative items of eastern manufacture were the lightweight patterned Indian chintzes, which were used as furnishing fabrics at least as much as items of fashionable dress.[30] One of the early mentions of chintz as an item of interior decoration appears in Pepys's diary when he describes how he went with his wife to a shop in Cornhill, 'and after many tryalls bought my wife a chintz, that is, a painted Indian calico, for to line her new study, which is very pretty'.[31] Queen Mary had a bed covered in chintz at Windsor Castle and, by the first decade of the eighteenth century, there is evidence that chintz was widely available. The fabric lightened the appearance of the domestic interior, providing a welcome contrast to heavier silks and brocades. As Defoe wrote in his *Weekly Review* on 31 January 1708, chintz 'crept into our houses, our closets and bedchambers, curtains, cushions, chairs, and at last beds themselves, were nothing but calicoes and Indian stuffs, and in short everything that used to be made of wool or silk, relating to the dress of the women or the furniture of our house, was supplied by the Indian trade'.[32] Swift likewise satirized the taste of a country squire for things Indian, writing in 1712 how he was now likely to long for 'Mangos, Spices, and Indian Birds' Nests etc., and could not sleep but in a Chintz Bed'.[33]

The second symbol of the Orient in the home was porcelain, which was arranged on the mantelpiece or in corner cupboards. Collecting porcelain as a pastime was not restricted to the nobility, as indicated by the inventory of John Sherwood, a drysalter in London who died in 1703 owning 200 pieces of china and so-called 'tonquin' (a reference to the short-lived factory set up by the East India Company at Tongking on the coast of north Vietnam).[34]

A further addition to the element of exoticism in the early

eighteenth-century interior was japanned furniture. This was now reasonably common, and patterns were sent out to the Far East for British furniture types to be copied. As with chintz and porcelain, japanned furniture must have heightened the awareness of the cultural meanings which might be attached to goods. Where choice of goods is highly restricted, there is not likely to be an awareness of the signals that property could convey; but both porcelain and japanned furniture were purchased to make a statement about the interior in which they were displayed. The volume of trade in japanned furniture is indicated by a petition from the Joiners' Company to Parliament in 1700 to prevent this trade:

> the following Goods, Manufactured in *India*, have been Imported within these four Years, viz. Two Hundred Forty Four Cabinets, Six Thousand five hundred eighty two Tea-Tables, Four hundred twenty eight Chests, Seventy Trunks, Fifty two Screens, Five hundred eighty nine Looking-Glass Frames, Six hundred fifty five Tops for Stands, Eight hundred eighteen Lacquer'd Boards, Five hundred ninety seven Sconces, and Four thousand one hundred twenty Dressing, Comb, and Powder Boxes.[35]

As with the social commentary of Swift and Defoe, these figures should probably be taken with a pinch of salt; but with such a volume of importation, it is hardly surprising that an item of so-called 'Indian' furniture had become a common item in the inventories of the period.

Goods which had been brought to London in the great merchant ships of the East India Company were advertised for sale in the newspapers and sold from the company headquarters at East India House in Leadenhall Street. During the first two decades of the century there were already a number of dealers who specialized in East India wares, many of them based in the New

Exchange in the Strand or in shops on Ludgate Hill and in Fenchurch Street. They sold lacquered cabinets and tea tables, together with tea, chocolate and snuff.[36]

The appearance of the domestic interior was diversified not only by the arrival of luxury goods from the Orient, but also by goods which were manufactured in England. Domestic manufacturers were under pressure to compete with increasingly high standards of production and a more sophisticated awareness of the characteristics of goods.

The most striking change in goods for the home was the availability of silks made in England, which could be used for curtains, wall hangings and bed-coverings.[37] Although not many of the Huguenots who established the silk industry in Spitalfields had worked in the French industry, since the Grandes Fabriques in Lyons were not open to Protestants, they rapidly acquired the necessary skills and, by the beginning of the eighteenth century, home-produced silks were available for sale from the mercers in Cheapside and Covent Garden and on Ludgate Hill. According to a pamphlet published in 1713,

> The Silk Manufacture that was hardly known in *England* Forty Years ago, is, by the Encouragements from the Crown, and Parliament, in Prohibiting the Weaving of *East-India* Wrought Silks, but chiefly from the Interruption of Trade with *France*, now brought to that Perfection, and increas'd to that Degree, that it not only employs a vast Number of Families, Men, Women and Children, by the Throwing, Dying, Winding, Warping, Weaving, and Dressing of the same, but also on many other Accounts, is of very great Advantage to this Kingdom.[38]

Spitalfields grew rapidly as a result of this industry; and the silk industry, more than any other, fostered a consciousness of fashion, with a rapid change in the character of surface patterns and a separation of labour between the so-called 'pattern drawers' and silk weavers.[39]

Other industries which saw a substantial expansion in the first two decades of the eighteenth century were the making of high-quality silver and the more mundane metalworking trades, both of which underwent considerable expansion and specialization during these decades. As with silks, the making of silver was transformed by the skills developed by the Huguenots, skills which seem to have included not only a consciousness of fashion, but also considerable business acumen. Their technical expertise was also applied to other items of the domestic interior, including locks and clocks.

The centre of the metalworking trades in London was in Clerkenwell. In 1710 Zacharias Conrad von Uffenbach recorded how

In the afternoon we went to Cassel Street to a locksmith's, called Westerreich, who is Swiss and makes the best locks in England. I bought a handsome lock for a cabinet from him for two guineas. He showed us various impressions of elegant keys which he had made for gentlemen of high positions. That which he has made for the King of Prussia as Arch-Chamberlain was particularly handsome. He said that he had made twenty fine locks for some hundred and twenty guineas for Prince Eugene's house in Vienna. Finally we bought a contrivance that is very useful on journeys, since it will make fast all such doors as have no locks.[40]

In the Midlands, there was also a rapid expansion in a whole range of small metalworking industries.[41] According to John Crowley, writing in 1717, the iron industry was 'the second manufacture in the Kingdom'. Iron was used on a large scale to make the nails which were required for house construction; but much was also made into other household items, for example locks, brackets and hinges. Moreover, the Midlands metalworkers were also able to produce better-quality fashion items which were sent to London for export. Up until 1710 the majority of references in the metalworking trades are to nail, lock and buckle making; but from 1710 onwards, there is increasing evidence of diversification into other types of metalworking, including japanning and the making of toys and boxes.[42] A political pamphlet published in 1712 boasted of the development of an export trade in these more elaborate wares:

> The extraordinary late Improvement and Nicety in all Sorts of Brass Wares, great and small, in and about London, Birmingham, and divers other Parts of England; and the Capacity and Genius of the English Artificers, is obvious to every common Understanding in England, but has acquired a singular Reputation Abroad, particularly in France, where our English Watches, Clocks, Locks, Buckles, Buttons, and all Sorts of English Brass Toys, are in great esteem, and in Case of Peace we may expect an extraordinary Accession to the Consumption of our Brass Wares.[43]

The most significant change to the appearance of the interior in the first two decades of the eighteenth century was in the diversification of furniture types. In the seventeenth century the range of available furniture had been comparatively small. Inventories list a limited range of furniture types, principally chairs, tables and cupboards. But by the early part of the eighteenth century a whole range of different types of furniture of more specialized function was beginning to be developed. Mirrors of large size were now made in England. Chests of drawers were developed. Bureaux and desks made it possible for businessmen and the mercantile community to organize their working lives. Both tables and chairs proliferated in type and style.

Traditionally the centre of the furniture trade had been round

St Paul's Churchyard. For example, the firm of John and G. Coxed and Thomas Woster had premises at the White Swan in St Paul's Churchyard. Their trade card read:

G. Coxed and T. Woster At the *White Swan*, against the South-Gate in *St. Paul's* Church Yard, *London*, Makes and Sells Cabinets, Scrutoires, Desks and Book-Cases, Buro's Chests of Drawers, Wisk, Ombre, *Dutch* and *Indian* Tea-Tables; All sorts of Looking-Glasses, Large Sconces, Dressing Sets and Wainscot-Work of all sorts, at Reasonable Rates. Old Glasses New polished and Made up fashionable.[44]

Philip Hunt, at the sign of the Looking-Glass and Cabinet, likewise advertised 'Cabenetts, Looking Glasses, Tables and stanns [stands], Seretor, Chests of Drawers, And Curious inlaid Figures for any works'; and William Old and John Ody, cabinetmakers at the Castle, advertised that they made and sold 'all sorts of Cane & Dutch Chairs, Chair Frames for Stuffing and Cane-sashes. And also all sorts of the best Looking-Glass & Cabinet-work in Japan Walnut Tree & Wainscot'.[45] At the same time, it is evident that between 1700 and 1720 there was a marked shift in the location of the furniture trade to the back streets of Covent Garden, with shops in Long Acre and the Strand.[46]

From the trade cards, account books and diaries of the period, it is clear that the new commodities which began to be available in the early years of the eighteenth century were not restricted in their circulation only to the country houses of the nobility. As Peter Earle and Lorna Weatherill have abundantly demonstrated in their studies of domestic inventories, it was precisely in these two decades that a more diverse range of consumer goods began to penetrate into an increased social range of households. On the basis of a statistical analysis of a substantial sample of inventories, Lorna Weatherill has concluded that 'The decade of 1705–15 stands out as the one in which most change took place in both sets of inventories.'[47] Or, as Defoe was to write in 1713 of the house of a London merchant, 'Here I saw, out of a Shopkeeper's House, Velvet Hangings, Embroidered Chairs, Damask Curtains . . . in short, Furniture equal to what, formerly, suffis'd the greatest of our Nobility.'[48]

Attitudes to Luxury

The result of the widespread diffusion of luxury goods into households outside the range of the nobility was a widespread social unease about the moral consequences of increased wealth. Parsons from the pulpit, economic pamphleteers, and writers in the new form of periodical journal commented on, and mostly lamented, the fact that objects and property were no longer able to demarcate social boundaries. This unease inevitably had an impact on aesthetic ideas.

One way of mitigating the effects of such 'vice' was through the exercise of taste. The idea of taste as the means of expression of nobility of spirit is especially evident in the writings of Anthony Ashley Cooper, third Earl of Shaftesbury, an etiolated and asthmatic member of the peerage and an influential commentator on aesthetics.[49] Shaftesbury was the grandson of one of the most venal Restoration politicians. His tutor was the philosopher John Locke. After a spell as an MP in the late 1690s he retreated to his country estates in Dorset and developed a refined and idealized form of Platonism in opposition to Locke's more materialist views. As he wrote to his young protégé, Michael Ainsworth, ''Twas Mr. Locke that struck at all fundamentals, threw all order and virtue out of the world and made the very idea of them . . . *unnatural* and without foundation in our minds.'[50]

Shaftesbury's first work was *An Inquiry concerning Virtue, in Two Discourses*. His attitude to luxury and wealth is already evident in it:

We see the enormous Growth of Luxury in capital Citys, such as have been long the Seat of Empire. We see what Improvements are made in Vice of every kind, where numbers of Men are maintain'd in lazy Opulence, and wanton Plenty. 'Tis otherwise with those who are taken up in honest and sure Imployment, and have been well inur'd to it from their Youth. This we may observe in the hardy remote Provincials, the Inhabitants of smaller Towns, and the industrious sort of common People; where 'tis rare to meet with any Instance of those Irregularitys, which are known in Courts and Palaces, and in the rich Foundations of easy and pamper'd Priests.[51]

All Shaftesbury's writings, initially circulated in manuscript to his friends, were collected together in his *Characteristicks of Men, Manners, Opinions, Times* in 1711, the publication of which he himself supervised to minimize errors and satisfy his hyper-fastidious sensibilities. The *Characteristicks* demonstrates Shaftesbury's optimistic belief that everyone had an innate ability to recognize beauty in exactly the same way that they could moral truth; and that the way to truth might be through the appreciation of beauty.

Although taste was a concept which had been present in French seventeenth-century writings and had antecedents in the Renaissance concept of *gusto*, it was Shaftesbury who gave it an intense moral significance and brought it into the currency of eighteenth-century thinking.[52] As he wrote in the *Characteristicks*, 'The Accomplishment of Breeding is, To learn whatever is *decent* in Company, or *beautiful* in Arts: and the Sum of Philosophy is, To learn what is *just* in Society, and *beautiful* in Nature, and the Order of the World.'[53] For Shaftesbury the possession of taste was the mark of a gentleman, a clear indication of judgement, education and breeding.

The consequence of Shaftesbury's highly idealized view of aesthetics was a belief that both art and architcture should be ordered geometrically in order to obtain a form of harmony.[54] He wrote:

> The senseless part of mankind admire gaudiness: the better sort and those who are good judges admire *simplicity*. Thus in painting, architecture, and other such things, the greatest beauties are what the vulgar despises: and thus even in furniture, habits, instruments, and arms, plainness and simplicity are the most becoming, and are the greatest perfection. For where proportion and exactness are wanting, then it is that there is no need of those additional ornaments; but, where order is preserved and the perfection of art attained, the rest only does prejudice and is an eyesore.[55]

Elsewhere, Shaftesbury writes of 'the inward ornaments of houses, apartments, furniture, the ranging, order, disposition of these matters. What pains! what study! judgment! science!'[56]

It is always difficult to make a direct connection between aesthetic ideas and actual buildings; but it is likely that Shaftesbury's ideas, which were widely known, had an influence on the way people thought about interior decoration, and especially about its relationship to the moral virtues of good taste. In case the connection was not made, Shaftesbury himself wrote a 'Letter concerning Design', which he arranged to have included in the 1714 edition of *Characteristicks*, and in which he discussed the inadequacies of public buildings.

Shaftesbury planned a further set of reflections on the connections between morality and art, of which the 'Letter concerning Design' was to form a part; but he never got beyond a set of miscellaneous notes in which he jotted down his overheated reflections on the way an artist was able to catch 'these fleeting Forms (call 'em the *Effluvia* of *Epicurus* or the *ideas* of Plato)'.[57] Instead he concentrated his attentions on preparing an elaborate second edition of *Characteristicks*, which was published posthumously complete with engraved emblems. By this stage of his career ill health had compelled him to retreat to Naples, travelling through France with elaborate preparations being made for all the windows to be sealed. On 15 February 1713 he died in his house on Chiaia.

An alternative response to the increased materialism of the first two decades of the eighteenth century was not so much to retreat from it, as did Shaftesbury, but instead to attempt to describe it; and by describing it to tame it and give it some form of superior definition. This more ambivalent attitude to material goods, an ironic awareness that society was necessarily undergoing change, is clear in the writings of the periodical journalists Joseph Addison and Richard Steele.[58] The periodical form itself is a symptom of a different type of readership, the casual perusal of short pieces of social commentary in the congenial surroundings of the coffee house. As the first issue of *The Tatler* made clear, it was a vehicle of social instruction informing people how it was appropriate to act, which included the provision of advice on what to wear: 'The general purpose of this paper, is to expose the false arts of life, to pull off the disguises of cunning, vanity and affectation, and recommend a general simplicity in our dress, our discourse, and our behaviour.'[59] Addison and Steele developed this form of journalism with considerable literary skill, an ease and fluency of writing, a continual diversity of subject matter, and an ability to characterize human foibles with sententious irony. They mocked social pretentions. They described the way that individuals displayed themselves through what they owned. They absorbed the plurality of social types into an awareness of the potential range of polite society.

In *The Spectator* no. 299, Addison described the character of John Enville, Knight, who married a Lady Mary Oddley. She 'set her self to reform every Room of my House, having glazed all my Chimney-pieces with Looking-glass, and planted every Corner with such heaps of *China*, that I am obliged to move about my own House with the greatest Caution and Circumspection, for fear of hurting some of our Brittle Furniture.'[60] In *The Spectator* no. 336, Richard Steele described the behaviour of consumers in a china shop:

> I am, dear Sir, one of the top China-Women about Town; and though I say it, keep as good things, and receive as fine Company as any o' this end of the Town, let the other be who she will: In short, I am in a fair way to be easy, were it not for a Club of Female Rakes, who, under Pretence of taking their innocent Rambles forsooth, and diverting the Spleen, seldom fail to plague me twice or thrice a Day, to cheapen Tea or buy a Screen, *what else should they mean?* as they often repeat it. These Rakes are your idle Ladies of Fashion, who have nothing to do, employ themselves in tumbling over my Ware. One of these No-Customers (for by the way they seldom or never buy any thing) calls for a Set of Tea Dishes, another for a Bason, a third for my best Green Tea, and even to the Punch-Bowl, there's scarce a Piece in my Shop but must be displac'd and the whole agreeable Architecture disorder'd, so that I can compare 'em to nothing but to the Night-Goblins that take a Pleasure to over-turn the Disposition of Plates and Dishes in the Kitchens of your housewifely Maids.[61]

The satire is gentle, the tone one of amused detachment. Addison and Steele were adept at describing the early flowering of consumer psychology.

A third social commentator of the early 1700s who responded to the flood of new consumer goods into the home was the expatriate Dutch doctor Bernard Mandeville.[62] In his well known tract *The Fable of the Bees* he adopted a much more cynical interpretation of what was happening in society. The subtitle of *The Fable of the Bees* − *Private vices, public virtues* − encapsulated its philosophy. Mandeville believed that humans were essentially motivated by greed and pride, and that it was better to be realistic and acknowledge the fact than to be hypocritical and deplore it. *The Fable of the Bees* recognized that the increased luxury evident in early eighteenth-century England was merely a symptom of human industry, fuelled by desire.

These ideas were not entirely new. Economic writers in the 1690s had already begun to explore the links between the requirements of national trade and the desire for luxury. Nicholas Barbon, the great entrepreneur who was responsible for much of the reconstruction of London in the last decades of the seventeenth century, was one of the first writers to acknowledge that fashion might be a beneficial influence in the development of the economy. In his book *A Discourse of Trade* he wrote that

> Fashion or the alteration of Dress, is a great Promoter of Trade, because it occasions the Expense of Cloaths, before the Old ones are worn out: It is the Spirit and Life of Trade; It makes a Circulation, and gives a Value, by Turns, to all sorts of Commodities; keeps the great Body of Trade in Motion.[63]

What Mandeville did was to take up these ideas and to express them with a startling, and to most people highly distasteful, pungency.

Because Mandeville regarded vice as essential to the successful working of society, he did not deplore the display of luxury, but positively welcomed it. He admired the self-interested and hedonistic members of the 'beau monde'. He rejected the idea that there might be a correct standard for consumption. As he wrote,

> If the wants of Men are innumerable, then what ought to supply them has no bounds; what is call'd superfluous to some degree of People will be thought requisite to those of higher

Quality; and neither the World nor the Skill of Man can produce any thing so curious or extravagant, but some most Glorious Sovereign or other, if it either eases or diverts him, will reckon it among the Necessaries of Life; not meaning every Body's Life, but that of his Sacred Person.[64]

As a result of his ideas Mandeville welcomed the superfluity of material culture as a symptom of the social benefits of greed:

The greatest Excesses of Luxury are shewn in Buildings, Furniture, Equipage and Cloaths; clean Linnen weakens a Man no more than Flannel, Tapistry, fine Painting or good Wainscot are no more unwholesome than bare Walls; and a rich Couch, or a gilt Charriot are no more enervating than the cold Floor or a Country Cart.[65]

Thus a complex set of attitudes to the flood of new consumer goods into the home is reflected throughout the writings of the first two decades of the eighteenth century. It was the key issue for writers to come to terms with. As a result commodities became politicized, tokens of a whole attitude towards society. Instead of the interior being a neutral space for the display of private possessions, it became a public vehicle for a statement of the position of the individual in society. It was a conscious articulation of a moral idea.

1720–1740

Architectural Drawings

By 1720 a convention for the illustration of houses had been established. They were drawn in a cutaway section showing the decoration of the main rooms, including the panelling and where the pictures would hang, but not the furniture. This convention had been used by Colen Campbell in some of the plates of his architectural publication *Vitruvius Britannicus, or the British Architect*, the first volume of which was published in 1715, the second in 1718, and the third in 1725.[1]

Before *Vitruvius Britannicus* the standard way of illustrating country houses had been to show them in bird's-eye perspective, surrounded by their gardens and estates: the emphasis was on what the house looked like from a distance and on showing its relationship to its surroundings. The most important artist in this genre was Leonard Knyff, a Dutchman who settled in Westminster in 1690 and who travelled the country drawing houses, which were then engraved for publication by Jan Kip.[2] *Vitruvius Britannicus* marked a decisive shift in methods of reproduction, whereby houses were shown in a much more austere form of line engraving, demonstrating their qualities of geometry and proportion, as opposed to their location. This graphic convention indicated the extent to which architects were beginning to switch their attention both to a more rigid and linear form of composition in exterior façades and to a greatly enriched form of interior decoration.

During the early 1720s Campbell was employed in the design of Mereworth Castle in Kent for the Hon. John Fane, a former lieutenant-colonel of the Thirty-Seventh Foot, who had served at the battle of Malplaquet.[3] It was built in the style of a Palladian villa and Campbell submitted a drawing which shows the self-consciously architectural character of the interior, with an elaborate coffered dome in the central rotunda and severe doorcases. According to John Loveday, an antiquarian who visited Mereworth in 1730,

> Colonel Fane, Brother to the Earl of Westmorland, has built an Italian House at Merryworth, with great expence. You ascend to it by a great flight of Stone Steps, under which are part of the Offices. A vast Portico on every side the House, so that there are four Fronts exactly alike, but Steps up to only one. The Windows are very small. A Cupolo very large, seemingly too large for the size of the House, as are also the Porticos. The Rooms below are lofty, above very low. The Servants lie in the four Rooms over the Porticos. Above there are some of the Bed-Chambers, others below Stairs. The Passage, and Hall under the Cupolo, have a Floor of Red Plaister. There is no Grand Stair-Case; two go up from the Hall and lead you to a Gallery round it, in which are the Passages to the Rooms. You see no Chimnies on the Outside, for the Smoke is conveyed through Leaden Pipes, which are as Ribs to the Cupolo; at the top of which the Smoke of the whole House goes out.[4]

This description demonstrates the extent to which the decision to model buildings on strictly Palladian lines introduced a transformation in the way that interiors were laid out, with more complex arrangements of rooms dictated by the rigidity of having to imitate Italian prototypes.

More important than Campbell in developing a suitable ornamental vocabulary for the decoration of neo-Palladian villas was William Kent. During the 1720s Kent turned from the practice of decorative painting, in which he had an indifferent talent, to the design of furniture and rooms, at which he was extremely skilful.[5]

Kent was born in Yorkshire in the mid-1680s. According to George Vertue, he 'unexpectedly demonstrated his youthfull inclination to drawing' and is said to have been apprenticed to a house painter. On account of his evident talent, he was taken up by the local gentry and sent to Italy in company with John Talman. In Rome he trained as a painter in the studio of Benedetto Luti and, on 23 May 1713, he came second in the second class for painting in the prizes awarded by the Academy of St Luke. He then worked as an agent on behalf of members of the nobility on their Grand Tour, purchasing modern paintings, prints and books and Antique statuary and arranging for their shipment back to England. He did not return to England until 1719, by which time he had a more cosmopolitan knowledge of Rome and Italian painting than most of his English contemporaries, and had already demonstrated a conspicuous ability to ingratiate himself with members of the peerage.[6]

On his return to England Kent took up residence in Burlington House in Piccadilly, where he taught Lady Burlington to draw and entertained Lord Burlington's friends with his absurdly affected Italianate manners, as well as assisting Lord Burlington in his various architectural projects. Kent's aristocratic connections gained him the commission to paint the interiors of Kensington Palace, instead of Thornhill. His figurative paintings were fairly atrocious, but he also did a certain amount of decoration in what was described as the 'grotesque' style, that is, in imitation of an ancient Roman style of decoration, which had been revived in

Renaissance Italy by Raphael, Vasari and Giovanni da Udine and was known especially from the Vatican *loggie*. Perhaps recognizing his limitations as a painter, Kent soon turned to the practice of architecture, and especially to the design of interiors.

The first indication of Kent's work as a designer appears in the accounts of Kensington Palace, where between 1723 and 1725 James Moore the elder carried out William Kent's designs for furniture in the so-called 'new apartment'. In 1727 Kent was asked to prepare proposals for the interiors at Kensington Palace, which was to include 'drawing the sides of the Drawing room with all the pictures sketched in their proper colours, designing and drawing the moulding and ornaments for all the picture-frames, glasses, etc., for drawing the gallery with all the pictures sketched in proper colours, the frames drawn with their orna-ments at large'.[7]

At some time around 1726, Kent was asked to provide advice on the interior decoration of Sir Robert Walpole's great new mansion in Norfolk, which had been designed by Colen Campbell and built under the aegis of Thomas Ripley, the Master Carpenter in the Office of Works. Among Kent's surviving drawings for Houghton is a preliminary design for the Cabinet Room, which shows the walls of the room folded out so that it is possible to see their relationship to the coffered ceiling. Houghton set new standards of interior magnificence and was much visited and admired by contemporaries. According to Lord Hervey writing to Frederick, Prince of Wales on 14 July 1731,

The base, or rustic story, is what is chiefly inhabited at the Congress. There is a room for breakfast, another for supper, another for dinner, another for afternooning, and the great arcade with four chimneys for walking and quid-nuncing. The rest of this floor is merely for use, by which your Royal Highness must perceive that the whole is dedicated to fox-hunters, hospitality, noise, dirt and business. The next is the floor of taste, expense, state and parade. The first room is a hall, a cube of 40 foot finished entirely with stone, a gallery of stone round it and the ceiling of stucco, the best executed of anything I ever saw in stucco in any country. The ornaments over the chimney and doors are bas-reliefs of stone; round the sides marble bustos, and over against the chimney the famous group of Laocoon and his two Sons. Behind the hall is the salon, finished in a different taste, hung, carved and gilt large glasses between the windows, and some of his finest pictures round the three other sides of the room (this room looks to the garden). On the left hand of the hall and salon, this floor is divided into a common eating room, a library, a dressing room, a bed-chamber, and with-drawing room for ordinary use; and on the right hand (which is the only part yet unfinished) is to be the great dining room, and the State apartment. The furniture is to be green velvet and tapestry, Kent designs of chimneys, the marble gilded and modern ornaments. Titian and Guido supply those that are borrowed from antiquity. The great staircase is the gayest, cheerfulest and prettiest thing I ever saw; some very beautiful heresies in the particulars, and the result of the whole more charming than any bigotry I ever saw. The upper or attic story is divided all into lodging-rooms.[8]

Lord Hervey's meticulous and detailed description of the layout of the interiors at Houghton, coupled with his sardonic epistolary style, makes it possible to imagine the original effect of the Houghton interiors. Kent's work at Houghton was illustrated in Isaac Ware's *Plans, Elevations and Sections of Houghton*, published in 1735.

In 1727 Kent was responsible for the publication of *The Designs of Inigo Jones*, which had been commissioned by Richard Boyle, third Earl of Burlington. To the authentic designs of Inigo Jones, Kent added a number of his own and Lord Burlington's, including the side of a cube room and the octagonal hall at Chiswick.

Work on a new villa at Chiswick had begun in 1726. On 7 May 1727 Sir John Clerk of Penicuik wrote in his diary that he

> went with my cousin Mr Aikman to Chiswick and was very kindly entertained by my Lord Burlington at dinner. His Lordship's good taste appeared here in many Shapes. He is building a new house 70 foot square, all in the ancient manner, of which there is a drawing published. Yet this house is rather curious than convenient.[9]

By 1728 Sir John Evelyn was able to write that 'his Lordship has lately built but not finish an Italian house with a Cupolo, Portico, & Octagonall hall near his old house'.[10] Compared to the restrained exterior façades at Chiswick the interiors are extraordinarily ornate, with richly coffered ceilings and heavy door surrounds. There is a sense that at least as much effort was expended on the interior disposition of space, on how people would move through and react to the rooms, as on the composition of the façades. The Italianate style of the decoration and its ornate character were the responsibility of William Kent.[11]

During the 1730s Kent continued to advise members of the nobility on the layout of their houses and on the design of individual pieces of furniture. As he wrote to Theophilus, Earl of Huntingdon on 3 August 1734, 'if I can be of service, I shall always be ready to give my advice . . .'[12] His designs were richly overloaded with classical imagery and were criticized by the Earl of Oxford as consisting of 'a great deal of gilding, very clumsy over-charged chimneypieces to the great waste of marble'.[13] This is a fair characterization of his work, as published in John Vardy's *Some Designs of Mr. Inigo Jones and Mr. William Kent* in 1744. But the importance of Kent historically is not so much in the individual work which he designed as in his role as an artistic adviser to the members of the nobility – an oleaginous Yorkshire-man who thought that he knew how interiors should be laid out better than they did themselves. He can be regarded as an interior decorator interposing himself between client and decoration.

The Origins of the Conversation Piece

The most significant development in the two decades from 1720 to 1740 was not any change in the conventions of architectural drawing, but the new vogue for the conversation piece, a system of representation which showed individuals in their social environment.

The conventions of portraiture in the first two decades of the eighteenth century, associated most obviously with the work of Sir Godfrey Kneller, had dictated that the persons represented were placed in the foreground in a style that was hieratic and mainly concerned with showing the individual in the guise of social authority. The conventions of representation did not extend into an investigation of the background scene.[14]

The first suggestions of any change to this convention of a nonspecific social setting comes in paintings of artists' studios. In 1695 an unknown artist who was clearly influenced by Dutch paintings of interiors depicted the room in which he received and painted sitters;[15] and in 1716 the Flemish artist Peter Tillemans painted his studio.[16] The Tillemans clearly belongs to a different convention of portraiture from the standard images of the early eighteenth-century nobility and gentry: it is the self-portrait of the artist advertising the accoutrements of his trade, with miscellaneous pieces of statuary strewn around the room. It is particularly interesting to note the contrast and comparison of the two modes of showing curtains, the fictive curtain revealing the scene and the much more realistically depicted draw-curtain pulled sideways across a sash window, with the heavy glazing bars characteristic of the period.[17]

The other artist who began to explore a different convention of illustration in the first two decades of the eighteenth century was the younger Marcellus Laroon, whose father was a painter of the same name, described by Bainbridge Buckeridge as 'fam'd for Pictures in Little, commonly call'd Conversation-Pieces'.[18] After travelling on the Continent, the younger Laroon entered the army, first with the Foot Guards and subsequently as a lieutenant in the Royal Scots regiment.[19] When his regiment was disbanded in 1712 he returned to London and received instruction at the newly established Academy of Painting in Great Queen Street. In 1715 he went back into the army, but continued to produce occasional sketches, particularly, according to Vertue, 'painting & drawing. conversation. in small with much variety & pleasant entertainment of musick'.[20]

The most interesting painter of conversation pieces in the 1720s was another Flemish artist, Joseph van Aken, who was born in Antwerp in about 1699 and came to England at some time around the year 1720, with his brothers Arnold and Alexander.[21] Van Aken became one of the leading drapery painters in the 1730s and 1740s. According to George Vertue, writing in 1737, he excelled in painting 'particularly the postures for painters of portraits who send their pictures when they have done the faces, to be drest and decorated by him. in which he has a very ready Talent'.[22] Horace Walpole commented more sarcastically that 'as in England almost every body's picture is painted, so almost every painter's works were painted by Vanaken'.[23] Before he discovered that it was considerably more lucrative to work for other painters – or possibly as a diversion from his everyday work – van Aken painted a number of genre scenes in an obviously Dutch style. They are all customarily dated to *c.* 1720, but given that van Aken only came to the country around then, the date provides no more than a *terminus post quem*. His work is intriguing, and much more visually engaging than the run-of-the-mill portraits of the period.

Van Aken's *oeuvre* includes an *Interior of an Alehouse*, a luminous depiction of an eighteenth-century interior, full of genre details such as the serving woman standing in her booth, the group of gentlemen playing what appears to be backgammon, and the solidly constructed table and chair, completely outside the stereotypical idea of furniture of this period; and the better-known *English Family at Tea* in the National Gallery, which gives a good idea of the mode of grouping round a tea equipage, as well as showing the various items of the tea service, including the pot and its stand and the handleless cups, in microscopic detail. He also painted a number of scenes of ordinary domestic interiors, as distinct from those of the nobility and gentry. The best of these, entitled *Grace before a Meal*, shows all the trappings of such an interior: the pewter plates balanced rather precariously on a small wooden table; the two-pronged fork and a knife for cutting up the meat; some earthenware bowls ranged round the room; the stone floor. Although it may be idealized and follows the conventions of previous Dutch art, it does help one to imagine the appearance of interiors away from the country house circuit.

By the early 1730s there were a number of artists specializing in the genre of the conversation piece; but, unlike van Aken, they worked to commission and concentrated on the representation of the nobility. The most popular was Charles Philips, who in 1730 painted a tea party at Lord Harrington's house. William Stanhope, first Earl of Harrington, was a successful diplomat, who had served as ambassador to Spain in the early 1720s and been raised to the peerage in 1729. The painting shows his friends assembled in his house 'in ye Stable Yard, St. James's', sitting at different tables, playing cards or drinking tea.[24] The figures are all of a curiously different scale, like dummy-boards stuck into an empty stage scene.

Another artist specializing in the genre in the 1730s was Gawen Hamilton, a Scottish artist, born near Hamilton, trained under an obscure bird painter called Wilson, and who then set up as a portrait painter in London at some time around 1730. According to George Vertue, writing on Hamilton's death in 1737, he specialized in 'family peeces'. The characteristics of his style are shown by two group portraits in the Yale Center for British Art, one being *The Brothers Clarke with other Gentlemen Taking Wine* and the other *A Group Portrait of the Raikes Family*. They share an identical composition, with both groups sitting round a small circular table covered in a green baize cloth and drinking wine. In the picture of the Brothers Clarke a servant is fetching an additional bottle of wine from a large wine cooler under the side table in the corner of the room; in the portrait of the Raikes family a servant is opening the wine. The faces are devoid of character. Instead, the scenes are animated by the social action, the way that in both a curtain is lifted to the right of the painting to reveal a small tableau of a group acting out a particular form of social relationship. The focus of artistic interest has been transferred during the course of the first three decades of the eighteenth century from the representation of dominant individuals in the trappings of rank to that of social groups in an accurately rendered situation.

Hogarth was clearly instrumental in fostering the fashion for this genre of group portraits in an appropriate domestic setting. In January 1729 Vertue commented on 'The daily success of Mr Hogarth in painting small family pieces & Conversations with so much Air & agreeableness Causes him to be much followd, & esteemd. whereby he has much imployment & like to be a master of great reputation in that way'.[25] Between 1728 and 1731 he is reckoned to have painted at least two dozen such pictures.

Hogarth's most famous work in this idiom is *The Assembly at Wanstead House*. According to the Hogarth manuscripts in the British Museum this picture was commissioned on 28 August 1729, but was still unfinished on 1 January 1731, the length of time taken presumably being due to the number of portraits which were to be incorporated into the scene. It shows the Tory plutocrat Sir Richard Child, Viscount Castlemain, sitting on a tremendously elaborate carved and gilt chair, in the style associated with William Kent, in front of a slightly preposterous silvered tea table. It is not known how accurate a depiction this is of the interior of Sir Richard Child's famous mansion at Wanstead, but it demonstrates the nature of the decoration of its state apartments, described by John Macky in his *Journey through England in Familiar Letters from Gentleman Here to his Friend Abroad*: they included four sets of apartments on the ground floor, one for Lord Castlemain, one for his wife, and a third 'for the Entertainment of their Friends'; while upstairs there was a Great Hall and a Saloon facing the garden, with five rooms of state on either side.[26] Presumably Hogarth's portrait had to be sufficiently realistic to satisfy the patron; but, as with many of Hogarth's paintings, his ostensibly serious work teeters on the brink of social satire.[27]

Other works by Hogarth in this genre include a group portrait of the Wollaston family, described by Vertue as 'really a most excellent work containing the true likeness of the persons, shape aire & dress – well disposd. genteel, agreable. – & freely painted & the composition great variety & Nature'.[28] William Wollaston did not belong to the same social category as Viscount Castlemain, but came from a family of wealthy Suffolk gentry, descendants of Elizabethan wool merchants; in 1728, he married Elizabeth Fauquier, daughter of the Deputy Master of the Mint and Governor of the Bank of England. He was prosperous enough not to mind being represented in a room with Corinthian pilasters and a painted ceiling, from which hung a silver candelabrum; ornate, squat, round-backed chairs; a portrait bust over the chimneypiece; and a marginally less ornate silvered tea table than is represented in the Wanstead Assembly.

In 1732, Hogarth painted *The Cholmondeley Family* and began work on *The Performance of The Indian Emperor or The Conquest of Mexico by the Spaniards*, which was still not complete in 1735. These two paintings show how Hogarth was able to exploit a restricted pictorial convention and animate not only the sitters, who are very much more like social actors than stuffed dummies, but also the setting which is, on the one hand, made to articulate the pictorial space and, on the other, to define in an emblematic way the status and character of the sitters. There is a successful fusion of group with setting. Nor was Hogarth working in a bourgeois convention. George Cholmondeley, Viscount Malpas, was the heir to the earldom of Cholmondeley and to Cholmondeley Castle in Cheshire, and described by Horace Walpole as 'a vain empty man, shoved up too high by his father-in-law, Sir Robert Walpole, and fallen into contempt and obscurity by his own extravagance and insufficiency'. The performance of *The Indian Emperor or The Conquest of Mexico by the Spaniards* took place in the household of the Master of the Mint, John Conduitt. According to Dr Clarke, writing to Mrs Clayton on 22 April 1732,

> Mr. Conduit came into this country with Sir Andrew Fountain for two days in Easter-week, but I did not see him. I am told he is going to have a conversation-piece drawn by Hogarth, of the young people of quality that acted at his house; and if I am not mistaken he hopes to have the honour of the Royal part of the audience in the picture.[29]

The child actors include Lord Lempster, heir to the Earldom of Pomfret, and the daughter of the Duke of Richmond, Lady Catherine Lennox; while amongst the audience are the Duke of Richmond and the Earl of Pomfret, and the royal children, William, Duke of Cumberland, and the Princesses Mary and Louisa, a reasonably glittering assembly, dressed appropriately for the occasion, seated on ornate, low-back chairs, in a room with pictures hung in a curiously arbitrary way across the panelling.

Having identified the characteristics of a highly specific and significant shift in the nature of the artistic representation of the individual's relationship to the physical and social ambience, it is worth considering the question of why this particular genre of the conversation piece came into fashion when it did, around the year 1730.

There are several possible answers. The first is to attribute the popularity of conversation pieces to the vigour and artistic enterprise of Hogarth himself, as an entrepreneur in a new field of artistic endeavour, exploiting the market for art with a fresh pictorial commodity. There is plenty of evidence to support this explanation, which is the one favoured in the secondary literature, since it conforms both to Hogarth's own forceful self-image of a lone and heroic individual battling against the forces of established artistic convention, and to the traditional preference of art historians to view the development of art as a teleology in which great individual painters make significant entrances, thereby adjusting the range of artistic possibilities.

It is possible to argue that Hogarth was able to escape from the established genre of artistic representation because of his unconventional training as an engraver of ornament on silver. He had been apprenticed in 1712 to Ellis Gamble, of Cranbourne Street in Leicester Fields who, according to his trade card, 'bought and sold plate, rings, jewels etc.', but who seems to have operated primarily as an outworker for the more established goldsmiths whose marks were entered at Goldsmiths' Hall. This early experience would have given Hogarth a realistic sense of the social connotations of artefacts, and of the motivation which led aristocratic customers to purchase elaborately engraved silver; so, by extension, he would have known what were the social signals of artefacts displayed in a London house. In the early 1720s Hogarth was forced to scratch a living as a hack engraver of book illustrations and trade cards and of ornament, so that he must have had an unusually astute perception of the precise resonances of different styles of artefact, which made him well equipped to introduce a greater element of social realism into the representation of the relationship of commodities to their owners. This is the explanation provided by Vertue, who wrote in his notebook in 1729 that

> Mr. William Hogarth first learnt to grave armes on Silver. plate &c. from thence study'd in the Accademy St. Martins lane, some time having a quick lively genius made several Charica-tures. prints etch'd afterwards the designs & plates of Hudibras. but finding it more agreable to his mind, took up the pincill & applyd his studyes to painting in small conversations. or fancyes. wherein he now has much reputation.[30]

According to Vertue, the origin of conversation pieces lay in individual whim and the movement of Hogarth out of book illustration into a version of portrait painting in which character was represented by physical surroundings. Hogarth himself described how dissatisfaction with engraving 'made him turn his head to painting portrait figures from 10 to 15 inches high, often in subjects of conversation. It had some novelty . . . it gave more scope to fancy than the common portrait.' Here, the key words are 'fancy', in the sense popularized by Addison in *The Spectator* to mean the pleasures of the imagination, and 'novelty', a word with a powerful currency in the commerce of the early eighteenth century.

The second explanation as to why conversation pieces came into fashion in the late 1720s lays stress less on the dynamic impact of Hogarth's intervention in St Martin's Lane Academy and more on the long-term evolution of artistic convention. The exploita-tion of the conversation piece is seen not so much as a novelty, but more as a logical extension of existing artistic precedents, whereby Hogarth merely took up and applied ideas and artistic practices which were already generally current. This was George Vertue's argument when he came to survey the development of the conversation piece in October 1737 by relating it to 'conversations done above a hundred years ago – by Teniers

Brower Breugil Watteau and some of those flemish Masters of the Schoolars of Rubens Vandyke and indeed some painters lately here'.[31] This, in Vertue's characteristically random and haphazard way, outlines all the major artistic precedents which lie behind the British convention of the conversation piece: the small-scale family groups which had been painted throughout the seventeenth century in Flanders and Holland; the informal group portraiture popularized by Watteau in France in his *fêtes galantes*; and the way these two artistic conventions were imported into England by immigrant artists such as the Flemings Egbert van Heemskerk and Peter Angellis, and by the French Huguenot Philippe Mercier, who came to England from Berlin and who painted conversation pieces in England in 1725.[32] These are the artistic antecedents traced in the one substantial monograph on conversaion pieces, Ralph Edwards's *Early Conversation Pictures;*[33] and this is the argument which has been reiterated in the art-historical literature ever since: that conversation pictures are an amalgam of two artistic traditions, Dutch social realism and French *fêtes galantes*, which were popularized by foreign artists working in England in the early 1720s.

So there are two rival accounts of the origin of the conversation piece, one relating it to individual initiative, the other to artistic precedent. Both accounts, doubtless, contain a measure of truth and they are not completely discrepant; but both are, in different ways, unsatisfactory as complete explanations of a particular artistic phenomenon. First, it is clear that Hogarth was not alone in exploiting this genre of group portraiture, so that any explanation which lays too much stress on his individual initiative is liable to be found wanting when it comes to investigating the wider ramifications of the fashion; it may explain why Hogarth began to produce small group portraits, but it does not in any way help one to understand why people commissioned, purchased and presumably enjoyed such works. Second, although there were clearly diverse international precedents for the British convention of conversation pieces, this does not explain why, at a particular historical juncture, native-born artists picked up these strands of artistic practice and synthesized them into a novel version of the convention, one which was sufficiently distinct from the work of foreigners for Mrs Pendarves (later Mrs Delany) to write to Mrs Granville on 13 July 1731:

> I am grown passionately fond of Hogarth's painting, there is more sense in it than any I have seen . . . I have released Lady Sunderland from her promise of giving me her picture by Zinck, to have it done by Hogarth. I think he takes a much greater likeness, and that is what I shall value my friend's picture for, more than for the excellence of the painting.[34]

This passage indicates that the desire for representations of individuals in appropriate surroundings was not just an invention of artists, but indicates a new interest on the part of their sitters. There was a new and insistent public demand around the year 1730 for realism in the depiction both of character and of social setting.

New Buildings

There are several ways of seeing a change in the material environment which might help to account for the change in its perception. The first is in the sheer amount of building which was going on during the 1720s.

In 1959, in the first attempt to quantify building, Sir John Summerson identified the early 1720s as a period of boom in the building of country houses. He wrote: 'It is quite easy to compile a list of about 150 large country houses built in England between 1710 and 1740, the majority being securely dated and their builders and sometimes their designers known. If we arrange these houses in chronological order (date of commencement being preferred to date of completion) we are faced at once with a most striking phenomenon. Out of 148 houses, 21 are datable to 1710–14, 22 to 1715–19, but no fewer than 50 to 1720–24.'[35] The increase in building projects was not simply a proliferation of grandiose villas or pseudo-country houses into an extended metropolitan area. In Shropshire, for example, many of the old-established county families were embarking on new building projects: John Kynaston, the head of an ancient Shropshire family and leader of the Shropshire Tories under Queen Anne, commissioned a new house at Hardwick; the Revd Richard Hill, who inherited valuable estates at Hawkstone, built a new house during this decade; William Lacon Childe, another Tory Member of Parliament, commissioned Francis Smith to build Kinlet Hall in 1727.

The broad pattern of country house building during the 1720s is reasonably clear. Members of the peerage were substantially involved in building: George Lee, the second Earl of Lichfield, for whom Ditchley in Oxfordshire was built; the fourth Earl of Scarsdale, for whom Sutton Scarsdale in Derbyshire was designed in 1724 by Francis Smith; and Richard Boyle, third Earl of Burlington, who designed Chiswick for himself, if this is to be included in the category of country houses. Equally striking is the extent to which the new building projects were by peers of recent creation, such as Robert Bertie, first Duke of Ancaster, for whom Grimsthorpe in Lincolnshire was built, and John Wallop, who was made Earl of Portsmouth after his building of Marlow Place in Buckinghamshire; also, how many of these building projects by members of the nobility were not flamboyant, large houses at the centre of landed estates, but more modest and more self-consciously architectural houses, like Sudbrook Park in Petersham, designed by James Gibbs for the Duke of Argyll. What one is witnessing is a subtle, but distinctive, shift away from the hegemony of the landed élite exercising their power through the House of Lords.

This same process of a shift of the locus of power away from the old nobility is reflected in the substantial number of members of the House of Commons who built houses in the 1720s, including such professional politicians as Henry Pelham, who employed Nicholas Dubois, described as 'the French son of a bitch', to design Stanmer House outside Brighton in Sussex; Horatio Walpole, who employed Thomas Ripley to plan a new house at Wolterton in Norfolk; and Sir Robert Walpole himself, who built Houghton.

Continuing this social analysis of the people who were engaged in country house building during the 1720s, there is a small but significant increase in the amount of new money which was spent on new building projects. This category includes Henry Hoare, of the great London banking family, for whom Colen Campbell designed the Palladian villa at Stourhead; John Lade, a prosperous Southwark brewer and a director of the South Sea Company, who built Cralle Place at Warbleton in Sussex; Benjamin Styles, who built Moor Park in Hertfordshire; Sir Gregory Page, who inherited a vast fortune from his father, made in trade with China and the East Indies, and spent it in the building of Wricklemarsh in Blackheath; and John Morse, the bachelor London banker, who built Woodperry House in Oxfordshire.

This boom in the building of country houses in the early 1720s, parallel to and presumably sparked off by the financial speculation surrounding the South Sea Bubble, was accompanied by an equal and rapid boom in London speculative housing.[36] In 1717 Lord Burlington was permitted by a private Act of Parliament to develop his estate bordering Piccadilly. It included General Wade's house and Queensbury House at the corner of Savile Row and Burlington Gardens. The area round Hanover Square was being developed by Lord Scarborough, and much of the Grosvenor estate was laid out during this period. North of Oxford

Street, Edward Harley, second Earl of Oxford, was involved in a large area of building around Cavendish Square. When Defoe came to survey London for his *Tour through the Whole Island of Great Britain*, first published in 1724, he was amazed by the extent to which it had grown in living memory and especially in recent years:

> The increase of buildings here, is really a kind of prodigy; all the buildings north of Long Acre, up to the Seven Dials, all the streets, from Leicester-Fields and St. Martin's-Lane, both north and west, to the Hay-Market and Soho, and from the Hay-Market to St. James's-street inclusive, and to the park wall; then all the buildings on the north side of the street, called Picadilly, and the road to Knight's-Bridge, and between that and the south side of Tyburn Road [Oxford Street], including Soho-Square, Golden-Square, and now Hanover-Square, and that new city on the north side of Tyburn Road, called Cavendish-Square, and all the streets about it. This last addition is, by calculation, more in bulk than the cities of Bristol, Exeter and York, if they were all put together; all which places were, within the time mentioned, meer fields of grass, and employ'd only to feed cattle as other fields are.[37]

What this rapid boom in property speculation produced was a large chunk of London, all of which was brand new, demonstrating a sharp contrast between the old street patterns of the City and the ostentation of the new West End.

This was the period when the classic form of English town house developed, with origins in the housing developed after the Fire of London.[38] Its characteristic feature was its strongly vertical organization of space, with a differentiation of the functions of the house into separate layers. All houses, whatever their scale, tended to have a narrow street frontage and to be at least two storeys high, plus a cellar for storage and a garret used either for work or for servants' bedrooms. They were also almost invariably built on the principle of having two rooms on each floor, a relatively large one at the front and a smaller one at the rear. The extent to which the staircase was used as the principal means of access to rooms meant that expense was often lavished on it. The rooms, in comparison to the stateliness of the staircase, are apt to appear surprisingly small.

The vertical division of space in these London houses compels a correspondingly sharp division of activities between eating, sleeping, work and entertainment. The most usual arrangement of an ordinary house, as shown by a study of inventories, was to use the ground floor as shop or work space, with convenient access out into the street and to a yard behind, and the first floor for kitchen and dining room, and to have at least one other floor for bedrooms. Some people needed only one work room on the ground floor, in which case the room at the back was likely to be used as a kitchen. Inevitably there was a certain amount of variation in the use of rooms, particularly as some were likely to be let to lodgers.[39] The quality and character of new building in London was commented on by foreign visitors. César de Saussure remarked on the occasion of his visit to England in 1725:

> I must own that Englishmen build their houses with taste; it is not possible to make a better use of ground, or to have more comfortable houses. It is surprising to see in what a small space they will build, and in what an incredibly short time. The houses are [made] of bricks; the walls are thin, most of them having only one foot and a half thickness. The finest houses sometimes have cornices and borders to divide the floors, and round the doors and windows you occasionally see a sort of polished marble. In all the newly-built quarters the houses have one floor made in the earth, containing the kitchens, offices, and servants' rooms. This floor is well lighted, and has as much air as the others have. In order to accomplish this a sort of moat,

five or six feet in width and eight or nine deep, is dug in front of all the houses, and is called the 'area'. This moat is edged on the side next the street with an iron railing. The cellars and vaults where coal is stored are very strongly built beneath the streets, and to reach them you cross the area. Hangings are little used in London houses on account of the coal smoke, which would ruin them, besides which woodwork is considered to be cleaner and prevents damp on the walls. Almost all the houses have little gardens or courtyards at the back.[40]

New building projects were not confined to London. This is the period which Peter Borsay has described as 'the English urban renaissance', when new urban and civic values were expressed in a more polite form of architecture.[41] Throughout the country houses were being built to a more consistent standard of design, with a greater awareness of what Richard Neve described as the 'Principal Qualities' of the modern method of building, 'viz. *Compactness, Uniformity*, and *Conveniency*'.[42]

These developments in housing construction were fuelled by a proliferation in the number of publications devoted to the arts of building during the 1720s and 1730s, which brought a greater awareness of the principles of building and inevitably a greater self-consciousness in the choice of how houses could and should be laid out.[43] As Batty Langley wrote in his *The City and Country Builder's and Workman's Treasury of Designs*, published in 1745,

The great Pleasure that Builders and Workmen of all Kinds have of late Years taken in the Study of Architecture; and the great Advantages that have accrued to those, for whom they have been employed; by having their Works executed in a much neater and more magnificent Manner than was ever done in this Kingdom before; has been the real Motive that induced me, to the compiling of this Work, for their further Improvement.[44]

The changes in urban building were not confined to the superimposition of a more ordered classical façade, but extended to the layout and organization of the interior as well, with a more marked differentiation of social space: as in London, but developing slightly later in provincial cities, a greater number of rooms allowed for more privacy and more specialization in the ways rooms were used. In the seventeenth century rooms had tended to be of uneven size, and ground-floor rooms had combined the functions of living, eating and sleeping. By the 1720s it is clear from house advertisements in provincial newspapers that even small houses in provincial towns often had separate kitchens, parlours, and sometimes dining rooms as well. John Wood wrote of the changes which were taking place in the interiors of the houses in Bath during these years:

As the new Buildings advanced, Carpets were introduced to cover the Floors, though Laid with the finest clean Deals, or *Dutch* Oak boards; the Rooms were all Wainscoted and Painted in a costly and handsome Manner; Marble Slabbs, and even Chimney Pieces, became common; the Doors in general were not only made thick and substantial, but they had the best Sort of Brass Locks put on them; Walnut Tree Chairs, some with Leather, and some with Damask or Worked Bottoms supplied the Place of such as were Seated with Cain or Rushes; the Oak Tables and Chests of Drawers were exchanged, the former for such as were made of Mahoggany, the latter for such as were made either with the same Wood, or with Wallnut Tree; handsome Glasses were added to the Dressing Tables, nor did the proper Chimneys or Peers of any of the Rooms long remain without well Framed Mirrours of no inconsiderable Size; and the Furniture for every chief Chimney was composed of a Brass Fender, with Tongs, Poker and Shovel agreeable to it.[45]

It was this changed landscape of urban and country house building that the new genre of conversation piece registered, demonstrating the ways in which the domestic environment could be controlled as a psychological extension of the character of the owner. Domestic space was not a neutral envelope for multifarious daily activities, but was much more highly specified in its functions, determining how individuals thought about their private lives.

Topographical Description

In any attempt to comprehend attitudes towards the domestic interior in the two decades between 1720 and 1740, it is important to recollect that this was the period that saw the establishment of the novel as a popular form of literature. The literary form of the novel stimulated the imagination of the reader into conjuring an appropriate location for the events which were described; it used settings as a way of reinforcing both narrative and character. Ian Watt has written of the novel's concept of space: 'Defoe would seem to be the first of our writers who visualized the whole of his narrative as though it occurred in an actual physical environment. His attention to the description of milieu is still intermittent; but occasional vivid details supplement the continual implication of his narrative and make us attach Robinson Crusoe and Moll Flanders much more completely to their environments than is the case with previous fictional characters. Characteristically, this solidity of setting is particularly noticeable in Defoe's treatment of movable objects in the physical world: in *Moll Flanders* there is much linen and gold to be counted, while Robinson Crusoe's island is full of memorable pieces of clothing and hardware.'[46]

Although Watt cites *Robinson Crusoe* and *Moll Flanders* as his evidence of a new awareness of the role of location in Defoe's novels, the tendency is most evident in *Roxana*. Much of the narrative of Roxana's life is animated by the description of her possessions and the changing physical settings in which she found herself. Material goods are the token of the intentions of characters in the plot. When Roxana decides to entertain some gentlemen in her apartments in Pall Mall, the rooms are described in circumstantial detail:

> I had a large Dining-Room in my Apartments, with five other Rooms on the same Floor, all which I made Drawing-Rooms for the Occasion, having all the Beds taken down for the Day; in three of these I had Tables plac'd, cover'd with Wine and Sweet-Meats; the fourth had a green Table for Play, and the fifth was my own Room, where I sat, and where I receiv'd all the Company that came to pay their Compliments to me.[47]

This narrative, which appears commonplace to us, was unusual in the 1720s in providing an exact physical sense of where an action took place, like the listing of an inventory. The following Tuesday she planned to have more company, and this time there were to be certain improvements:

> I made Provision of about twelve Dozen of fine Damask Napkins, with Table-cloaths of the same, sufficient to cover all the Tables, with three Table-cloaths upon every Table, and Side-boards in Proportion; also I bought a handsome Quantity of Plate, necessary to have serv'd all the Side-boards, but the Gentlemen would not suffer any of it to be us'd; telling me, they had bought fine China Dishes and Plates for the whole Service.[48]

When, later in the narrative, Roxana chooses to lodge with some Quakers in Hackney much attention is again devoted to describing the domestic setting: she sits in a chamber upstairs until a Gentleman arrives, who is taken into 'a very handsome Parlour below-stairs'; when she discovers it is someone she does not wish to see, her maid nips into the closet for a cordial; Roxana then descends 'down a Pair of Back-stairs with her, and into a Dining-Room, next to the Parlour in which he was'.[49] Clearly this action could not have taken place if there was not already by this date a considerable specialization of rooms and their function, even in the house of a Quaker in Hackney. Indeed the importance of room setting to the narrative of Roxana is indicated by the frontispiece of the first edition in which Roxana ushers the reader into her private apartments.

Defoe's ability to define and describe imaginary domestic space is clearly related to his interest in precise topographical description. His work as a novelist coincided with his work as a topographical journalist, recording the physical and social characteristics of the nation for his *A Tour through the Whole Island of Great Britain*, first published in three volumes between 1724 and 1726.[50] Defoe had travelled a good deal as a merchant in the 1680s, and again as a government agent working for Robert Harley in the reign of Queen Anne. There is evidence in the *Tour* that he undertook further journeys specifically in order to describe them.

In his *Tour* Defoe is alert to the implications of changes in the character of building. Whereas he displays much less interest than Celia Fiennes in the exact character of individual houses, he is more concerned with trying to understand changes in the character of the urban landscape, in order to interpret political and social changes in the nation. This gives his writing a more analytical character than had previously been evident in topographical writing, and is further evidence of the way changes in style were being interpreted in the 1720s. Occasionally he discusses the use of rooms, if it is in some way unusual: he describes the lodgings of the merchants at Morden College as consisting of 'two apartments in each stair case, with cellars for their conveniences, coals, beer, &c. and each apartment consists of a bed-chamber, and a study, or large closet, for their retreat, and to divert themselves in with books, &c.';[51] and he is alert to the conventions of social usage, as in his detailed description of a day at Epsom, including how

> After the morning diversions are over, and every one are walk'd home to their lodgings, the town is perfectly quiet again; nothing is to be seen, the Green, the Great Room, the raffling-shops all are (as if it was a trading town on a holiday) shut up; there's little stirring, except footmen, and maid servants, going to and fro of errands, and higglers and butchers, carrying provisions to people's lodgings.[52]

Here are the characteristics of Defoe's excellent descriptive journalism, capable of encapsulating what a place is like by a few deft phrases.

If one considers the full range of topographical writing, it appears that everybody in the 1720s was on the move, rushing round England to see and record the new houses which were being built, full of curiosity about the ways that England differed from her Continental neighbours, and interested in the architectural novelties of the previous thirty years.[53] Throughout the 1720s the Earl of Oxford travelled round England in company with his chaplain. Both of them kept detailed records of the houses they visited. The Earl of Egmont kept letter books in which he described the appearance of the houses he visited in considerable detail.[54] Sir John Evelyn, the son of the diarist, kept a diary during the 1720s which also contains accounts of the houses he visited.

From these descriptions it is possible to gain an impression of the attitudes of leisured members of the nobility or gentry, how they spent their time, and what they admired in the interiors of the houses of their friends. It is abundantly clear that there was a well developed visual culture, in which a member of the gentry

1. Samuel Pepys's library, attributed to Sutton Nicholls, 1687.

2. Design for a state bedchamber, by Daniel Marot, *c*. 1698.

3. The Saloon at Blenheim, attributed to Sir John Vanbrugh, *c.* 1707.

4. A scheme for the Saloon at Blenheim, by Sir James Thornhill, *c.* 1714.

5. An English family at tea, by
Joseph van Aken, c. 1725.

6. Grace before a meal,
by Joseph van Aken, c. 1725.

7. The Brothers Clarke and other Gentlemen Taking Wine, by Gawen Hamilton, *c.* 1730–5.

8. The Cholmondeley Family, by William Hogarth, 1732.

9. The Cutting of Flour, by Francis Hayman, *c*. 1741–2.

10. Mr B. finds Pamela writing, by Joseph Highmore, 1742–3.

11. The family of John Bacon, by Arthur Devis, *c.* 1742–3.

12. Children in an interior, by Arthur Devis, *c.* 1742–3.

13. The dining room at Kirtlington Park, by John Sanderson, 1747.

14. A chinoiserie saloon, by Timothy Lightoler, 1757.

could read the signs of an interior and interpret it in terms of the level of education of the owner, the evidence of Continental travel, and the sophistication with which the different parts of a collection had been put together. This amounted as a whole to a judgment of the owner's taste. Interiors were visited and assessed as aspects of their owner's personality.

The Influence of the Antique

The third cultural change during the 1720s and 1730s which engendered a sharper consciousness of the nature of domestic space was a different awareness of time, and of how the present was situated in history. This change in cultural consciousness is most clearly registered in attitudes towards classical scholarship.

Different views of classical scholarship had been evident in the important debate about the relationship of ancient to modern learning.[55] This had been sparked off by the publication by Sir William Temple of his book *Ancient and Modern Learning* in 1692, in which he maintained the great superiority of the ancients in every branch of learning on the basis of an obscure classical text, the 'Epistles of Phalaris'. In 1695 the 'Epistles' were published in a new edition by a young scholar of Christ Church, Oxford, the Hon. Charles Boyle, in which he complained that the Royal Librarian, Richard Bentley, had not given him an adequate opportunity to inspect a copy of the text. Richard Bentley was able to point out in an essay which he contributed to William Wotton's *Reflections on Ancient and Modern Learning*, published in 1697, that the 'Epistles of Phalaris', far from being a great monument of classical learning, were forgeries. In January 1698 Boyle, with the encouragement and assistance of a group of friends at Christ Church, published his *Dr. Bentley's Dissertations on the Epistles of Phalaris and the Fables of Aesop, examin'd by the Honourable Charles Boyle*, in which he attacked Bentley not on the basis of his scholarship, which could not be impugned, but more on his lack of gentility, that 'he was born in some Village remote from Town, and bred among the Peasantry while Young'.[56] This publication was commended by Sir William Temple for its 'pleasant Turns of Wit, and the Easiness of Style'.[57] In 1699 Bentley published his *Dissertations on the Letters of Phalaris*, in which he completely crushed Boyle's pretensions to scholarship with an unsurpassed display of critical and philological learning.

Evident in this battle between rival scholars is a conflict as to whether the classical past should be regarded as a source of polite accomplishment, a mark of gentility; or whether it should be treated as a subject of necessarily specialist, and possibly pedantic, learning. Although Richard Bentley clearly won the battle over the authenticity of the 'Epistles of Phalaris', he lost a more general battle concerning the study of the classical past. What is striking in the culture of the 1720s and 1730s is the extent to which the attitudes of the Christ Church group of scholars were accepted. A knowledge of the classical past was seen as a polite accomplishment which distinguished the nobility and the gentry and provided them with models of both literary and architectural style.

This change in the nature and tenor of classical scholarship can also be seen in the study of antique remains. As in the study of Greek and Roman literature, the first two decades of the eighteenth century had been an important period for the active study of Romano-British and Anglo-Saxon archaeology. These were the years when Sir Hans Sloane was assembling the collections which were to become the basis of the British Museum, including stuffed animals, Indian costumes and rare books, coins and stones. Dr John Woodward, a slightly crackpot virtuoso, likewise combined an interest in fossils with what Ralph Thoresby described as 'a curious collection of Roman antiquities, not only of urns, but gems, signets, rings, keys, stylus Scriptoriis, res turpiculae, ivory pins, brass fibulae, &c.'[58] William Nicolson, the learned Bishop of Carlisle, managed to advance the study of

Anglo-Saxon remains alongside his episcopal duties.[59] Thomas Hearne who, like John Woodward, was slightly eccentric in his attitudes to scholarship, was guarding the riches of the Bodleian Library, which he studied with single-minded zeal. Ralph Thoresby, who maintained a correspondence with all these scholars, made a major study of Roman antiquities and English coins in Leeds. There is a sense in the writings of these collectors of a passionate, if sometimes mildly crazy, enthusiasm for the study of the British past.

In 1717 the Society of Antiquaries was established.[60] As so often happens, the effect of the institution was to kill off much of the activity which it had been set up to promote. Although there were important antiquarian scholars during the 1720s and 1730s, of whom the most notable was William Stukeley, new research died out.[61] Collections of classical statuary were assembled not for the purposes of academic study, with eclectic enthusiasm, but more as a mark of taste. Between 1720 and 1740 the deep enquiries of individual students of the classical past were replaced by a culture which was permeated with an imitative form of classicism, influenced by the widespread belief that England's wealth, expanding naval empire and political laws should produce a corresponding cultural flowering at least equal, if not superior, to that of Augustan Rome.[62]

It is this aspect of classicism as a mark of gentility, a badge of an individual's taste, which dictated the character of interiors during the 1720s and 1730s. Young members of the nobility were sent off on the Grand Tour to acquire a suitable patina of learning.[63] In Rome they had an opportunity to buy as well as to study the great monuments of the classical past and, assisted by a variety of *ciceroni*, restorers, and disreputable sharks, they acquired ancient and modern statuary which was then shipped off in trunkloads to England. In the country houses of the nobility this statuary was displayed in appropriately classical surroundings.

The most prominent person in establishing this taste for

authentically classical surroundings, modelled on the architectural precepts of Vitruvius and Palladio, was Richard Boyle, third Earl of Burlington.[64] Lord Burlington had been born into the Anglo-Irish peerage and inherited extensive estates in Ireland, which he was quite happy to fritter away in indulging his considerable appetite for the arts. He first travelled to Italy in 1714, returning in the summer of 1715; soon after his return, the poet Alexander Pope wrote to the artist, Charles Jervas, how 'His Gardens flourish, his Structures rise, his Pictures arrive, and (what is far nobler and more valuable than all) his own good Qualities daily extend themselves to all about him'.[65] In 1719 he returned to Italy, partly to study the buildings of Vicenza and Genoa and partly, it has recently been suggested, to indulge in Jacobite espionage. On his return to England, he was acknowledged as the leader of a whole circle of artists, architects, writers, poets and musicians, all of whom were interested in Italian ideas and the concept of establishing a more cosmopolitan culture in England. Burlington, more than anyone, was responsible for establishing a taste for more austere and more strictly classical interiors. Over the door at Chiswick was a bust of Augustus; the cornice was modelled on that of the Temple of Castor and Pollux, the Corinthian capitals on those of the Temple of Jupiter Stator; inside was housed Burlington's enormous collection of classical statuary. The house was conceived as an antique shrine.

Around Lord Burlington, and following his example, were a group of other peers, who were intoxicated with the idea of reproducing the glories of Rome across the English countryside. For example, at Holkham in Norfolk, Thomas Coke, who became Lord Lovell in 1728 and Earl of Leicester in 1744, embarked on the construction of a great house which was a deliberate attempt to emulate the Antique.[66] Coke had been on the Grand Tour between 1712 and 1718, where he had met William Kent and developed a precocious interest in collecting works of art, acquiring a wealth of paintings, drawings, books and manuscripts. On his return he would have liked to start building a new house at once, but was delayed by financial losses in the South Sea Bubble. When, with the assistance of Kent and Burlington (their exact role is disputed), he did make plans, they were on the grandest possible scale. They involved manufacturing a particular type of yellow brick, because that was what Vitruvius had advocated; and both the ground plan of the house and its details were deliberately copied either from Antique examples or from the work of Palladio. Matthew Brettingham wrote in his description of the house that it was 'all decorated with admirable propriety from the purest models of antiquity' which produces 'an effect that perfectly corresponds with our ideas of Vitruvian magnificency'.[67] The house was filled with Antique statuary and plaster casts of other pieces, many of them supplied by the younger Matthew Brettingham, who went to Rome on Lord Leicester's behalf in the 1750s. When Lord Leicester had his portrait made, it was in the guise of a Roman senator. Nothing could be a clearer indication of Coke's dream of incarnating Antique values in eighteenth-century England.

Another member of the peerage who was obsessed by the Antique was Henry Herbert, ninth Earl of Pembroke.[68] Violent, intemperate, exceptionally athletic and a vegetarian, he had a fervent, if slightly erratic, enthusiasm for architecture and antiquity. Born in 1693, he was educated at Christ Church, Oxford. Following a visit to Italy in 1712 he returned to England and held a succession of minor court offices, for which he was temperamentally unsuited. He preferred the company of antiquarians, accompanying William Stukeley on visits to Stonehenge, and in 1722 he became a member of the Society of Roman Knights. In 1717 he acquired the lease of Pembroke House in Whitehall which, according to Horace Walpole, was 'as madly built as my lord himself was'.[69] In 1724 Herbert advised Lady Suffolk on the design of Marble Hill, and his name is likewise associated with the White Lodge in Richmond New Park, begun in 1727 and completed the following year. Together these works suggest that Lord Herbert had a good, if simplistic, knowledge of Palladian architecture. This was sufficient at least for Robert Morris, in 1728, to describe him, alongside Lord Burlington and Sir Andrew Fountaine, as one of 'the principal Practitioners and Preservers' of ancient architecture. Lord Chesterfield, in the same year, was less polite, writing to Mrs Howard that a room designed by Lord Herbert would 'have five great faults, which are five great windows, each of them big enough to admitt intolerable light';[70] and the Duchess of Marlborough in 1732 described Lord Herbert's house at Blackheath as 'the most ridiculous thing that ever I saw in my life . . . One can't help thinking soon after one gets into the house that it must have been built by somebody that is mad'.[71]

During the 1730s Lord Herbert, who succeeded his father as Earl of Pembroke in 1733, continued to be involved in a variety of architectural schemes, including the Column of Victory at Blenheim and a house for the Duchess of Marlborough. However, his major monuments were the Palladian Bridge at Wilton, the prototype of many subsequent copies and a perfect example of austere, rectilinear classicism; and his encouragement of the Swiss engineer, Charles Labelye, in the construction of Westminster Bridge.

A final example of this attempt to reincarnate the semblance of the Antique during the 1720s and 1730s was Narford in Norfolk, the house of Sir Andrew Fountaine. Fountaine was described by Bishop Nicolson as 'a bigotted Creature of ye Dean of Christ Church', who assembled an 'admirable collection of medals, Greek, Roman, Saxon, and Norman'.[72] In 1723 he was appointed Vice-Chamberlain to the Princess of Wales, a prominent court appointment; but he was principally known as a man of taste. According to Jonathan Richardson, he proved himself 'one of the keenest virtuosi in Europe and out-Italianized the Italians themselves'; Colen Campbell, in the third volume of *Vitruvius*

Britannicus, described how he was 'distinguished by his universal Knowledge in all the Polite Arts' and had 'given Marks of his good Taste and Affection for Architecture';[73] according to Lord Hervey his house at Narford was 'the prettiest trinket I ever saw. My Lord Burlington could not make a better ragoust of paintings, statues, gilding and virtû!'[74] The best description of Narford comes from the second Earl of Oxford, who described it as follows:

> It is a pretty box, a great deal of gilding and painting done by very bad hands; many pictures, most copies. The library is very smart and beauish, there are round the room the heads of several learned men, but very ill done. The joiners' work as well as the painters' is very bad; in short, all parts are most vilely furnished by all workmen. There are some very pretty things over his cabinets in his library. What he could not sell of his chaps [i.e. his statuary] in London, he has brought down here to ornament this fine gimcrack of a house.[75]

This description, and the vocabulary it uses to describe the house, reveal the change in taste between the first and second quarter of the eighteenth century: attitudes to interior decoration were becoming much more finicky, fastidious, and contrived. The key words of aesthetic description here are 'smart and beauish', balanced by 'gimcrack' in scorn of the amount of novelty in interiors of the period, when furniture and decoration were viewed as a backdrop for collections of classical remains.

1740–1760

Hayman, Highmore and Richardson

In the 1730s the genre of conversation piece was limited in its depiction of character. Except in the works of Hogarth, there was little sense of narrative and the objects in the interior were shown like items in an inventory, stark in their surroundings. However, in the 1740s a number of artists explored in much greater depth the communication of social identity through illustration.

The first of the artists to develop the conventions of painting in this way during the 1740s was Francis Hayman, who was born in Devon in 1708, was apprenticed in 1718 to a minor decorative artist, Robert Browne, and in the early part of his career painted scenery for the theatres at Goodman's Fields and Drury Lane.[1] By all accounts he was a highly congenial character, who made friends with the group of artists engaged in teaching life drawing at the St Martin's Lane Academy, who met in Old Slaughter's Coffee House nearby.

The exact role of this group has been much discussed in recent years: it was not a formal group, but a loose association of like-minded, mostly impoverished artists of the same generation, who needed work, enjoyed each other's company and were bored by the limited conventions which governed the art of the time.[2] For anyone with an artistic temperament, the opportunities for painting in London were restricted and involved either drudgery in the theatre or subservience to rich patrons. Moreover, the opportunities for grand decorative painting were dying out with the change in taste in interiors. This was in sharp contrast to artistic practice on the Continent, which provided a much greater range of activity to the painter, including opportunities for proper training and a higher professional status. The two *émigré* Frenchmen in this group of artists – the sculptor Louis François Roubiliac, and the illustrator and engraver Hubert Gravelot – presumably made the discrepancy between conditions in London and Paris clear.

Gravelot, in particular, appears to have been influential in introducing a French style of drawing to England. He came to England in 1732 to help with the engravings of an English edition of Picart's *Ceremonies* and stayed in London until 1746, turning out book illustrations, including illustrations to Gay's *Fables* in 1738 and a new edition of Shakespeare in 1740. He also produced trade cards, book plates and cartouches, in which he demonstrated the possibilities of a more fluent style of decoration.[3] He and Roubiliac both encouraged the artist Joseph Highmore to visit Paris, and furnished him with letters of introduction on his trip in 1734.[4] Together, this group of artists stimulated one another to experiment with new artistic genres. They wanted to give art a higher academic status, and were determined that British art should be more European.

Towards the end of the 1730s Hayman began to extend his repertoire beyond the painting of scenery for the theatre. Lord Radnor wrote to Dr Macro on 12 July 1741: 'I realy think him a Genius, and if He Had not fool'd away many years at the beginning of life painting Harlequins, trap doors, &c. for the playHouse, he would certainly by this time be the greatest man of His Age.'[5] In 1740 he was commissioned to paint a group portrait of the family of Jonathan Tyers, the entrepreneur who had been responsible for transforming Vauxhall Gardens from an open-air brothel into one of the major sites of popular entertainment in London.[6] As a social type Tyers was distinct from the previous people who had been represented in conversation pictures. He was a self-made businessman, with a genuine interest in art. Hayman shows him at ease with an elbow carelessly placed on the table, while his wife is pouring him out a cup of tea. Although the grouping is clearly arranged, there is a feeling of animation, of the sentiment as well as the tensions of family life. Instead of individuals being represented in purely social roles, there is an awareness of personality and of family relationships.

At around the same time Hayman also painted the Gascoigne family. The same characteristics are evident as in the group portrait of the Tyers: although the likenesses are not particularly good, since all Hayman's sitters tend to have similar expressions, there is a coherent pictorial narrative, of the son reading a letter in the background, the father looking with pride towards his daughter, another son lounging at his ease. Of course, it is highly contrived; but in comparison to previous conversation pieces there is considerable solidity. The sitters are not just marionettes.

Hayman's subsequent work in the 1740s does not substantially develop the conventions which he adopted for these two early group portraits; but it includes, for example, a fine double portrait of Thomas Nuthall and Hambleton Custance, now in the Tate Gallery, which shows them not in the genteel surroundings which were normal for conversation pieces, but instead in a spartan room, with diamond-shaped window panes and straight-backed country chairs, relaxing after going out shooting. Even more than in his early portraits, it is not the social status of the sitters which was important to Hayman, nor conveying a good likeness, but illustrating individuals in an appropriate form of recreation, at ease in their shooting box.

While Hayman continued to paint group portraits, he was also involved in one of the biggest and most interesting commissions of the 1740s. Thanks to his knowing Jonathan Tyers, he was asked to provide a set of subject paintings for the 'supper boxes' in Vauxhall Gardens. The implications of this commission were that the works would be seen by a larger and more diverse audience than those which were painted for the country houses of the gentry and nobility. Hayman had to invent a genre of public painting without any of the religious or mythological overtones which had previously been standard in large-scale decorative art.

The preparatory drawings for these paintings principally consist of outdoor scenes, such as flying a kite and fishing; but there is also one of a man and a servant girl playing with battledore and shuttlecock indoors and another of a curious game, described in one of the early guidebooks as 'placing a little ball at the top of a cone of [flour] into which all are to cut with a knife, and whoever causes the ball to roll from the summit must take it out with their teeth'.[7] These drawings are completely different in style and subject matter to anything which had previously been seen in England. They are genre scenes, quite possibly studied from life, which show individuals at leisure, so that people could enjoy looking at versions of themselves as they strolled down the long alleyways of Vauxhall Gardens.[8]

It is not always possible to relate changes in visual convention to those in literature. But in the case of the greater consciousness of the way individuals could be depicted in the early 1740s and the increased interest in narrative in art, there is an obvious relation to the interest in characterization inspired by the publication of Samuel Richardson's novel *Pamela* in two volumes on 6 November 1740. Richardson explored the developing sensibility of his heroine Pamela through a series of scenes, recorded in her letters. Each of these scenes is akin to a conversation piece in the way that it is a framed narrative event, composed by the author and full of details about the attributes of characters and what they were wearing, in order to give the events which are described a sense of reality. More than in the works of Defoe, Richardson's narrative is dependent on an imagined location which, although it is never possible to define in detail, none the less is effectively communicated, so that the characters have a physical substance as well as a psychological one. Right at the beginning of the novel, the supposed reality of the letters is emphasized by a description of the way that they were to be folded up in a small pill box, and the location is described as 'my late lady's dressing room'.[9] Action is locked into its surroundings. At an early stage, the future moral problems that Pamela is going to have to face are communicated through the gift of material objects:

> He called me up to my late lady's closet, and pulling out the drawers, he gave me two suits of fine Flanders laced head-clothes, three pair of fine silk shoes, two hardly the worse, and just fit for me (for my lady had a very little foot), and the other with wrought silver buckles in them; and several ribands and top-knots of all colours; four pair of fine white cotton stockings, and three pair of fine silk ones; and two pair of rich stays.[10]

Right at the beginning, consumer desire (neatly expressed by the pleasurable recognition that the silk shoes fit Pamela so well) is going to have to compete strenuously with the demands of moral probity. This was the dilemma of people in the 1740s as they had to engage and come to terms with an ever increasing flood of luxury items, titillating wants which had not previously been known. It is this tension between the moral consciousness of the individual and the surrounding world of luxury goods that Richardson's novels so effectively explore.

In case this connection between the emerging form of the novel and the conversation piece appears far-fetched or nothing more than a convenient analogy, it is important to note that, soon after the publication of *Pamela*, Richardson took the unusual step of commissioning a set of illustrations for the book; an indication of the importance which he attached to the visual aspect of the narrative.[11] On 29 December 1740 Aaron Hill wrote to Richardson: 'The designs you have taken for frontispieces, seem to have been very judiciously chosen; upon pre-supposition that Mr. Hogarth is able (and if any body is, it is he), to teach pictures to speak and to think.'[12] The idea that Richardson should want the illustrations 'to speak and to think' is the clearest evidence of the demands which were being placed on artists to provide a realistic, rather than idealized, version of events. As it happened it was not Hogarth who provided the first illustrations for *Pamela*, but Hayman, in association with Hubert Gravelot. One of Hayman's preliminary drawings for the series survives, and it demonstrates the relationship between the imagined world of the novelist and the projected image of the artist.

There is further evidence of this relationship between fiction and the pictorial image in the friendship between Richardson and Joseph Highmore. Highmore was slightly older than Hayman. He was born in 1692, educated at the Merchant Taylors' School and trained as a lawyer, which gave him, according to George Vertue, 'a good Voluble speech with a Stedfast assurance, of which he has benefitted'.[13] He learned to paint at Kneller's Academy in Great Queen Street and established himself as a portrait painter. He also made the drawings for the illustrations to Cheselden's *Anatomy of the Human Body*, published in 1722; Pine's *Installation of the Knights of the Bath, of* 1726; and Croxall's *Select Novels*, of 1729. Like Hayman, he was one of the group of artists associated with Old Slaughter's Coffee House in St Martin's Lane. He improved his knowledge of French painting and, especially, of the work of Rubens by visiting Paris in 1734.

Joseph Highmore began a set of paintings after the story of Pamela some time in late 1742 or 1743. On 22 February 1744 he placed an advertisement in the *London Daily Post and General Advertiser* to the effect that he was able to sell

Twelve Prints, by the best French Engravers, after his own Paintings, representing the most remarkable Adventures of *Pamela*. In which he had endeavour'd to comprehend her whole Story as well as to preserve a Connexion between the several Pictures; which follow each other as Prints successive, and dependent, so as to compleat the Subject.[14]

This set of prints brought Highmore into contact with Richardson, who was presumably anxious to meet an artist who had taken so much care with the visual interpretation of his book; and they became and remained friends, Highmore being present at Richardson's death in Fulham in 1761. According to Richardson, writing in a letter to his friend, Lady Bradshaigh:

Mr. Highmore is an eminent painter in Holborn-Row, Lincolns-Inn Fields, the same who published Twelve Prints of Pamela, of which he has the Drawings, and which he had finished before I had the Pleasure of knowing him. He has drawn Clarissa at whole length and in the Vandyke Taste and Dress. Had finished the Piece before I saw it, or knew of it, and before Clarissa was printed, having seen only some parts of the Work in Manuscript. His own imagination was his principle guide, and he has given it great intelligence, sweetness and dignity. As you propose to see it I will say no more of it.[15]

In this letter, with its acknowledgement of Highmore's abilities to portray the world of Richardson's novels, there is the clearest possible evidence of the shared moral and didactic world of these two branches of art in the early 1740s. Painters, like writers, were attempting to communicate an increased consciousness of the moral dilemmas of their subjects, in order that their works might appeal to a larger audience. Richardson undoubtedly succeeded in this: both *Pamela* and *Clarissa* inspired a cult following. Painting was slower to adapt to the demands of a mass public, but Hayman and Highmore recognized that it had this potential.

The Work of Devis

In any analysis of the way interiors were represented in the mid-eighteenth century, the work of Arthur Devis assumes pre-eminent importance. It is Devis who has informed the popular idea of an eighteenth-century interior: bare, sparsely furnished and sterile; a husband and wife sit upright, hardly communicating, as if a vacuum pump had drained the interior of any movement. Yet these conversation pieces should be read for what they are: particular works of art by an idiosyncratic artist, observing stylistic conventions and not necessarily showing interiors realistically.

Devis was born on 19 February 1712 in Preston, Lancashire, the son of a carpenter who later became a partner in a local firm of printers.[16] It is thought that he moved to London in the early 1730s, where he worked under the Flemish artist Peter Tillemans, and was trained as a copyist of Italian landscapes. His earliest known portraits date from the beginning of the 1740s.

Around 1740 Devis painted an unidentified gentleman leaning against a desk in his library. This picture establishes at once the characteristic features of his style, the hyper-fastidious sensibility, the minuscule brushstrokes, and the air of unreality. From then onwards Devis specialized in the genre, accepting commissions from the lesser gentry and content to work in a style which bore increasingly little relation to the artistic currency of the time, as if he knew exactly the limitations of his abilities. There is no feeling of character in the figures, nor of animation in the fine, carefully drawn outlines. He remained in the studio of his house in Great Queen Street, surrounded by the most fashionable artistic neighbourhood in mid-eighteenth-century London, and by all sorts of new developments in pictorial fashion to which he was entirely immune.

A more elaborate interior than usual appears in the background of Devis's portrait of John Bacon and his family, painted at some time in the early 1740s. The interesting feature of this interior is how it shows Bacon's scientific interests by the inclusion of a transit quadrant set up in front of the window to track the movement of the sun and, in front of it, a telescope standing on a side table. But, as in all Devis's work, there is no variation in style or finish across the whole surface of the canvas, so that the pattern of the carpet is painted with the same precision as the faces of the children building their house of cards on the low table in the foreground.

At roughly the same period Devis also painted an unidentified group of children in an interior. In the foreground a boy holds the tail of a kite, which is propped up against the wall in the background; sitting down on the other side of the table is a girl, presumably his sister, holding some item from her sewing basket; behind the table another girl has just been interrupted from her game of building a house of cards; the youngest member of the group is riding a gold-topped cane. It is a provocative image, challenging and at the same time defying explanation. It is possible that Devis had seen an engraving of a work by Chardin, who exhibited at the Salon in 1741 *The Son of M. Le Noir amusing himself by making a house of cards*.[17] Certainly the air of concentration is in many ways Chardinesque, although here it is represented less self-consciously.

There has been much discussion in recent years about supposed changes in attitudes to family affection in the eighteenth century. Lawrence Stone's *Family, Sex and Marriage in England 1500–1800*, published in 1977, suggested that the mid-eighteenth century marked a shift in the perception of childhood. Although this idea has now been discredited in the secondary literature, Devis's portrayal of children does mark a change in artistic treatment. He can scarcely be said to show them affectionately; rather they are young adults, occupying a space and a world of their own.

A third, and equally remarkable, painting from the early 1740s is Devis's portrait of William Atherton and his wife Lucy. William Atherton was, like a number of Devis's early patrons, a leading figure in Preston. He had twice served as Mayor, remained an alderman, and had a house in the Market Square. Yet they are depicted as if at home in a country seat, with a view out of the window in the background into a garden. Again, the minute precision with which the scissors and the sewing basket are represented on the table is Chardinesque. Objects, property and surroundings assume exactly the same importance as the ownership of a dog or a wife. Everything has its place in the order of the composition. When these images are considered together with those of Francis Hayman of the same few years, it is clear how much the vocabulary of art was changing in the early 1740s.

Yet, instead of developing this genre, Devis went on painting in exactly the same way, year in, year out. Sitters arrived at his house in Great Queen Street, and returned to their homes with a memento which did not challenge the viewer by being self-consciously artistic, but satisfied a non-artistic desire for realism. His work marks the extension of the availability of art to a new type of buyer, the wealthy citizens of a country town, who were proud to have their portrait painted, but were glad that the artist was born in Preston.

In 1747 Devis painted Mr and Mrs Richard Bull of Ongar in Essex. It was the year of their marriage, and Richard Bull is shown relaxing at home. As in all Devis's portraits, there is no evidence to connect this interior with the Bulls' own house in Ongar, one of the many small villages to the east of London where prosperous citizens were building new houses, not too far from the counting-house but far enough away from the smog. As in the majority of these portraits, the interior appears to have been made up; it gives an impression of domestic space, but at the same time does not divert too much attention away from the sitters. The features which are particularly interesting are the fine turkey carpet and the neat array of porcelain along the mantelpiece with two ornamental birds, suggesting the fashion for ceramic figures which were being turned out from the factories at Chelsea and (not far from Ongar) at Bow.

Devis's pictures provide a persuasive image of how rooms looked during the 1740s. They are the most ostensibly realistic depictions of interiors that survive; and their very precision commands a belief in their realism. One is seduced into thinking that this is what a mid-eighteenth-century interior would have looked like. Yet as evidence of the appearance of actual interiors, they need to be treated with circumspection.

Two of the most conspicuous features of Devis's paintings are the bareness of the floorboards and the sparseness of the furnishings. Yet it was in the 1740s that carpets began to be more widely available and interiors were filled up with a mass of furniture of different types. Devis's work may be just as much evidence of a psychological resistance to the increasing clutter of the domestic interior as a true representation of its appearance. There is not a straightforward equivalence between art and domestic life: Devis was not strictly a provincial painter, although he was born in Preston; he was not a naive painter, but someone satisfying the demands of a market; his art is not a realistic portrayal of particular places, but an artful form of deliberately deceptive composition.

Wall Decoration

The impression given by Devis of rooms in the middle part of the eighteenth century is of bleak interior spaces. But if one considers the appearance of interiors in the two decades between 1740 and 1760 on the basis of evidence other than pictorial images, it appears that, on the contrary, their wall surfaces were diversified by a range of different types of ornamental treatment, in plasterwork, wallpaper, or paint.

During the early part of the century, the walls of rooms had often been covered in some form of wainscot. *The Builder's Dictionary*, published in 1734, had described wainscot as 'the Timber Work that serves to line the Walls of a Room, being usually in Pannels, and painted to serve instead of Hangings'.[18] Although the wood was painted, it gave the room a feeling of warmth, breaking up the austerity of bare walls. However, by the middle part of the century wainscoting had begun to go out of fashion; and by 1774 Thomas Skaife was able to write, in his *Key to Civil Architecture; or The Universal British Builder*, that 'Wainscotting, in this refined age, is quite obsolete, and seldom used, except in studies, or offices for servants, &c.'[19]

In the grander type of country house it became common to decorate the walls with some form of ornamental plasterwork. This was not a new fashion, since there was a long indigenous tradition of decorative plasterwork, stretching back to the strapwork panels of Elizabethan interiors and encompassing the ornate decoration of late seventeeth-century interiors, such as the ceiling of the Long Gallery at Sudbury in Derbyshire and the chapel at Belton House in Lincolnshire.[20] What was distinctive to the 1740s and 1750s was the way that Continental and English plasterworkers imitated French rococo patterns, both in their ornamental vocabulary and in individual motifs of birds, monkeys and other animals, so that the plasterwork was not simply a background form of ornament, but was itself a work of art. The specific properties of plaster as a material – the ease of shaping it both wet and dry, and its ability to cover large areas – lent itself to elaborate decorative schemes, which made use of the asymmetric motifs which had become fashionable. There are examples of this type of work in a number of houses in the Midlands which were decorated in the 1740s and 1750s, including Edgecote in

Northamptonshire, which is documented as being by John Whitehead, who was paid £581 'To Plastering & Stoco-work'; Honington Hall in Warwickshire, with its saloon full of mythological personifications of the elements, likely on stylistic grounds also to be by John Whitehead; Hagley Hall in Worcestershire; and Farnborough Hall in Warwickshire, the work of a Yorkshireman, William Perritt, who was paid a total of £434 4s 4d on 14 November 1750. In these houses it is possible to study the range of mythological and abstract motifs which plasterworkers of the period were able to employ.

If this style of plasterwork could not be afforded – and clearly it was an expensive luxury – then it was possible to have wallpaper as a cheaper alternative.[21] Like plasterwork, wallpaper was not new in the 1740s. Fragments of wallpaper of the early sixteenth century have been found on the walls of the Master's Lodge at Christ's College, Cambridge; and evidence of the extensive use of wallpaper begins in the late seventeenth century, when the stationers around St Paul's Churchyard in London began to market sheets of printed paper which could be pasted to the wall to form patterns. In 1680 George Minnikin, a stationer at St Martin's le Grand, advertised that he sold 'all sorts of colour'd paperhangings', and ten years later Edward Butling likewise advertised that he 'maketh and Selluth all sorts of Hangings for Rooms in Lengths or in Sheets, Frosted or Plain. Also a sort of Paper in Imitation of Irish Stitch, of the newest Fashion, and several other sorts, viz. Flock Work, Wainscot, Marble, Damask, Turkey Work' at the sign of the Old Knave of Clubs in Southwark.

By the 1740s wallpaper had ceased to be merely an economical substitute for more expensive textile hangings and had itself become a highly fashionable item, much discussed in contemporary letters and diaries. In 1741 the Countess of Hertford wrote to her friend the Countess of Pomfret:

Yesterday I was busy in buying paper, to furnish a little closet in that house, where I spend the greatest part of my time within doors ... The perfection which the manufacture of that commodity is arrived at, in the last few years, is surprising: the master of the warehouse told me that he is to make some paper at the price of twelve and thirteen shillings a yard, for two different gentlemen. I saw some at four shillings, but contented myself with that of only eleven-pence: which I think is enough to have it very pretty; and I have no idea of paper furniture being rich.[22]

The letter reveals the range of wallpaper patterns which were available and, more importantly, the range in price.

The sale of wallpaper had become a profitable trade and, in the anonymous *General Description of all Trades* published in 1747, it was written under the heading 'Papermakers' that 'There are likewise Hangings for Rooms made by colouring and Embossing of Thick Paper, the making and dealing in which has now become a considerable Branch of Trade.' In 1761, the profession of 'Paper-hangings maker' was described as being 'a very extensive business that has been lately much improved';[23] and Thomas Mortimer's *The Universal Director*, published in 1763, lists the names of ten prominent paper-hanging makers in London and adds that

The art of Painting and Staining of Paper of various patterns and colours, for hanging of rooms, is lately become a very considerable branch of commerce in this country, for we annually export vast quantities of this admired article; and the home consumption is not less considerable, as it is not only a cheap, but an elegant part of furniture, and saves the builders the expense of wainscotting; for which reason they have brought it in vogue, and most of the new houses lately erected are lined throughout with paper.[24]

At the same time, wallpaper was sometimes still used as a cheap way of decorating a room, since plastering a room for wallpaper was cheaper than for paint. In 1748 Lady Luxborough was resigned to having her main room 'only hung with sixpenny paper',[25] and two years later Mrs Montagu recommended that a friend could furnish her house 'in the present fashion, of some cheap paper and ornaments of Chelsea China or the manufacture of Bow, which makes a room look neat and finished'. By 1756, Isaac Ware was able to write in *A Complete Body of Architecture* that 'Paper has in great measure taken the place of sculpture . . . and the hand of art is banished from a part of the house in which it used to display itself very happily'; and in 1759, Thomas Gray wrote to his friend Thomas Wharton that 'I allow tapestry (if at all tolerable) to be a very proper furniture for your sort of house; but doubt, if any bargain of that kind is to be met with, except at some old mansion sale in the country, where People will disdain tapestry, because they hear, that Paper is all the fashion.'[26] So, by the middle part of the eighteenth century, wallpaper was readily available as a way of diversifying the appearance of a domestic interior.

Another way of decorating interiors was by using paint. Like the use of plasterwork and wallpaper, paint was not a new technology in the mid-eighteenth century. There had always been specialist painters who were capable of mixing colours for house painting. What changed around 1730 was that readymade paint began to be available, first marketed by Alexander Emerton, a colourman at the sign of the Bell near St Clement's Church in the Strand.[27] According to William Salmon in his *Palladio Londinensis; or, the London Art of Building*, published in 1734,

> it is well known, and daily experienced, since the Advertisement of *Alexander Emerton*, that several Noblemen and Gentlemen, have by themselves and Servants, painted whole Houses, without the Assistance or Direction of a Painter, which, when

examined by the best Judges, could not be distinguished from the Work of a professed Painter.[28]

Inevitably, the availability of ready-mixed paint damaged the expertise of the specialist trade, so that when Robert Campbell wrote of the trade of painter in his *The London Tradesman* of 1747, he complained:

As a House Painter, he is employed in Painting the Outside and Inside of Houses; which requires no manner of Ingenuity: The chief Secret lies in grinding, mixing, and compounding the Colours; as to the laying them on, it requires no Art, but an even Hand and to carry the Brush up and down according to the Grain of the Wood – This Branch is now at a very low Ebb, on account of the Methods practised by some Colour-Shops; who have set up Horse-Mills to grind the Colours, and sell them to Noblemen and Gentleman ready mixed at a low Price, and by the Help of a few printed Directions, a House may be painted by any common Labourer at one Third of the Expence it would have cost before the Ministry was made public. There are a vast Number of Hands that follow this Branch, as it may be learned in a Month as well as in seven Years: Plaisterers, Whitewashers, and every body that can but handle a Brush, now set up for House Painters. When it was the Taste to paint Houses with Landskip Figures, and in Imitation of variegated Woods and Stone, then it was necessary to serve an Apprenticeship to the Business, and required no mean Genius in Painting to make a compleat Workman; but since the mode has altered, and Houses are only daubed with dead Colour, every Labourer may execute it as well as the most eminent Painter.[29]

This tendency to paint interiors is confirmed by evidence from the American colonies, where, up until 1725, the majority of houses had unpainted interiors, owing to the scarcity of linseed oil and the expense of pigments. But so-called 'Painter's Colours' were imported. During the 1730s, houses for sale were often described as having painted rooms. A house was described in the Boston *News-Letter* as having its rooms 'all nicely painted', and another, in 1734, was advertised in the *New England Journal* as having 'Eight Fine Rooms, Two of which with Entries are very beautifully Wainscotted and laid in Oyl, and Four handsomely Painted'. In 1749 Peter Kalm wrote of the houses in New York City:

> The walls were white-washed within; and I did not any where see hangings, with which the people in this country seem in general to be but little acquainted. The walls were quite covered with all sorts of drawings and pictures in small frames. On each side of the chimnies they had usually a sort of alcove; and the wall under the windows was wainscotted, and had benches placed near it. The alcoves, and all the wood work, were painted with a bluish grey colour.[30]

As in England, it appears from the advertisements of house-painters that it was possible to purchase colours ready-mixed, and it is in the American colonies that one finds the most detailed descriptions of house-painting, as in the contract for painting the interior of a house in Salem, Massachusetts, on 31 January 1763:

> To paint the Entry Way throughout & back stare Rails & Banisters into the Garrit with a good Stone Collour four times over. To paint One Front Room Stone Collour the other Front Room Mahogany Collour one back Room Cedar or Stone Collour & the Kitching Lead Collour – One front Chamber Ceder, one front Chamber Green, one back Chamber Russian Blue & one Back Chamber Lead or olive Collour, to paint them all over 4 times except the two Rooms that is to

be Lead Collour which is to be done twice over, to paint the Dressers Chocolat Collour the Seats in all the Windows Mahogany Collour & to paint all the Closetts & to Size all the Upper Chambers with Spanish Browne & the Wash Boards black & to finish & Compleat it all to the Satisfaction of sd Orne on or before the 30 Day of April next & to find all the Oyl & Collours.[31]

The opportunities that were available for painting, plastering or wallpapering, suggest that rooms in the middle part of the century were not as austere or as bleak as they are depicted by Devis. On the contrary, it appears that it was increasingly common to diversify the appearance of rooms with a wealth of different types of wall decoration, drawing attention to the interior as a theatre of action, with a variety of different atmospheres. Rooms could be painted a range of pale colours, pearl, cream or stone; they might be a darker shade of chocolate, cedar or mahogany; or they might be vivified by the use of more expensive colours such as 'Sky-blue, orange, lemon, pink, blossom, straw, Prussian blue'.[32] The mid-eighteenth-century interior was anything but a monochrome box.

The Furniture Trade

It was not only in the wall surfaces of rooms that the mid-eighteenth century saw an increasing diversity of style, but also in the contents. By 1750, the furniture industry was able to supply an amazing diversity of types to a market which was hungry for novelty.[33]

At the top end of the market were the London upholsterers, who were responsible for supplying the full range of fittings for a new house. Robert Campbell wrote in *The London Tradesman*, published in 1747:

I have just finished my House, and must now think of furnishing it with fashionable Furniture. The Upholder is chief Agent in this Case: He is the Man upon whose Judgment I rely in the Choice of Goods; and I suppose he has not only Judgment in the Materials, but Taste in the Fashions, and Skill in the Workmanship. This Tradesman's Genius must be universal in every Branch of Furniture; though his proper Craft is to fit up Beds, Window-Curtains, Hangings, and to cover Chairs that have stuffed Bottoms: He was originally a Species of the Taylor; but, by degrees, has crept over his Head, and set up as a Connoisieur in every Article that belongs to a House.[34]

This account gives a good impression of the primacy of the upholsterer in orchestrating the contents of an interior, and suggests the extent to which it was not only the nobility who listened to advice about the layout of rooms.

One of the largest suppliers of both furniture and upholstery was William Hallett, who set up a shop in Great Newport Street in the mid-1730s and was able to supply the full range of household furnishings. For Cannon Hall in Yorkshire he provided a card table, a dining table, a mahogany writing table, chairs, a bookcase and sconces, as well as a bed covered in 'green Harateen'; for Wilton, he supplied '3 pair of candlestands, silvered nozzles, £5 8s od'; at St Giles's in Dorset, the seat of the Earl of Shaftesbury, he was paid for carved chairs, 'for making and putting up ye bed', for 'Mahogany Cisterns' and a mahogany commode; and for Strawberry Hill, the house of Horace Walpole, he supplied sofas, chairs and a pier glass in Gothic style for the Great Parlour or Refectory.[35] Hallett was able to provide more or less whatever was required in interior furnishings, whether it was upholstery or cabinetwork, and whatever the style.

A similar large-scale commercial operation was run by John Cobb and William Vile in St Martin's Lane. Vile had been trained by William Hallett and, in 1752, Hallett moved his shop next door to 'William Vile & Co.', suggesting an element of partnership and collaboration. Like Hallett, Vile and Company were able to supply the full range of furniture, including, for the Vyne in Hampshire, carpets, festoon curtains, beds and bedding, 'neat Mahogany Chairs Stuff'd in linnen', a variety of different types of table, 'a wallnuttree Buerow on Castors' and even bellows and a hearth broom. For Sir William Proctor in Bruton Street, Vile and Cobb supplied a mahogany dressing table 'with folding top & cabinet at top with doors & drawers with inside glass to draw forwards'; and for Lord Archibald Hamilton, they organized the sale of his furniture by auction, including a 'collection of rich Genoa Damask and other furnishings, in Red and W-cls, large Pier and Looking Glasses, Mahogany Tables, Chairs etc likewise his Coach, Chariot and Post-Chaise'.[36]

It is in the context of these large-scale suppliers of household goods that the firm of Thomas Chippendale must be understood. Chippendale was not a lone craftsman, turning out fine furniture in a workshop, but a successful entrepreneur.[37] He was born in Otley in Yorkshire on 5 June 1718, the son of a local joiner. After marrying in 1748, he took a house first in Conduit Street off Long Acre and subsequently in Northumberland Court off the Strand. It is likely that he was taught to draw by Matthias Darly, a prolific artist, draughtsman and printmaker, who is first recorded as a printseller in 1749, when he lived in Duke's Court, St Martin's Lane.[38] Darly took over the lease of Chippendale's house in Northumberland Court and collaborated with him in the preparation of plates for *The Gentleman and Cabinet-Maker's Director*, first published in 1754.

The Gentleman and Cabinet-Maker's Director was one of the most lavish folio volumes ever devoted to furniture. As its subtitle indicates, it was 'a large collection of the most Elegant and Useful Designs of Household Furniture in the Gothic, Chinese and Modern Taste'; and it applied some of the principles employed in architectural publications to the design of furniture, including the art of drawing in perspective and the appropriate use of the classical orders. It demonstrates the full range of furniture which was available at the time, from the bookcase to the tea caddy, from a girandole to a clothes press. Moreover, it shows the stylistic diversity which was considered admissible, including ribband-back chairs next to 'Chinese' ones, without any thought or worry about which was better.

As a result of the commercial success of the *Director*, Chippendale was able to go into partnership with James Rannie and open a shop in St Martin's Lane, described as 'The Cabinet and Upholstery Warehouse'. It consisted of three houses fronting on to the street with an entrance leading through to a yard, round which there were various sheds and workshops. The outbuildings housed journeymen cabinetmakers and upholsterers, with special rooms for veneering and drying deals. From these premises Chippendale was able to supply the nobility and gentry with a colossal range of fashionable goods, including curtains, carpets, wallpapers, loose covers and even coffins, either made on the premises or subcontracted to workshops nearby. As he stated in an advertisement for the *Director*, 'All Commissions for Household Furniture, or Drawings thereof, sent to the Cabinet and Upholstery Warehouse, at the Chair in St. Martin's Lane, will be most punctually observed, and executed in the genteelest Taste, and on the most reasonable Terms.'[39]

A fourth example of these large commercial firms which dominated the sale of furniture in London was that of William and John Linnell.[40] William Linnell had first set up a carving workshop in Long Acre in the late 1720s, where he gradually expanded his activities to cover the full range of carving and cabinetwork, including mouldings, picture frames, and a fine card table, which were supplied to Richard Hoare for Stourhead in 1740. By 1749 Linnell had been joined by his son John, and in 1750 they moved to larger premises in Long Acre and again, in 1754, to Berkeley

Square, where they were able to have a showroom alongside the workshops.

During the 1750s the Linnells provided a comprehensive service to their customers, including a substantial amount of carved work for Woburn Abbey, a table for Alscot Park, Warwickshire, described in the accounts as 'a six-legged table by a design of Kents', a magnificent chinoiserie bed for Badminton House in Gloucestershire, and 'six neat gothick chairs covered with Spanish leather' for Sir Nathaniel Curzon's London house in Audley Square. Something of the scale of their operation is indicated by the inventory taken at the time of William Linnell's death in 1763, which reveals that they had workshops on three floors in Berkeley Square, including rooms for carvers, joiners, turners and gilders, amounting in all to a workforce of about fifty people; and their stock-in-trade included 'magnificent large pier and other glasses, elegant carved termes, brackets and girandoles', as well as Siena and Derbyshire marble tables.

Although these big firms have dominated subsequent knowledge of furniture production, this was only a consequence of their skills at self-advertisement. London was filled with a network of smaller firms, which were able to provide a more specialist service or did work subcontracted by the larger firms; and it was possible to buy elegant furniture in a local provincial town. The list of subscribers to Chippendale's *Director* includes a vast number of names of cabinetmakers whose work is unknown; for example, in spite of being a metropolitan production, it lists three upholsterers in York: Robert Barker, who had a shop at the sign of the 'Sopha Dome Bed' in Petergate; Richard Farrer; and George Reynoldson, who in 1734 had advertised in the *York Courant* as follows:

George Reynoldson upholsterer, undertaker and sworn appraiser, in Stonegate, York. Makes all sorts of looking glasses and sconces, in gilt Mahogany or walnut frames and coach glasses, by wholesale or retail, at the *London* prices; where old glasses are cut, polished and silvered, very reasonably. He also makes and sells all sorts of Beds, of Mohair, Silk and worsted Damasks, Camblets, Harrateers, cheneys and printed stuffs; Feather Beds, Mattresses, Blankets, Quilts, Rugs and Coverlets, *Flanders* and *English* Ticks, Paper Hangings, imbosed, damasked or plain, Tapestry Hangings, Silk, Worsted Bed-Lace, *Turkey*, *Muscate*, *Persian* and *French* carpets, List, Hair or Painted Floor Cloths, *Dutch* and Floor Matts, Wax Candles, Flambeaux, single or double Brass Arms, Gallery Hall or Door Glasses and Lamps, Mahogany and Walnut Desks and Book Cases, Breakfast and Dining Tables, Chamber and Card Tables, Cases of Drawers, scaloped and round Tea Boards, shaving Stands, Night stools, Chairs of all prices, Folding and Fire Screens, gilt or plain etc.[41]

With this amount of furniture available for sale in a provincial centre, it was not necessary to go to London to purchase well made and up-to-date pieces.

The way in which a family of the gentry purchased furniture is demonstrated by the correspondence that survives for the Purefoys who lived in Shalstone Manor in Buckinghamshire.[42] They often bought furniture from local auctions, where they acquired all sorts of oddments such as quilts, a tablecloth, a pair of sconces and a tea tray, as well as larger items, including a bureau and a chest of drawers. In January 1742 Mrs Purefoy 'Paid at the Sale at Bidlesdon for a Buroy with glasse doors £7, for 2 Table cloaths £1, for a Tea Table £1 1s., for a card Table £1 5s., for a pair of Sconces 10s. in all'.[43] For grander purchases, she ordered furniture from London, writing on 8 February 1743 to John Belchier, a cabinetmaker who had premises on the south side of St Paul's Churchyard:

This desires Mr. Belchier to send mee a round neat light mahogany folding table with four legs, two of them to draw out to hold up ye ffolds. It must be four foot two inches wide. Send it (with the price thereof) by Mr. Zachary Meads the Bucks carrier who sets out of London on Monday nights & Friday nights.[44]

In 1746 Mrs Purefoy was trying to obtain a second-hand sedan chair; and on 18 July 1749 she complained to John Belchier: 'I have received the Desk, but wee can't open the Draw but do suppose it opens in the two Slitts down the Legs. I desire you will let mee have a [letter] next post how to open & manage it, as also what it comes to that I may order you payment.'[45]

As a result of the fierce competition in the supply of furniture, there were two developments which are important to the middle part of the eighteenth century. The first of these was the increasing magnificence of the shops, which were set out to tempt the casual customer. In the early part of the eighteenth century small items of domestic furniture and utensils were at least as likely to be sold by the travelling chapman as purchased in a local shop. But as competition for goods increased and the market expanded, so it became common for shopkeepers to have a permanent establishment, stocked with goods which were sent from London.[46]

Some of these shops could be extremely grand. According to Defoe,

It is a modern custom, and wholly unknown to our ancestors, who yet understood trade, in proportion to the business they carried on, as well as we do, to have tradesmen lay out two-thirds of their fortune in fitting up their shops. By fitting up, I mean, in painting and gilding, in fine shelves, shutters, pediments, columns of the several orders of architecture, and the like; in which they tell us now, it is small matter to lay out two or three, nay, five hundred pounds, to fit up what we may call the outside of a shop.[47]

Although Defoe is animated by a strong sense of moral disapproval for what he saw as a frivolous misuse of capital investment, it was clearly a trend of the mid-eighteenth century to spend large sums of money on shop fittings, and on shop windows to attract the casual passer-by. Of London shops, André Rouquet wrote in 1755:

The London shops of every kind, make a most brilliant and most agreeable show, which infinitely contributes to the decoration of this great city. Everything is rubb'd clean and neat; every thing is inclosed in large glass shew glasses, whose frames, as well as all the wainscot in the shop, are generally fresh painted, which is productive of an air of wealth and elegance that we do not see in any other city. The signs to their houses are very large, well-painted, and richly gilt; but the costly iron work they hang by, is so clumsy and heavy, that their weight seems to threaten the thin brick wall to which they are fastened.

And yet they are not satisfied with all this decoration of merchandises, with these shew glasses, with these paintings, and gaudy signs. Within these few years the custom has been introduced of dressing the front of their shops, particularly the mercers, with some order of architecture. The columns, the pilasters, the freeze, the cornich, every part in fine preserves its proportion, and bears as great a resemblance to the gate of a little temple as to that of a warehouse. These shops they make as deep as possibly they can; the further end is generally lighted from above, a kind of illumination which joined to the glasses, the sconces, and the rest of the furniture, is in regard to those who are passing by, frequently productive of a theatrical effect, of a most agreeable vista. It is in this extremity of the shop that the English dealer burns that ill placed and tiresome incense with which he almost smothers his customers; here it is that, from too officious a greediness, he oftener disgusts than persuades.[48]

There was a well developed appetite for the display and promotion of consumer goods; shopkeepers were already adept at seducing their customers by the way they arranged and displayed their goods.

A second consequence of the increased competition between suppliers of different types of household goods in the mid-eighteenth century was diversification into stylistic pluralism: if one was supplying essentially the same type of table or chair as a rival firm, one way to differentiate it was to make it in a pseudo-Chinese or Gothic form. It was in these two decades, between 1740 and 1760, that firms began to experiment with a range of different styles in furniture, thereby encouraging people to buy new furnishings to demonstrate their knowledge of the latest fashions.

This stylistic pluralism is evident throughout writings on the applied arts during these years. Indeed, there were periodicals which were established specifically to keep people in touch with the latest ideas in taste. Of many examples of writings which describe, while ostensibly also deploring, the whirligig of new fashions, an item in *The World* on 20 September 1753 describes a newly renovated country house:

In about four months my house was entirely new furnished, but so disguised and altered that I hardly knew it again. There is not a bed, table, a chair, or even a grate, that is not twisted into so many ridiculous and grotesque figures, and so decorated with the heads, beaks, wings and claws of birds and beasts, that Milton's 'Gorgons and hydras and chimeras dire', are not to be compared with them. Every room is completely covered with Wilton carpet, I suppose to save the floors, which are all new laid, and in the most expensive manner. In each of the rooms is a pair or two of stands, supported by different figures of men or beasts, on which are placed branches of Chelsea china, representing lions, bears and other animals, holding in their mouths or paws sprigs of bay, orange or myrtle, among the leaves of which are fixed sockets for the reception of wax candles, which, by dispersing the light among the foliage, I own, make a very agreeable appearance. The upper apartments of my house, which were before handsomely wainscotted are now hung with the richest Chinese and Indian paper, where all the powers of fancy are exhausted in a thousand fantastic figures of birds, beasts and fishes, which never had existence. And what adds to the curiosity is that the fishes are seen flying in the air, or perhaps perching upon trees.[49]

This stylistic eclecticism, with furniture in the strangest and most contorted shapes, is the most marked feature of the middle decades of the century. It should be understood not just in terms of the whims of individual designers, but as part of the drive to find new markets for fashionable goods.

The Rise of the Designer

Closely associated with the changes in the pattern of furniture retailing was the increasing role of the designer, who operated separately from the making of furniture and simply provided drawn designs.[50]

The *Oxford English Dictionary* cites the first use of the word 'design', in terms of the ability to improve the economic competitiveness of commercial goods through their visual appearance, in Bishop Berkeley's work of applied economics, *The Querist*, published in 1735. In this work, Berkeley asks a whole series of analytical questions about the operation of the Irish economy, which include the following:

64. Whether those same manufactures which England imports from other countries may not be admitted from Ireland? And, if

so, whether lace, carpets, and tapestry, three considerable articles of English importation, might not find encouragement in Ireland? And whether an academy for design might not greatly conduce to the perfecting those manufactures among us? 65. Whether France and Flanders could have drawn so much money from England for figured silks, lace and tapestry, if they had not had academies for designing? 66. Whether, when a room was once prepared, and models in plaster of Paris, the annual expense of such an academy need stand the public in above two hundred pounds a year? 67. Whether our linen-manufacturers would not find the benefit of this institution? And whether there be anything that makes us fall short of the Dutch in damasks, diapers, and printed linen, but our ignorance in design? 68. Whether those who may slight this affair as notional have sufficiently considered the extensive use of the art of design, and its influence in most trades and manufactures, wherein the forms of things are often more regarded than the materials?[51]

In these rhetorical questions are many of the problems concerning design which were prominent in the more familiar discussions of the nineteenth century and have been recurrent ever since: whether an academy should be founded to train artists whose work could then be applied to commercial goods, in particular to the decoration of textiles, in order to make them more competitive in an international market; whether the production of luxury goods (such as tapestry and carpets) could compensate for the loss of overseas markets in more staple goods (such as wool); how far the government should intervene in the promotion of design; and whether the consumer judges the desirability of domestic commodities according to the material, the ways things are made, or according to their visual appearance, the surface shape and decoration.

In fact, although the *Oxford English Dictionary* cites this single use by Bishop Berkeley of the word 'design' as it applies to trade and manufacture, it is quite clear that these statements form part of a wider discourse on design which was generally current from the 1730s and continued to gather momentum through the middle of the century. Ephraim Chambers defined design in relation to the manufacture of silks in the first edition of his *Cyclopedia*, published in 1728:

> DESIGN, in the Manufactories, the Figures wherewith the Workman enriches his Stuff, or Silk; and which he copies after some Painter. In undertaking such Kinds of figured Stuffs, 'tis necessary, that before the first Stroak of the Shuttle, the whole Design be represented on the Threads of the Warp.[52]

In October 1731 the *Gentleman's Magazine* published an advertisement for 'A Delineation of the most beautiful and uncommon flowers growing in distant parts, or native of our own clime, disposed in 12 Copper Plates', which collection, it was said, 'will assist the Fancy of Carvers, Pattern-drawers, Embroiderers, Painters, Enamellers and Designers'.[53] In July 1733 an advertisement appeared in the *Daily Post* for the sale of goods belonging to an otherwise obscure cabinetmaker, Francis Croxford, which stated, 'To be sold . . . all the entire stock in trade of the ingenious Mr. Francis Croxford, chair and cabinet-maker, eminent in his profession for his many new and beautiful designs, neatness of workmanship etc.'[54] It is quite clear from these fleeting references in the periodicals of the day that the concept of design as an activity independent from, but intrinsic to, the manufacture of consumer goods was beginning to enter the common currency. Design consciousness emerges in the everyday vocabulary.

By the time of the publication of Campbell's *London Tradesman* in 1747 a good knowledge of drawing was being recommended for the practice of a number of trades, so that it would be possible to invent, rather than just follow, fashion. Of the cabinetmaker, Campbell wrote that

A Youth who designs to make a Figure in this Branch must learn to Draw; for upon this depends the Invention of new Fashions, and on that the Success of his Business: He who first hits upon any new Whim is sure to make by the Invention before it becomes common in the Trade; but he that must always wait for a new Fashion till it comes from Paris, or is hit upon by his Neighbour, is never likely to grow rich or eminent in his Way.[55]

Campbell, moreover, described pattern drawers as belonging to a completely separate branch of commercial activity. According to him, they were 'employed in drawing Patterns for the Callico-Printers, for Embroiderers, Lace-workers, Quilters, and several little Branches belonging to Women's Apparel'.[56] And he acknowledged the need for proper facilities for training, lamenting the fact that 'We have but one Academy, meanly supported by the private Subscription of the Students, in all this great Metropolis: There they have but two Figures, one Man and a Woman; and consequently there can be but little Experience gathered, where there are neither Professors nor Figures.'[57]

During the decade following the publication of Campbell's *London Tradesman*, this demand for proper methods of teaching artisans how to draw became increasingly insistent, alongside the realization of the commercial advantages to be gained. In 1749, John Gwyn, an obscure carpenter-turned-architect, published his *Essay on Design, including proposals for erecting a Public Academy to be supported by Voluntary Subscription*, in which his plans for the establishment of a national academy were supported not merely on the grounds of providing training in the fine arts, but also because 'there may be great pecuniary Advantages, such as ought to engage the Attention of the mere Merchant, obtained from our

Improvements in the Art of Design'.[58] He recognized that 'All Men whose Employment is in the fashioning of Earth, Wood, Metal, or Stone, or in ornamenting the various Utensils of Life which are fashioned from these, must acknowledge that *Drawing* turns greatly to their Account; and that if they can form no Designs of their own, they are constantly obliged to copy those of better Artists';[59] and he documented 'the Complaints of Persons engaged in [those] Parts of the Weaving Trade, where *Design, Invention*, or, as they term it, *Fancy* are concerned'.[60] According to Gwyn,

> These Men have long been convinced of the Necessity of *Drawing* in those Branches, and it is with great Concern that they lament, that notwithstanding the Perfection to which the Silk Manufacture is brought in *London*, particularly in *Spittlefields*, our greatest Artists, for want of Skill to delineate, and thereby improve their own Conceptions, are, in the Article of brocaded Silks in particular, reduced to the Necessity either of calling in the Assistance of the better instructed, though not more ingenious, *French*, who reside among them, or of servilely imitating their less elaborate Performances.[61]

In 1751 Malachy Postlethwayt, in his introduction to his edition of *The Universal Dictionary of Trade and Commerce*, described how

> the increase of trade and navigation greatly depends, not only upon the increase of husbandry and agriculture, but also on the increase of ingenious working artists of every kind, in order to improve the perfection and delicacy of our Old Manufactures, and to discover such New Trades and Manufactures, as will enable us, at least, to keep pace in wealth and power with our rival nations, if we cannot go beyond them.[62]

In 1752 the anonymous author of *Reflections on Various Subjects*

Relating to Arts and Commerce: Particularly, The Consequences of admitting Foreign Artists on easier Terms again called for the establishment of 'An Academy for the Fine Arts' on the grounds that it 'might give us a prospect of some Perfection in the Branches of Tapestry-weaving, Painting, Sculpture and Statuary, and all the lower Trades of Elegance depending on fine Design'.[63]

Meanwhile, several people were putting the requirement for proper training in the arts of design into practice. The history of the provision of art training in the eighteenth century has generally been written in relation to its influence upon the fine arts; but there is ample evidence to demonstrate that there was a strong awareness of its immediate, practical application to various trades. The best known of the various places where it was possible to learn to draw was, as has already been described, the Academy of St Martin's Lane. The Academy was almost certainly not just a place for life drawing but somewhere where jobbing artists could learn the skills required for a highly competitive market in luxury goods. Nearby in Meard Street, the architect Batty Langley and his brother Thomas opened a School of Architecture, where they also taught draughtsmanship to carpenters and other artisans. In 1753 Peter Parisot opened his factory for making carpets and tapestries at Fulham under the patronage of the Duke of Cumberland and, beside it, set up an establishment for tuition in drawing, because, as he claimed, 'Drawing and painting being the arts on which all the fine productions of this manufacture are to be founded, particular care will be taken to educate in these arts, the young people designed to be employed in these manufactures.'[64] In 1755 William Shipley founded the Society of Arts, which had, alongside it, Shipley's own drawing school. In a letter to the *Gentleman's Magazine*, published in January 1756, Shipley very clearly explained his purpose as being to provide financial encouragement and training for the improvement of manufactures, rather than being just to promote the fine arts. He wrote:

The money given for the encouragement of boys and girls to apply themselves to drawing has not, 'tis hoped, been misemployed, since drawing is necessary in so many trades, that the general knowledge of it must conduce greatly to the improvement of our manufactures, and give them an elegance of air and figure, which a rival nation (where drawing is much encouraged) has found, to its great advantage, capable of setting off even indifferent workmanship and mean materials . . . The Society would not be misunderstood to aim at raising numbers of what are usually called painters; but it is earnestly sollicitous to produce among the boys ingenious mechanics, such as carvers, joiners, upholsterers, cabinet-makers, coach makers and coach painters, weavers, curious workers in all sorts of metals, smiths, makers of toys, engravers, sculptors, chasers, calico-printers &c. . . . Nor is it less sollicitous to produce amongst the girls ingenious milliners, mantua makers, embroiderers, pattern drawers, fan-painters, and good workwomen in many other sorts of business where fancy and variety are required.[65]

So by the middle part of the eighteenth century there was an acute awareness of the relationship of a highly competitive international market in luxury goods to their visual appearance and of how design (in the sense of the prior conception and invention of fashionable models) might play a significant part in the chain of sale and production. When Bishop Berkeley came to publish a later edition of *The Querist* in 1750, he added as a postscript: 'Since the first publication of this Query, the art of design seems to be more considered and countenanced among us.'[66] In 1758 Robert Dossie wrote in his book *The Handmaid to the Arts* that,

as several circumstances both of our oeconomical and political condition, by inhancing to a very high degree the price of common necessaries, and introducing more expensive modes of life, are depriving us of the share we had of the grosser manufactures that depend on labour, it particularly behoves us to exert ourselves in cultivating those of a more refined nature; where skill and taste (in which we by no means seem naturally wanting) are required to give a higher value to the work, and stand in the place of a greater proportion of manual operation.[67]

In 1763 Mortimer's *Universal Director* listed, among others, Peter Babel, who was described as 'Designer and Modeller' of 'Long Acre, near James Street', who was said to be 'One of the first Improvers of Papier Mache Ornaments for Cielings, Chimney-pieces, Picture-frames &c. an invention of modern date';[68] and Richard Landcake, who was described as a 'Pattern-drawer for the Manufactories dependent on Design', resident in Gough Square.[69] By that date the independent profession of designer had already been born, and a number of people who can accurately be described as designers could be found lurking in precisely what is still their habitat, the streets of Soho and Covent Garden.

Having established that there was already in existence by the mid-eighteenth century an independent profession of what were described at the time as designers, it is worth trying to answer the question of why it was in the years approximately between 1740 and 1760 that the concept and consciousness of design in its relation to the market of manufactured goods emerged; and why it was particularly in London that this revolution in design awareness took place.

The first reason, which is given constantly by contemporary commentators, as to why it was necessary actively to foster the training of designers was nationalism. There was a constant worry about the extent to which the top end of the market was seduced by French fashion. As Joshua Gee wrote in his book *The Trade and Navigation of Great-Britain Considered*, published in 1729:

England takes from *France* Wine, Brandy, Linnen, Fine Lace,

Fine Cambricks and Cambrick Lawns to a prodigious Value, Brocades, Velvets, and many other rich Silk Manufactures, which are either run in upon us, or come by Way of *Holland*; the Humour of some of our Nobility and Gentry being such, that altho' we have those Manufactures made as good, if not better than the *French*, yet they are forced to be called by the name of *French*, to make them sell.[70]

This was the reason given by Bishop Berkeley for his idea that an Academy for Design should be established in Ireland: that is, the volume of British imports of expensive foreign luxury goods, combined with a realization of what the French government had done under Colbert to promote the training of designers for these industries. A similar reason was given by John Gwyn for his call for the establishment of a national academy in his *Essay on Design*: that British manufacturers were far too dependent on French refugees for the invention of fashionable design; that there were no facilities for training comparable to those in France; and that the French Academy was part of the glory of the nation, which the British ought to be able to emulate. To this extent, the awareness of design in the years 1740 to 1760 reflects the highly ambiguous attitude of the British in these years towards things French: the realization that Paris was the origin of so much that was fashionable; and that fashion was an essential element in marketing, especially of expensive commodities which had a high profit margin.

The second major reason why it was in these years that there was an increased consciousness of the meaning of design is that it relates to an intellectual milieu in which there was an active engagement in problems of political economy. Bishop Berkeley's call for the establishment of an Academy for Design was not an isolated or particularly idiosyncratic statement, but emerged from a context in which there was much public discussion about how to improve the condition of Irish manufactures, which led, in

1731, to the establishment of the Dublin Society for Improving Husbandry, Manufactures, and other Useful Arts and which prompted Berkeley himself to establish a spinning school for children in his diocese at Cloyne. Some of the discussion about how to improve industrial output through design seems to have come from individuals associated with Freemasonry. Ephraim Chambers had been apprenticed to the globe maker and printer John Senex, who had been prominent in the establishment of the Freemasons' Grand Lodge. Batty Langley is well known to have been an active Freemason. It is also worth pointing out that William Shipley's Society for the Promotion of the Arts was first established in 1755 in the Bedford Coffee House, associated with one of the London masonic lodges, and that the first president of the Society was the then Grand Master, the Earl of Morton. In a sense, this is not so much an explanation for the interest in design, as a significant conjunction in intellectual activities, which derived from the search for an applied quasi-scientific understanding of practical affairs, and which likewise led to the many writings on economics during this period. For this reason the desire to set up an Academy for Design, and the many individuals who advertised their services as drawing masters, can be seen as part of the general movement at the time to establish small teaching and training establishments, such as the mathematical schools which proliferated in Spitalfields, Hackney, Wapping and Soho. Design as an activity derives from the desire to order and systematize the form of commodities: it must therefore be seen as associated with the development of an analytical frame of mind and a more general interest in the nature of consciousness. To this extent, design belongs to the broader intellectual history of the period.

The third major reason why design emerged as an active factor in the circumstances of production in the middle part of the eighteenth century was the vastly increased circulation of print. It is well known that during this period there was an immense growth in provincial newspapers, and in the advertising which went with them. There was also a great increase in the publication and circulation of sometimes rather gimcrack source books of designs, of ornament, and of models for artefacts. For example, in 1754, Matthias Darly published *A New Book of Chinese Designs*, in which he collaborated with the ornithologist George Edwards to produce fashionable chinoiserie illustrations to be copied on cotton and porcelain.[71] Darly subsequently advertised his services as 'Professor of Ornament to the Academy of Great Britain', and one of his surviving trade cards describes him as

> DARLY/Engraver in General/No.39 facing New Round Court Strand/Engraves/Coats of Arms, on Gold, Silver or Copper/Visiting Tickets &c Tradesmen's Bills/Frontispieces & Devices for Authors/Plates for Linnen and other/MANUFAC-TURERS/Old Engravings repair'd/& Printing neatly done/ DRAWING TAUGHT on EVENINGS/Drawings made for Gentle-men, Mechanics &c.[72]

A person such as Matthias Darly is symptomatic of a highly competitive market economy in which there was a widespread appetite for novelty in engravings, both engendered and served by an active print trade. As Darly declared polemically in his final book, *The Ornamental Architect, or Young Artists Instructor*, published in 1771:

> Ornamental Drawing has been too long neglected in this Trading Country, and great Losses have been sustained in many of our Manufactures, for want of studying it. On the knowledge of true Embellishment Depends the Improvement of every Article that tends to Ornament or Use, and I do Aver that this Kingdom is more Indebted (as a Commercial State) to Langcake than to a Sr. Godfrey Kneller.[73]

This provides three interconnected reasons for the growth of design consciousness in the middle part of the eighteenth century: the first, a chauvinistic competitiveness with French fashion; the second, a desire for an intellectual analysis of techniques for improving production; the third, a saturation in two-dimensional print which fostered an awareness of three-dimensional design. Yet the most significant questions concerning this issue of the emergence of the designer in the eighteenth century are: what the connection is, if any, between the emergence of an interest in design in the mid-eighteenth century and the state of the national economy; the nature of the hypothetical model of the interrelationship of design and industry in a given historical period; and whether there is any link between the emergence of the designer and the early history of England's industrial economy.

Although there has been a marked shift in the interests of historians towards the nature of consumption – a shift first evident in the volume of essays edited by Neil McKendrick, *The Birth of a Consumer Society* – there is still no agreement amongst either historians or sociologists as to why a shift in the appetite for consumption might have occurred. Any answer to this question is further complicated by the fact that there are two widely divergent interpretations of the state of the economy during this period, 1740 to 1760.[74]

The first interpretation of the economy during these years is essentially pessimistic, a view propounded in several of the current general surveys and which appears in its fullest and clearest form in Anthony Little's *Deceleration in the Eighteenth-Century British Economy*. Little argues, as the title of his book suggests, that, during the second quarter of the eighteenth century, the rate of economic growth slackened as a result of the fall in agricultural prices. The essential elements of this argument are: (1) a series of epidemics in the 1720s produced a short-term reverse in the rate of population growth; (2) a run of good harvests in the 1730s and 1740s, combined with a static population, produced a surplus of grain and low agricultural prices; (3) low agricultural prices caused difficulties in the economy of the countryside, evident in vacant holdings and rent arrears; (4) problems in the agricultural sector in turn led to stagnation, or even contraction, in the home demand for manufactured goods; (5) this was paralleled by problems in the overseas markets, due to the widespread imposition of protective tariffs and increased competition in third markets. These factors are held to have combined to produce a downward turn in the rate of economic growth, if not an actual recession.

This essentially pessimistic view of the economy has implications for how one regards the emergence of a self-conscious interest in design. According to this interpretation, the rise of design would constitute a response to poor trading in international markets, a way of increasing the competitiveness of export goods as well as a means of import substitution. The increased interest in the production of luxury goods, such as silks, hats and toys, would then appear as a search for an alternative to the traditional reliance on the woollen trade, which did not have the same high profit margins and for which an awareness of fashion was not a particularly important concern. Design, then, is seen as a form of response to a stagnant economy.

The alternative view of the economy during the years 1740 to 1760 is the opposite, a basically optimistic and favourable interpretation. According to this argument, (1) the idea that the epidemics of the 1720s had a significant effect on the rate of population growth is thought to be misconceived: on the contrary, the latest and most authoritative estimates of population change suggest that a brief fall during the 1720s was followed by a slow, but reasonably steady rate of increase in succeeding decades, producing an estimated percentage change of 0.62 in the 1730s, 0.42 in the 1740s and 0.66 in the 1750s; (2) the great bounty of good harvests in the 1730s and 1740s is still held to have produced a surplus of grain and low agricultural prices, but this is thought to have been to the great benefit of the bulk of the population, since cheaper prices of staple foodstuffs released funds in the average domestic budget for the purchase of manufactured goods; (3) the relatively rapid population growth and the rising real incomes resulting from falling agricultural prices are thought to have been met by a rapid increase in agricultural output, through cost-reducing innovations; (4) as the population grew, so did aggregate incomes and aggregate demand, producing a buoyant and less risky environment for investors and entrepreneurs; (5) the export market is thought to have accounted for a relatively low proportion of industrial output, in contrast to the important changes in home demand for manufactured goods. These factors combined, it is now believed, to create not a stagnant, but, precisely the opposite, a booming domestic economy, in which the gross national product increased from £57.5 million in 1720 to £64.1 million in 1740, a rise of 11.5 per cent.

This argument about the rate of economic growth in the second quarter of the eighteenth century is relevant to the status of the interest in design. A favourable interpretation of the economy during these years has important implications for a possible connection between design and changes in the demand for manufactured goods. On the one hand, there seems to be good evidence for suggesting that there was a rise in the real income of a large proportion of the population: that is, there were more people who had more money in their pockets available for the purchase either of more expensive or of a more diversified range of manufactured goods. On the other hand, there was an increasing interest among commentators on the economy in the promotion of design, that is, an interest in the creation of a more highly differentiated range of products. It would seem to be reasonable to suggest that there may have been some causal relation.

The rising economic prosperity of the country is clearly reflected in the changing material conditions of life in England in the middle decades of the eighteenth century. Abbé Le Blanc wrote of the conditions of prosperity for the farmer:

The fruits of his labour are not only sufficient for his necessities, but also enable him to procure that sort of superfluidity which makes what we term, the *pleasure of life*, and which varies according to men's different conditions; all of which we may say, have their luxuries. In England as well as in Holland, the villages are neater and better built than in France; every thing in them declares the riches of the inhabitants. One perceives by the houses of the English farmers, that they are in easy circumstances enough to have a taste for neatness, and that they have likewise time enough to satisfy it.[75]

By 1757 Tucker was able to write of the material conditions of the English:

England being a free Country, where Riches got by Trade are no Disgrace, and where Property is also safe against the Prerogative either of Prince or Nobles, and where every Person may make what Display he pleases of his Wealth, without incurring a higher *Taille*, Poll, or Capitation the next Year for so doing; – the Manufactures of the Kingdom accomodate themselves, if I may so speak, to the Constitution of it: That is, they are more adapted for the Demands of Peasants and Mechanics, in order to appear in warm Circumstances; – for Farmers, Freeholders, Tradesmen, and Manufacturers in middling Life; – and for wholesale Dealers, Merchants, and all Persons of Landed Estates, to appear in genteel Life; than for the Magnificence of Palaces, or the Cabinets of Princes. Thus it is, according to the very Spirit of our Constitution, that the *English* of these several Denominations have better Conveniencies in their Houses, and affect to have more in Quantity of clean, neat Furniture, and a greater Variety (such as Carpets, Screens, Window Curtains, Chamber Bells, polished Brass Locks, Fenders, &c.&c. Things hardly known Abroad among Persons of such a Rank) than are to be found in any other Country in *Europe, Holland* excepted.[76]

Long before the so-called industrialization of England, large sections of the population were able to enjoy conditions of considerable comfort and prosperity, spending their income on a whole range of manufactured goods; and the professional designer emerged to improve the diversity of appearance of commodities for sale.

Architectural Drawings

In comparison to the immense changes in the physical appearance of consumer goods in the middle decades of the eighteenth century, the 1740s were a dull period in the history of architecture, when the energy and enthusiasm for the restoration of architecture through the study of antique ideals had been dissipated. Instead, worthy but unimaginative architects turned out buildings of rather similar design. Le Blanc commented in his *Letters on the English and French Nations*:

> My lord Burlington, who has joined example to precept, by the fine house which he has built for himself at London, and some things which he has published concerning architecture; has endeavoured to give his countrymen a taste for it. But these models have not made the English architects more expert; for whenever they attempt to do any thing more than barely to copy, they erect nothing but heavy masses of stone.[77]

Perhaps partly in rebellion against the constraints imposed by the strict classical vocabulary employed on the exteriors of buildings, interior decoration became increasingly inventive.

Elizabeth Montagu, the 'bluestocking', wrote to the Revd Mr Friend in 1749:

> Thus has it happened in furniture; sick of Grecian elegance and symmetry, or Gothic grandeur and magnificence, we must all seek the barbarous gaudy goût of the Chinese; and fat-headed Pagods, and shaking Mandarins, bear the prize from the finest works of antiquity; and Apollo and Venus must give way to a fat idol with a sconce on his head.[78]

This shift in the conventions of decoration is evident in the architectural drawings of the period. In 1747 the architect John Sanderson, was called in to complete the design of Kirtlington Park in Oxfordshire. Architectural plans for the house had been supplied by James Gibbs in 1741; construction had begun on 5 April 1742, when, according to a small pocketbook belonging to the owner, Sir James Dashwood, workmen 'began to dig foundations of new house'; on 22 April the foundation stone was laid; in August 1746 Sir James and his family moved in and port and champagne were ordered to celebrate their arrival; but the interiors remained to be decorated.[79] The designs which were submitted by John Sanderson were, in their outlines, similar to the standard type of rooms of the previous twenty-five years, with heavy door surrounds and a compartmented ceiling; but in their ornament they show evidence of an inventive use of plasterwork, pioneered by the Italian *stuccatori* Giovanni Bagutti and Guiseppe Artari.

A similar style of representation was employed by the prolific country house architect James Paine, in plans he drew for the dining room at Gopsall Hall in Leicestershire.

In contrast to the restricted conventions of drawings for complete rooms around the year 1750, it was a period when architects began to experiment with, and indulge in, slightly wild fantasies in the individual features of interior decoration. For example, at some time in the 1750s, Sir Robert Taylor, normally a very correct and conventional architect, prepared a book of designs for chimneypieces which contains an eccentric collection of ornamental motifs, one with vines surrounding a mirror, another with bloated fish falling out of reeds on either side of the mirror surround.[80]

These drawings reflect the many, sometimes *outré*, plates of elements of the interior which were published in pattern books during the 1750s.[81] Although Abraham Swan, who was responsible for several books of designs during this decade, stuck to conventional and conservative models, on the grounds presumably that he was consciously aiming at the middle market, others were more adventurous. Most notably, in William and John Halfpenny's *The Modern Builder's Assistant*, published in 1757, there are plates which show rooms in chinoiserie style, with mandarins popping their heads out from behind ornamental foliage.

Towards the end of the 1750s the routine conventions of architectural drawing were reinvigorated by James Stuart, known as 'Athenian' Stuart. Stuart was born in London, the son of a Scottish sailor. He is assumed to have been trained as a draughtsman by the fan painter Lewis Goupy, and developed the ability to draw in pen and ink with attractive washes, and to paint in bodycolour.[82] He also taught himself Latin in order to read 'what was written under prints published after pictures of the ancient masters' and travelled to Rome on foot, keeping himself by painting fans. In 1748 a group of young enthusiasts for the classical past, all of them working in Rome as guides, decided that, in order to understand the classical past properly, they should not rest content with Rome but ought to visit Athens; among them were James Stuart and Nicholas Revett who, in the same year, together issued 'Proposals for publishing an Accurate Description of the Antiquities of Athens'. According to the 'Proposals',

Athens, the mother of Elegance and Politeness, whose magnificence scarce yielded to that of Rome, and who for beauties of a correct style must be allowed to surpass her, as much as an original excels a copy, has been almost completely neglected, and unless exact drawings from them be speedily made, all her beauteous Fabricks, her Temples, her Theatres, her Palaces will drop into oblivion.[83]

A group of rich young members of the Society of Dilettanti in Rome decided that the project was worth undertaking and that they would pay for it. In the early part of 1751 Stuart and Revett travelled to Athens, a city which was at that time unfamiliar to the eyes of western Europeans because of its long occupation by the Turks. They were able to make extensive drawings of the surviving antiquities, and returned to England in 1755 to prepare the drawings for publication.

On their return to London, Stuart and Revett were much in demand to provide advice and drawings for schemes of interior decoration, and for more substantial projects. They had the unique cachet of having been in Athens, which, now that travel to Rome was becoming common, marked them out as having a superior form of expertise. Moreover, James Stuart was able to use his abilities as a skilled draughtsman, able to convey the essential features of an interior with an attractive fluency.

In 1757 Stuart prepared drawings for the hall and dining room at Wimbledon Park in Surrey, which had been inherited by John Spencer, subsequently the first Earl Spencer.[84] Stuart's designs show the essential features of his style: vividness and the ability to convey three-dimensional animation in ornament and decorative features. The closet at Wimbledon Park, which was decorated by Stuart, was not appreciated by Horace Walpole, who described it as 'ornamented and painted by Mr. Stewart. the ornaments in a good antique taste. a Hymen, the Allegro & Penseroso, on the cieling & in compartments, villainously painted'.[85]

Towards the end of 1758 Stuart was called in to advise on the decoration of Kedleston in Derbyshire by Sir Nathaniel Curzon, a Derbyshire landowner, who had inherited substantial estates and a baronetcy in that year, and was reputed to have an annual income of £12,000 and to employ 10,000 coalminers.[86] A set of drawings survives which demonstrates Stuart's intense sensitivity to the atmosphere of a room – a sensibility which found its appropriate form of expression in the delicate wash applied to the designs for wall decoration. For the saloon, he provided proposals for the layout of pictures, to be hung symmetrically behind a line of chairs to create an appropriate pattern on the wall. On the end wall a substantial jasper urn, sent not long before from Sicily by the sculptor Richard Hayward, was to be placed under a table, flanked by further urns standing on appropriate bases; above the table, a shallow niche was to be decorated with curlicues and plasterwork swags. The significance of these drawings has long been recognized. What is striking about them is not so much that they indicate precisely how and where the pictures were to be hung, but more in the sensibility applied to the arrangement of the different components of a room, the feeling that if one part were displaced, the whole ensemble would lose its effect.[87]

In 1759 James Stuart provided designs for the interiors of John Spencer's town house in St James's Place, which had been built to the plans of John Vardy. Stuart's drawing for the painted room upstairs is in the so-called 'grotesque' style of decoration, pioneered by William Kent in the interiors of Kensington Palace. At Spencer House Stuart used the style with much more vigour, and a complete conviction in the way the ornament is arranged. As in his other drawings of interiors, Stuart demonstrates a refinement of aesthetic appreciation which is highly attractive.

Having seen the benefits to be gained from a more careful appreciation of how a room was to be arranged, other architects of the period swiftly began to follow Stuart's example. In 1759 William Chambers attempted to entice Edward, Duke of York, with a proposal for a grand town house in Pall Mall. The drawings he presented, which show the house as if it has been accidentally sliced in half and with the beginnings of a Piranesi-like decay creeping into the skyline, introduce a new level of realism to architectural drawings. The house is a doll's house, locked in time, with wallpaper still on the walls and the afternoon sun making shadows on the walls of the central staircase.[88]

The conventional way of explaining the transformation in graphic style which the drawings of James Stuart and Sir William Chambers represent is by tracing it to its origins in Rome. During the 1740s and the early part of the 1750s a number of artists in Rome had embraced a pictorial view of the classical past, admiring the remains not only for the information that they could provide, but as vivid reminders of history: classical monuments were no longer drawn in isolation, reconstructed as they would have been, but were admired for their state of decay, as fragments to be depicted *in situ*. This reinvigorated classicism, whose adherents viewed antiquity idealistically as a source of inspiration, was to dominate interiors in the succeeding two decades.

1760–1780

The Impact of Adam

If the first great stylistic revolution of the eighteenth century was the self-conscious importation of Palladian ideas of architecture and decoration from around 1715 onwards, the second was the profound effect that the architectural practice of Robert and James Adam had on the layout of interiors.

Robert Adam's father, William Adam, was himself a successful architect, described by John Clerk of Eldin as 'a man of distinguished genius, inventive enterprise and persevering application, attended with a graceful, independent and engaging address'.[1] William Adam married in 1716 and had four sons: the eldest, John Adam, was born in 1721 and carried on his father's firm, becoming, like his father, Master Mason to the Board of Ordinance and laird of Blair Adam, the family seat; his second son, Robert, was born in 1728 and started his career in partnership with his elder brother until, in 1754, he had the resources to embark on a Grand Tour, intending to establish himself as an architect in London on his return; the third son, James Adam, was born in 1732 and also went on a Grand Tour, from which he returned in 1763 to work in partnership with Robert; the fourth son, William, had an unsuccessful business career in the City.

Of these brothers Robert was the most able, as well as the most ambitious. According to Clerk of Eldin, he 'was from his infancy of a feeble constitution, which frequently seems the attendant of genius and refined taste. It was early discovered that in him they were united.'[2] He was educated at Edinburgh High School and then for two years at the University, before ending his studies at the age of eighteen in order to work with his father. In the years following he helped in the family firm with projects for the Board of Ordinance, and with the designs of Hopetoun House, outside Edinburgh, and Dumfries House, in Ayrshire, until, in 1754, he was invited to accompany the Hon. Charles Hope, younger brother of the Earl of Hopetoun, on his Grand Tour.

Adam and Hope travelled down through France, buying finery in Paris, meeting the engraver Cochin, having fun in Montpellier, travelling to Genoa by sea, and arriving in Florence on 30 January 1755 in time for the carnival. In Florence Adam met a French artist, Charles-Louis Clérisseau, of whom he wrote, 'He draws in architecture delightfully, in the free manner I wanted. I hope to reap some instruction from him.' He quickly realized that Clérisseau was able to provide him with exactly the knowledge and instruction which he had come to Italy to acquire. On 13 February he wrote:

I hope to have my ideas greatly enlarged and my taste formed upon the solid foundation of genuine antiquity. I already feel a passion for sculpture and painting which I before was ignorant of, and I am convinced that my whole conception of architecture will become much more noble than I could ever have attained by staying in Britain.[3]

This letter indicates Adam's slightly naive preconceptions of how foreign travel might benefit him and how he had recognized the desirability of a scenic view of antique remains. Six days later he was able to write of Clérisseau:

He raised my ideas. He created emulation of fire in my breast. I wished above all things to learn his manner, to have him with me at Rome, to study close with him and to purchase of his works. What I wished for I obtained. He took a liking to me.[4]

Soon afterwards Adam moved on to Rome. He fell out with Charles Hope, installed himself and Clérisseau in a house above the Spanish Steps, and embarked on an ambitious programme of self-instruction, including the purchase of 'all the books of architecture, of altars, chapels, churches, views of Piranesi and of all gates, windows, doors and ornaments that can be of service to us'.[5] He met Piranesi in June of that year and reported to his family in Edinburgh that

Piranesi, who is I think the most extraordinary fellow I ever saw, is become immensely intimate with me and as he imagined at first that I was like the other English who had a love of antiques without knowledge, upon seeing some of my sketches and drawings was so highly delighted that he almost ran quite distracted and said I have more genius for the true noble architecture than any Englishman ever was in Italy.[6]

It was from Piranesi and Clérisseau that Adam acquired his drawing skills. He was to spend the following two years in a campaign of self-improvement, constantly looking over his shoulder to see how his progress compared with that of William Chambers, who was also in Rome at the time and whom Adam rightly saw as his principal potential rival. He succeeded in everything he set out to do and returned to London in January 1758 with a specially made trunk full of architectural drawings, and with numerous old master paintings which he proposed to sell at a fat profit in London. He had gained a good knowledge of antique ornament, and the dedication of Piranesi's *Antichità romana* to 'Roberti Adams Scot'.

On his return to London Adam set himself up in considerable style, first in rooms in Cleveland Court, St James's, and subsequently in a house in Lower Grosvenor Street, so that he could show off his skills to prospective clients. As he had written rather cynically in Italy, it was essential 'to blind the world by dazzling their eyesight with vain pomp'.[7] This comment is a fair encapsulation of the skills which Adam brought to the arts of decoration: the ability to dazzle the eye with vivid surface ornament which made no pretence to great originality except in the way it was employed.

One of Adam's first clients was Fanny Boscawen, wife to Admiral Edward Boscawen. The Admiral was a tough, bellicose Cornishman, known as 'Old Dreadnought' to his sailors; Fanny was an independent-minded woman, who had been forced to look after her children during her husband's long absences at sea and had consciously developed an interest in interior decoration. When she furnished their London house in South Audley Street in 1748, she corresponded with her husband about her choice of wallpapers and fabrics, describing how

> I have tried at china ornaments for my chimney-pieces, which demand them in great quantities, but I have not been able yet to raise myself to the price of anything good and I don't care for a parcel of trumpery – like some chimney-pieces we know of.[8]

She was perplexed about the colour match of the hangings in the so-called bow window room:

> I consulted nobody about either – not one single person having seen either the paper or the linen till both were made up. Everyone commends each separate, but dislike them together and maintain I must have coloured linen to my coloured paper. I agree so far with them that I bestow my old chintz gown as

fast as they wear out, but till then I shall not give up my taste and opinion that 'tis now extremely pretty.[9]

In general, she was pleased with her abilities, and she set herself up as an arbiter of taste, advising others about their choice of furniture and ornaments on the grounds that 'Taste I have always pretended to and must own I shall be greatly disappointed if you do not approve that which I have displayed in Audley Street.'[10]

In 1755 the Boscawens bought a house at Hatchlands in Surrey and set about rebuilding it. It was ready for roofing in 1757. In 1758 or early 1759 Fanny Boscawen invited Robert Adam to advise on the interior decoration. He produced a design which shows his style in embryo, with flat painted motifs confined to panels and flanking a view of a classical ruin.

Soon afterwards, Adam was approached by Sir Nathaniel Curzon to provide advice on the interiors of Kedleston. He seized the opportunity to vilify the contribution of James Stuart, declaring that his work was 'pityfulissimo'. As a result he was able to replace Stuart as the principal architect involved in the schemes for the interior. He achieved this probably as much through his forceful personality and skill in organization as the aesthetics of the style he had to offer. But Curzon was justified in the decision by the fact that Adam went on to design a whole series of remarkable interiors, with wonderful coloured drawings, which were neater and more precise than those of Stuart.[11]

As a result of the success of his work at Kedleston, and thanks to continual hustling, Adam began to secure other major commissions.[12] He produced designs for the interiors of Shardeloes in Buckinghamshire for William Drake in 1759; for Harewood House in Yorkshire for Edwin Lascelles, also in 1759; and for Croome Court in Worcestershire for the sixth Earl of Coventry in 1760. In all these commissions, Adam was not the originating architect, but was called in to provide a high-class, ornamental vivacity to the interior arrangements of houses which had already been designed by more pedestrian architects.

Adam demonstrated his supreme abilities at revitalizing interiors in two houses near one another a few miles to the west of London, Syon House at Isleworth and Osterley Park. Syon was redesigned for one of the grandest members of the nobility, Hugh Percy, Duke of Northumberland, and his energetic wife, who regarded herself as something of an expert on interior decoration.[13] They kept up a lavish style of life, throwing gigantic parties at Northumberland House in the Strand, and were described by Horace Walpole as living 'by the etiquette of the old peerage'.[14] At Syon Adam had the opportunity of developing the interiors of an old house, for a patron who was both sympathetic to what he proposed and had a plentiful supply of funds. As a result, the house is one of the most effective monuments to Adam's abilities, and was recognised as such by its inclusion in his published *Works*, where he wrote that, 'as the idea was to me a favourite one, the subject great, the expence unlimited, and the Duke himself a person of extensive knowledge and correct taste in architecture, I endeavoured to render it a noble and elegant habitation'.[15] He certainly succeeded in providing a set of fantastically ornate, but carefully differentiated interiors, so that it is possible to move round the house in a circuit, being overwhelmed by the diversity of ornamental effect. It is a sequence of rooms which show Adam operating a very sensitively attuned instrument with all the stops out, a tremendous *tour de force* of high colour and surface ornament.

At Osterley Adam was able to provide a very different client, Sir Robert Child of the banking family, with interiors of similar, sustained magnificence, each one contributing to the cumulative effect. What Adam was adept at doing was articulating a sequence in which each room is distinguished by means of colour tones, surface decoration, and, in some houses, the furniture as well. Horace Walpole wrote: 'There is a hall, library, breakfast-room, eating-room, all *chefs d'oeuvre* of Adam, a gallery one hundred and thirty feet long, and a drawing-room worthy of Eve before the Fall. Mrs Child's dressing-room is full of pictures, gold filigree, china and japan. So is all the house.'[16] This was just the kind of breathless rapture which the Adam brothers' interiors were planned to induce.

When these interiors are examined, it is clear why Robert Adam – who was now assisted by his younger brother James, returned from Rome – was so successful. Previous architects who had dealt with interiors, even including Kent, had tended to operate with a single decorative vocabulary; but the Adam brothers were able to adjust the decorative effect room by room, so that every interior had a different character. Later in their career, this ability to treat each interior separately turned into a formula and their surface effects became increasingly two-dimensional; but in the early stages of their career, when they were busy making their reputation, they were able to orchestrate an impressive range of stylistic effects.

Although the bulk of Robert Adam's early work was the design of interiors in country houses, some of the best of the brothers' later work appears in their refurbishment of London houses. They received commissions in the early 1760s from the Earl of Bute, whom they had been assiduously cultivating ever since they returned from Rome, for the design of Shelburne House on the south side of Berkeley Square; and from Sir Lawrence Dundas, another member of the Scottish ascendancy in London, who had made a fortune from army contracts during the Seven Years' War. At the end of the 1760s they designed Kenwood, a substantial villa on the edge of Hampstead Heath, for William Murray, a great Scottish lawyer and orator, who in 1756 had been made Lord Chief Justice of the King's Bench, with a seat in the House of Lords as Earl of Mansfield.[17] Here, as at Syon and Osterley, it is possible to appreciate the way the Adams articulated the physical experience of moving through the house, the transitions between the rooms, the different room shapes, and the contrasting temperatures of their decoration.

In the early 1770s the Adam brothers designed 20 St James's Square for Sir Watkin Williams Wynn; Derby House in Grosvenor Square for Lord Stanley, later twelfth Earl of Derby; and Home House for the rich old Countess of Home in Portman Square. These town houses reveal another facet of their skills: their ability to contrive sharply distinguished interior spaces in a confined area, exhibiting a sense of spatial as well as decorative control.

That the Adam brothers were fully conscious of the effect that they were trying to achieve is evident from the preface to their *Works in Architecture*, in which they boast:

> We have adopted a beautiful variety of light mouldings, gracefully formed, delicately enriched and arranged with propriety and skill. We have introduced a great diversity of ceilings, freezes, and decorated pilasters, and have added grace and beauty to the whole, by a mixture of grotesque stucco, and painted ornaments, together with the flowing rainceau, with its fanciful figures and winding foliage.[18]

It is clear from the comments on plans that they paid much attention to the use of rooms, and to distinguishing the ornamental character of rooms according to their function. As they wrote,

> To understand thoroughly the art of living, it is necessary, perhaps, to have passed some time amongst the French, and to have studied the customs of that social and conversible people. In one particular, however, our manners prevent us from imitating them. Their eating rooms seldom or never constitute a piece in their great apartments, but lie out of the suite, and in fitting them up, little attention is paid to beauty of decoration.

The reason of this is obvious; the French meet there only at meals, when they trust to the display of the table for show and magnificence, not to the decoration of the apartment; and as soon as the entertainment is over, they immediately retire to the rooms of company. It is not so with us. Accustomed by habit, or induced by the nature of our climate, we indulge more largely in the enjoyment of the bottle.[19]

In working on their interiors the Adams were able to call upon the services of a whole army of skilled assistants, including draughtsmen whom they brought over from Italy to work in their office, a range of decorative painters, and specialist suppliers of furniture, including Chippendale and the Linnells. According to David Hume in a letter to Adam Smith of 27 June 1772, they had at least 3,000 dependent on them for work, which, even if it is an exaggeration, indicates something of the scale of their operation. Mrs Montagu described their arrival in a letter to the Duchess of Portland on 20 July 1779:

[Mr Adam] came at the head of a regiment of artificers an hour after the time he had promised: the bricklayers talked an hour about the alterations to be made in a wall; the stonemason was as eloquent about the coping of the said wall; the carpenter thought the internal fitting up of the house not less important; then came the painter, who is painting my ceilings in various colours according to the present fashion.[20]

As in the case of other designers of the 1760s and 1770s, notably Wedgwood and Boulton, Adam is significant not simply as an innovator in what he had to offer, but for the energy with which he promoted his activities. Like them, he was an entrepreneur of taste.

It is tempting sometimes to think of the work of the Adam brothers as facile, or even meretricious. They were too adept at pinching commissions from other architects, too brazenly aware of their own abilities. Certainly they concentrated the bulk of their attention on the more superficial aspects of decoration, rather than on the more solid characteristics of architecture. Yet it is impossible not to be overwhelmed by the sheer bravura skill of the best of the Adams' interiors, the range of their decorative effects, the beauty of their preparatory drawings, and their ability to take a room and make it into something polished and novel.

The Work of Zoffany

Closely akin to the Adam brothers' ability to distinguish the unique character of a room and, if necessary, to manufacture it, are the aesthetic qualities of the work of Johann Zoffany, whose paintings provide the most detailed characterization of interiors at this period. Zoffany was serving the same clientele: rich, frequently noble, leisured, conscious of the movement of fashion, and wanting to keep abreast of it. The immense success of Britain at war, the expansion and consolidation of her overseas empire, the profits of trade, and the improvements which had been made in agriculture, had created a social élite which, in the early 1760s at least, was self-confident, assured of the superiority of the British political system, and wanting to be artistically commemorated at home. Its members liked to go to exhibitions of paintings, to enjoy musical performances at Vauxhall Gardens, and to worry about whether their drawing rooms were in fashion. Of course the time had its political troubles, not least in the popular protests associated with John Wilkes; but the impression conveyed by the art of the period is of an élite determined to demonstrate its place in the world.

Zoffany provides the best record of the interior life of this social élite. He was German by birth, was born in Frankfurt on 13 March 1733 and, like Robert Adam, spent much of the 1750s in

Rome.[21] Piranesi dedicated one of the plates of his *Vasi, candelabri, cippi* to him. Returning to Regensburg in 1757, Zoffany began decorating rooms in the palace of Clemens August, Prince-Archbishop and Elector of Trier. Perhaps realizing the greater opportunities for practising his art in England, he came to London in 1760, but was initially forced to scratch a living as a drapery painter for an inferior artist, Benjamin Wilson. He was rescued from this drudgery by the actor David Garrick, who commissioned Zoffany to paint him performing in *The Farmer's Return* and lounging at his weekend villa on the banks of the Thames.[22] Soon afterwards Zoffany was asked by Lord Bute to paint his family, at exactly the time that Robert Adam was at work on the designs for Lansdowne House; he was probably introduced by Bute to Queen Charlotte.

For Queen Charlotte, Zoffany painted two of the best known scenes of eighteenth-century interiors. The first was a portrait of George, Prince of Wales and his younger brother Frederick, later Duke of York, playing with a spaniel in one of the drawing rooms at Buckingham House.[23] The painting is significant not only for the extent to which it represents the children enjoying their own imaginative space, suggesting a new sensibility towards childhood, but also for the way in which the picture space is dominated by the room and the sitters occupy only a small area, not at the centre. Indeed the surroundings are painted with at least as much care and precision as the sitters themselves, including the patterned wall-to-wall carpet, the embroidered firescreen, the tongs propped up against the mantelpiece, and the elaborate carved overmantel whose mirror reflects the door surround behind. It is all painted with an extraordinary degree of fastidious attention to carved ornament and fabric, as if goods and chattels were at least as interesting as the personalities of the sitters.

The second picture painted by Zoffany for Queen Charlotte in 1764 shows her sitting at her dressing table and the same two sons, the elder dressed up as Telemachus and the younger as a Turk.

Once again, this picture is notable not for its characterization, which is fairly inert, but for the attention which is paid to every detail of the surroundings: the child's drum on the armchair on the left, the sumptuous lace covering of the toilet table, every bottle and jar of Queen Charlotte's toilet service. It is a picture which makes one feel as if one is in the room and can breathe its air – but not, curiously, engage in any form of discussion with the sitters, who evaporate on contact. It is more enticing to travel away from them down the corridor. There is an interesting dislocation of subjects from setting; the setting has become the focus of interest, and the image in the mirror is more real than the sitters.

As a result of his success at fulfilling the demands of these early, and unusually advantageous, royal commissions, Zoffany went on to paint a whole series of portraits of the nobility and their offspring at play, and of actors aping their behaviour. For example, in 1768 he painted Mrs Abington in *The Way to Keep Him*, a play by Arthur Murphy, in a work which is a composite of his two earlier royal portraits, with Mrs Abington standing in front of a toilet table, which is similar to Queen Charlotte's, and a fireplace and firescreen which bear a marked resemblance to those of Buckingham House.

In 1769 Zoffany was commissioned by Sir Lawrence Dundas to record the appearance of the library of his house at 19 Arlington Street, which had been redesigned by the Adams. Throughout the 1760s Dundas had been acquiring furniture from the leading cabinetmakers of the day, including bookcases, for which Chippendale was paid £80, and a library table costing £37.[24] An inventory of the year before lists the contents of the library as:

A Chimney Board
A Turkey Carpet
2 Morine Window Curtains
A Pier glass in a gilt frame

A large mahogany Library table
A smaller Do.
A large mahogany pediment Book Case and an alabaster vauze
on Do.
A smaller Book Case
2 Mahogany Presses
A Mahogany 2 flap table
a large gilt 5 flap Screen
a french Elbow Chair in horse hair
5 Back stools in leather
A Wind Dial
4 Pictures
2 Branches screw'd to the Chimney
A Square Trunk.

Zoffany depicts the room with the same precision as the inventory, including the turkey carpet, the moreen curtains (moreen was a worsted cloth made in Kidderminster and recommended for the use of libraries), and the mahogany two-flap table. It is an intriguing image, showing the Commissar to the army, described by Boswell as 'a cunning shrewd man of the world', transformed into a benevolent grandfather and connoisseur, without any hint of the gambling and profiteering which had made his fortune. For his labours Zoffany was paid £105.

The last of Zoffany's major paintings of interiors was of the collector Charles Townley, sitting in the library of his house in Park Street, now Queen Anne's Gate.[25] Townley was a Lancashire Catholic, who had inherited a substantial estate outside Burnley. In 1765 he decided to leave England to live in Rome, where he developed an interest in collecting classical statuary. He returned to London in 1772, where he continued to acquire works for his collection through agents in Italy, and purchased a derelict house in Park Street which he converted especially to contain his collection. According to J.T. Smith, 'The library was highly interesting: it was lighted from above, and was in every respect an excellent room for study. The Marbles in it were not so numerous as those in the dining-parlour, but they consisted of some choice specimens.'[26] Here, and in the dining room which looked out over St James's Park, Townley used to entertain the eminent artists and collectors of the day. He remained a bachelor and used to refer to the bust of Clytemnestra (shown on the table in Zoffany's painting) as his wife.

Zoffany depicts Townley sitting at his ease in an armchair with his dog Kam (short for Kamchatka) lying at his feet. Beyond him, the French scholar Pierre Hugues, better known as d'Hancarville, has a book open on the table, presumably the catalogue he was compiling of the collection, while in the background two antiquaries, Charles Greville and Thomas Astle, converse. The sculptures are not shown as they were arranged in the house. Instead, as J.T. Smith describes, 'It was a portrait of the library, though not strictly correct as to its contents, since all the best of the marbles displayed in various parts of the house were brought into the painting by the artist, who made it up into a picturesque composition according to his own taste.'[27] The painting provides the archetypal image of the late eighteenth-century connoisseur, enjoying a life of cultivated leisure in the company of busts, bas reliefs, marble gods and his fellow antiquaries.

In this painting, as in his other work, Zoffany is not especially interested in the sitter. It was intended rather as a record of the collection. Indeed, when the painting was exhibited at the Royal Academy in 1790 it was described simply as 'A Nobleman's Collection'. In 1792 Zoffany was happy to add the Discobolus on the left-hand side of the painting, after Townley's acquisition of it in 1791.

Zoffany was able to record an interior with a curiously bland precision. His view of the role of the portrait painter was entirely different from what had been considered appropriate in the first half of the eighteenth century, and was totally contrary to the recommendations of his friend and contemporary Sir Joshua Reynolds. Instead of concentrating on character and elevating it, Zoffany was quite content to invent compositions which deliberately aimed to reproduce the appearance of reality.

Technology in the Home

One of the features shared by the work of Adam and Zoffany is their sense of precision. In his work, Adam identifies the functional and decorative requirements of a room and fulfils them with exactitude. Zoffany takes the whole picture surface and treats every aspect of it, down to the last door knob and fender, with the same care. Both show a feeling for the significance of the domestic environment which, for Adam, is worthy of substantial, even if essentially cosmetic, improvement and, for Zoffany, deserves the most detailed pictorial record. In the art of both there is a strong element of almost mechanical ingenuity, focusing on the conditions of domestic life. This precision engineering of the domestic interior can be related to the changes which were taking place in British manufacturing at the time.

Traditionally the period from 1760 to 1780 has been regarded as marking the take-off of industrialization. It was in these years that major improvements were made to the processes of textile manufacture, including the invention of Hargreaves's spinning jenny, which enabled a single person to spin on several spindles simultaneously, around 1764; and of Arkwright's water frame, patented in 1769. They were decades of fertile scientific experiment, with improvements in the understanding of the processes of steam and its application to pumping engines; of rapid development of the road system, with a whole series of Turnpike Acts; of legislation for the construction of canals, including the Grand Trunk, or Trent and Mersey, agreed by Act of Parliament in 1766 and constructed by 1777; and of expansion of the towns, particularly in the industrial parts of the Midlands and the north.

Of course, it is easy to exaggerate the impact of these developments. In retrospect, changes in the systems of manufacture are apt to appear more significant than they did at the time. Indeed, one of the benefits of examining the changing appearance of the eighteenth-century interior is that it is possible to shift the emphasis in the observation of historical change away from the circumstances of production – the factories, the craftsmen who specialized in the making of goods, and their outworkers – and to focus instead on the place where the goods were consumed. Instead of looking at industrialization in terms of the accumulation of capital, the chronology of technical inventions, and the organization of labour, it is possible to investigate the fashions which determined the acquisition of new goods in the home. For the home was the eventual location of many of those goods which are traditionally associated with industrialization: the ceramics which were made at Wedgwood's factory in Etruria, and then shipped round England on the new system of canals; the decorated doorknobs which were marketed in the pattern books of Matthew Boulton's factory at Soho; the papier-mâché boxes and japanned furniture made by Henry Clay in Birmingham; the wine bottles of Newcastle; and the locks, bolts and nails which were the staple products of the Midlands iron industry.

By concentrating on products as they entered the home, one can discern that the changes in the patterns of domestic consumption in the eighteenth century were of more gradual origin than a revolutionary model of industrialization would suggest. There was not a sudden, certainly not a revolutionary, change in the appearance of interiors in the two decades between 1760 and 1780. There were already many goods which were associated with new methods of production, including larger mirrors and window panes, better made locks, and porcelain. The domestic interior had been the scene of a long, slow cultural change, of shifts in the patterns of fashion and consumption, beginning at least in the latter part of the seventeenth century and continuing throughout the early and middle part of the eighteenth.

Yet, just as it is important not to exaggerate the impact of new processes of manufacture, it is at the same time possible to discern changes in the methods of manufacture of certain household goods during the two decades between 1760 and 1780. A good example of the way industrial processes changed the appearance of domestic interiors is the manufacture of carpets.

The use of carpets was not a novelty in the second half of the eighteenth century. They had long been imported from the Near East, especially Turkey, as luxurious furnishings for grand households.[28] Seventeenth-century inventories list carpets as a form of table covering; but by the early eighteenth century it was becoming sufficiently common to have carpets on the floor for the *Daily Courant* of 27 November 1711 to advertise:

> At Captain Parker's Warehouse, in Merchant Taylor's Hall in Threadneedle Street, near the Royal Exchange, are exposed for sale, a Parcel of Turkey carpets, just arrived by the Fleet from Turkey, viz. Twelve fine Moschet carpets proper for Ladies Chambers or Dressing Rooms, and ninety two Pike [i.e.pile] Carpets, some fit to cover Drawing Rooms and Chambers, others of a small Size to put under Beds and Tables, in Dining Rooms and Parlours, or by the Chimneys to sit on.[29]

This advertisement indicates the extent to which imported carpets were used to ornament particular rooms, those of the highest quality being reserved for ladies' chambers. Clearly they were beginning to be used as a form of floor covering: but Nathan Bailey's *Dictionarium Britannicum: or a Compleat Universal Etymological English Dictionary* of 1730 still defines the word as 'a covering for a table'.[30]

Because of the cost of imported carpets, attempts were made in England to provide substitutes. Carpets began to be made in Kidderminster at some time in the late seventeenth century. In 1699 a charter was granted by William III for the manufacture of carpets at Wilton; the charter was renewed in 1706 and again in 1725.[31] Initially Wilton carpets were comparatively badly made, and the Earl of Pembroke is reputed to have taken steps to introduce weavers from France in order to improve them. Then in 1741 a patent was granted to Ignatius Couran, a London merchant, John Barford, an upholsterer of Wilton, and William Moody, a Wilton clothier, for 'our new invention of making carpeting commonly called French carpeting or Moccadores and in France *moucades* or *moquets*'. In 1761 Joseph Collyer, in *The Parent's and Guardian's Directory*, wrote that 'The weaving of Carpets is chiefly performed at Wilton; and is an ingenious and profitable branch. These Carpets are sold in London at the Carpet warehouse and by the upholsterers.'[32] In 1769, when the factory at Wilton burned down, it was referred to as 'the great carpet factory' and was employing between 60 and 80 journeymen, earning wages of between 10s 6d and 12s per week (substantially more than a weaver).

In 1735 the first carpet factory was established at Kidderminster (earlier, carpets had been made by outworkers in their homes) and in 1751 Bishop Pococke wrote that 'That place is famous for carpets made without nap, like the Scotch, but now they make the same at Wilton, and it is said they are attempting to weave 'em in one piece.' In the 1750s the Royal Society of Arts was offering premiums for improvements in carpet manufacture, and in 1757 awarded one to Thomas Moore, who had set up a factory in Chiswell Street, Moorfields, on the grounds that his carpets were 'made in the manner of Turkey Carpets, and superior to them in Beauty and Goodness'.[33] Thomas Moore supplied many of the carpets which were such a characteristic feature of Robert Adam's interiors, including those at Syon and Osterley. In 1759 another premium of the Royal Society of Arts was awarded to Thomas Chitty, who had established a factory at Axminster two years before. Like Moore, Thomas Chitty was able to supply carpets of the highest quality.

The history of carpets demonstrates the gradual escalation of pace in the supply of new commodities, the increase in the number of factories, and the ways in which changes in fashion stimulated changes in the circumstances of production and manufacture: the changing demands of consumers led to increasing specialization and differentiation in the supply of goods. Carpets were not an innovation of the 1760s and 1770s; but they clearly became much more common during those years and were a feature frequently commented on and admired by foreign visitors, who were particularly impressed that stairs might be carpeted. Improvements in manufacture led to changes in the appearance of the home; and the desire for such changes must in turn have stimulated changes in manufacture.

A second improvement in the technology of the home during the 1770s was the first fully practical water closet, developed by Joseph Bramah. He was a Yorkshireman who started life as an apprentice to Thomas Allott, the village carpenter at Stainborough.[34] On moving to London he worked as a cabinetmaker. One of the technical problems he came across was the problem of how to flush a water closet effectively. In a patent granted on 27 January 1778, he was able to introduce the first substantially new mechanism for water closets since that invented by Sir John Harington for his house outside Bath in 1596. By 1797 Bramah had made and sold 6,000 water closets and was comparatively rich. Again, this change in the mechanics of domestic life is a clear indication of the way new technologies could be developed by the application of a craft mentality to a problem in everyday life. New technologies were not confined to factories in the north; and Bramah went on to apply the same technical intelligence to locks, also with long-lasting improvements to their method of operation.

A third example of improvements to the technical side of the home in the third quarter of the eighteenth century appears in the development of the mechanical stove, which cut down the amount of coal that was burned and improved the system of heating.[35] Mechanical stoves were already in use in many public buildings and in some affluent private houses in America early in the eighteenth century. The most common kind at that time was the so-called 'close stove', an upright enclosed box made of iron plates and mounted on a frame or legs. In October 1723 the *Boston Gazette* advertised 'a very good and large Holland stove. Enquire at the Post Office, or at Mr. Graffton Feveryear at the Sign of the Black Wigg, in First Street, Boston.'

But the essential improvements to the technology of stoves were provided by Benjamin Franklin. In 1742 he devised a more efficient type which had the form of an open fireplace with a descending flue at the back. As he wrote in his *Autobiography*:

Having in 1742 invented an open Stove, for the better warming of Rooms and at the same time saving Fuel, as the fresh Air admitted was warmed in Entering, I made a Present of the Model to Mr. Robert Grace, one of my early Friends, who having an Iron Furnace, found the Casting of the Plates for these Stoves a profitable Thing, as they were growing in Demand. To promote that demand I wrote and published a Pamphlet, Intitled, An Account of the New-Invented PENNSYL-VANIAN FIRE PLACES & c. This pamphlet had good Effect, Gov[erno]r Thomas was so pleas'd with the Construction of this Stove, as describ'd in it, that he offer'd to give me a Patent for the sole Vending of them for a Term of Years: but I declin'd it from a Principle, which has ever weigh'd with me on such Occasions, viz. That, as we enjoy great Advantages from the Inventions of others, we should be glad of an Opportunity to serve others by any Invention of ours; and this we should do freely and generously.[36]

By 1745 this type of stove was available for sale in Boston, as is evident from an advertisement in the *Boston News Letter* for 'New Fashion Fireplaces or Stoves from Philadelphia'; and in 1753 a Mr Durno of Jermyn Street, Piccadilly, imported one to London, which he adapted for the use of coal. He claimed that he was 'willing to give my machine gratis, if ever the least smoke is perceived in any room where it is erected, unless it may happen at the first lighting the fire'.

At some time around 1780 stoves began to be imported more regularly, and James Sharp issued a pamphlet in London, *An Account of the Principle and Effects of the Air Stove-Grate . . . Commonly known by the Name of American Stoves*, which advertised the fact that 'Many different Sizes and patterns of these Stoves may be seen at Mr Sharp's Manufactory, No. 133, Tooley Street, Southwark; or at his House, Leadenhall-Street, London.' As in the case of carpets and water closets, there was not a sudden or revolutionary change in technology after 1760; but there was an increase in the rate of development and in the supply of new types. Houses were beginning to have an appropriate set of gadgets.

If further evidence of the close interconnection between industry, fashion and interior decoration during these years is required, it can be equally clearly seen in the activities of Matthew Boulton and Josiah Wedgwood, the two best known industrial entrepreneurs of this period.

After his father's death in 1759, Matthew Boulton married a wealthy girl from Lichfield, whose dowry of £28,000 provided him with the capital to set up his famous factory at Soho.[37] To compete successfully with rival Birmingham manufacturers in what had become a cut-throat trade, he was determined to expand the range of goods he could supply, and to keep quality high and prices low. He wanted to remove 'the prejudice that Birmingham hath so justly established against itself'.[38]

In order to accomplish these aims and to ensure that his goods were in fashion, Boulton kept a constant and wary eye on what was going on both in London and on the Continent. His friends would keep him informed of what was on display in the shops of London. He himself travelled to Paris in 1765 to inspect the work of his French competitors. During the summer of 1767 he asked an agent to subscribe to the coloured plates illustrating Sir William Hamilton's collection of vases. In July of that year he wrote to the agent:

> I am fond of all those things that have a tendency to improve my knowledge in mechanical arts, in which my manufactory will every year become more and more general, and therefore wish to know the taste, the fashions, the toys, both useful and ornamental, the implements, vessels & c. that prevail in different parts of Europe, as I should be glad to work for all Europe in all things that they may have occasion for – gold, silver, copper, plated, gilt, pinchbeck, steel, platina, tortoise shell or anything else that may become an article of general demand.[39]

In 1768 Boulton was again in London, busily acquiring designs and objects which could be copied. In 1770 he bought the works of Sir William Chambers from his London bookseller; and in 1772 he wrote to Elizabeth Montagu:

> Fashion hath much to do in these things, and as that of the present age distinguishes itself by adopting the most elegant ornaments of the most refined Grecian artists, I am satisfyed in conforming thereto, and humbly copying their style, and makeing new combinations of old ornaments without presuming to invent new ones.[40]

The factory at Soho demonstrates how fashion was a substantial stimulant of an entrepreneurial mentality. A factory owner needed to be highly responsive not only to how things were made and how much they would cost, but also to how they would sell and how the consumer market would respond to changes in design. Just as Robert Adam was a broker in the fashion exchange, so too were successful manufacturers.

The same interest in the operation of fashion and how it could improve the sale of goods is even more evident in Wedgwood's commercial operations.[41] Josiah Wedgwood made no pretence of providing ceramics which were as cheap as those of his competitors, who continually copied his designs. Instead, he achieved success as a manufacturer by continually keeping abreast of fashion. He was one of the first people to exploit the taste of a market, which he described as being 'randy for antique', producing vases which were based on antique amphorae, decorated with classical swags and garlands. He wrote to Bentley in June 1779:

Fashion is infinitely superior to merit in many respects; & it is plain from a thousand instances that if you have a favorite child you wish the public to fondle & take notice of, you have only to make choice of proper sponcers. If you are lucky in them no matter what the brat is, black, brown, or fair, its fortune is made. We were really unfortunate in the introduction of our jasper into public notice, that we could not prevail upon the architects to be godfathers to our child.[42]

These contacts with the world of metropolitan fashion once again demonstrated how manufacturers could not afford to produce goods without regard to the potential market. They had to keep themselves well informed of minor adjustments in taste and fashion, following the market as fast as possible where they were not able to lead it. Looked at in this light, the manufacturers of the 1760s and 1770s appear not so much as the disciples of a new capitalist work ethic, but instead as sophisticated interpreters of novelty serving a market which was created by fashion.

Women and Decoration

Closely associated with the changing systems of manufacture in the decades between 1760 and 1780 were the beginnings of the domestic ideology which was such a feature of the nineteenth century. Once people began to go out to work and the home was no longer the location of manufacture, once wages did not need to be supplemented by paid domestic work, there was inevitably a change in the way home life was regarded, and a much clearer division between home and workplace.

There is evidence to suggest that it was in the third quarter of the eighteenth century that women began to view the household as their own special territory, a place to which they could retreat and over which they ruled.[43] It was in this period that women began to articulate more forcefully a privileged ability to comment upon the nature of fashion, to decide on the way that houses should be arranged, to make significant choices in the purchase and possession of domestic goods, and to develop a special form of visual sensibility. It is, of course, arguable that this was an ideology which was developed by men in order to keep women imprisoned at home; but equally it can be seen as an assertion of women's rights to maintain and develop an independent sphere of influence.

As with the changing patterns of manufacture, it is important not to exaggerate the nature of this change. It no doubt had a long trajectory of development; and the fact that women did not voice a special concern for household furnishings and their arrangement before the mid-eighteenth century does not mean that this interest did not exist. There is evidence in seventeenth-century women's wills that women made provision for the disposition of individual items, suggesting that they had a special feeling for the nature of particular objects. Yet if one searches the writings of women in the first half of the eighteenth century, their letters, autobiographies and diaries, there is not the same interest in how interiors were organized as is evident in those of the second half of the century.

It might be argued that Celia Fiennes demonstrates a forceful and in some ways a specifically female interest in the nature and organization of domestic space; but it is hard to relate the tough and idiosyncratic writings of someone riding round on horseback and suffering disgusting conditions of accommodation to a feminine viewpoint. She comments on fabrics and furniture, but she does not claim to have a special or privileged form of sensitivity to such matters. Equally, the wife of a country house owner, such as Sarah Duchess of Marlborough, might have held clear views on the nature of the interior furnishings; but, as with Celia Fiennes, she was such an odd and independent woman that it is hard to see her as a representative of her sex. In so far as she makes her views on interior decoration known, she was impatient of anything too contrived and disliked the fashions of Palladian decoration.[44]

In the second half of the 1740s it is possible to find a detailed interest in all the niceties of interior decoration in the letters which Lady Luxborough wrote to William Shenstone, after she had been compelled by her husband to stay in one of his family's houses in Warwickshire on suspicion of having an illicit affair in London. Shenstone and Lady Luxborough corresponded about stucco ornament and the way a Birmingham painter could simulate the appearance of stone. They swapped books which could act as sources for features in each other's house and garden. But it is striking that Lady Luxborough habitually consults, and is inclined to defer to, Shenstone's ideas.[45] There is no indication that she has a superior understanding of such matters or that there could be a switch in this relationship between the sexes.

In contrast to these few isolated examples of individual women demonstrating an interest in the arrangement and furnishing of rooms before 1760, after this date there is substantial evidence of women having a special interest in interiors. It appears in the way

Fanny Boscawen commissioned Robert Adam at Hatchlands. A similar sense that the organization of the household was a feminine prerogative is conveyed in the comments of the Duchess of Northumberland, who was also involved in working with Adam at Northumberland House in the Strand and at Syon, and who kept a diary recording her comments on other people's houses.[46]

One of the most significant arbiters of taste between 1760 and 1780 was Elizabeth Montagu, known at the time as 'The Queen of the Bluestockings' (a reference to the informal blue-grey woollen stockings which it was thought permissible to wear at her gatherings). As with the salon of Madame de Rambouillet in the early seventeenth century and probably consciously modelled on this French tradition, the setting was an important feature of her literary gatherings. As Madame du Bocage described Mrs Montagu's breakfasts, they brought together 'both the people of the country and strangers . . . in a closet lined with painted paper of *Pekin*, and furnished with the choicest moveables of *China*'.[47] Others were less complimentary about her gatherings, describing them as horribly stiff and inclined to make everyone feel uncomfortable, since they were forced to sit in a semicircle round the hostess. Either way, there is a sense of her presiding over a defined social space and of deliberately controlling it, using the surroundings of a social gathering in order to provide the appropriate form of organization. Initially Mrs Montagu, like so many of her friends, was going to commission Robert Adam to make improvements to the decoration of her London house; he had already worked for her in her house at Hill Street in Mayfair; but the great man kept her waiting an hour and brought 'a regiment of talking artificers'.[48] So she turned instead to James Stuart, on the grounds of 'his disinterestedness & contempt of money'.[49] She was exercising careful control in the nature and choice of her architect in order to ensure an appropriate atmosphere for her social gatherings.

Mrs Montagu was one of Matthew Boulton's correspondents,

15. The Dining Room at Kedleston, by Robert Adam, 1762.

16. Perspective view of the gallery at Syon, by Robert Adam, *c.* 1764.

17. Queen Charlotte with her two eldest sons, by Johann Zoffany, 1764.

18. Sir Lawrence Dundas with his grandson, by Johann Zoffany, 1769.

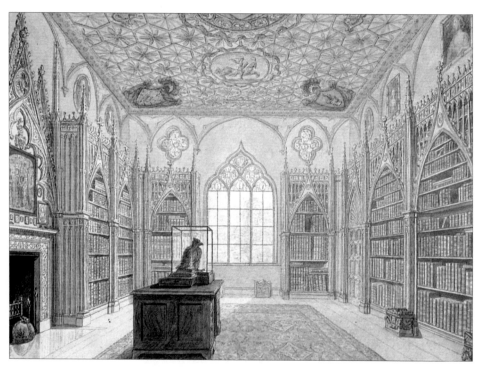

19. The Library at Strawberry Hill, by John Carter, 1788.

20. This is a sorry sight! by James Gillray, 1786.

21. The Miser's Feast, by James Gillray, 1786.

22. The Holbein Chamber at Strawberry Hill, by John Carter, 1788.

23. The staircase at Buckingham House, by Sir John Soane, *c.* 1792–5.

24. The Breakfast Room at 12 Lincoln Inn's Fields, by Joseph Michael Gandy, *c.* 1798.

and kept him informed of current tastes in fashion and decoration. In his letters Boulton deferred to her judgement, because he regarded her as a leader of style. She reciprocated by commending his wares to her friends. She wrote to him:

> I take greater pleasure in our victories over the French in our contention of arts than of arms. The achievement of Soho instead of making widows and orphans make marriages and christenings . . . Go on then, sir, to triumph over the French in taste and to embellish your country with useful inventions and elegant productions.[50]

Mrs Montagu's pronouncements demonstrate her view that fashion and taste were a female prerogative: that men might preside over the battlefield, but women should take control of the home. The tone of voice and the confidence are new.

Unlike Mrs Montagu and probably in deliberate contrast to her, Mrs Vesey, another member of this circle of bluestockings, used to organize the furniture at her gatherings much more informally. She deliberately scattered the chairs all round the room, especially liking to place them back-to-back, so that a whole range of different conversations could develop. She could then move round the room, eavesdropping with her ear trumpet. But, like Mrs Montagu, Mrs Vesey used the furnishings of her rooms consciously as props. Her gatherings were organized in such a way that men might be admitted, but only on sufferance and if they were amusing; as with Mrs Montagu, it is symptomatic of the way that women were beginning to commandeer social life for themselves.

The best remembered member of this circle, who also demonstrated a continuous interest in aspects of furnishing and decoration, was Mrs Delany, although she was slightly on the fringes of the bluestockings.[51] She had had a disastrous marriage to a drunken Cornish landowner. Luckily he died soon after and, following a period as a widow, she married an Irish clergyman. In her old age she travelled round England, writing long and detailed letters to a number of correspondents, the majority of them members of her family, in which she maintained a continuous barrage of comments about the character of interiors and how they might be improved. Again, this is no more than an isolated sympton of a trend; but it is significant how Mrs Delany's letters exclude any consideration of political affairs, and instead concentrate on the home as the centre of her concerns.

It might be argued that a group of well born ladies maintaining an interest in how their houses were laid out, including waspish comments on the taste of others, was not unusual. But these women were influential in establishing the idea of social gatherings to discuss literature. They forced themselves on to the consciousness of the period as being in some way different, more energetic and more independent in establishing a sphere of influence independent of men.[52] So the fact that they revealed such a close interest in their domestic arrangements suggests a shift in the relationship between the sexes, whereby women were thought to have a special awareness of their surroundings.

How far these ideas filtered down into the rest of society is not clear. There are hints of change in a variety of spheres. For example, it was in these years that special-interest magazines began to target a female market. *The Ladys Magazine* was first published in 1763 with a subtitle which described it as 'the first Miscellany expressly appropriated to the Fair Sex'.[53] It carried information about fashion and cookery, since these activities were regarded as appropriately feminine interests. It was followed by the publication in 1770 of *The Lady's Magazine or Entertaining Companion for the Fair Sex*, which opened with the statement that 'As your Sex is in this age more employed in reading than it was in the last, it is sometimes surprising that no periodical production should at present exist calculated for your particular amusement, and designed to improve as well as delight.'[54] In addition, it indicated that it would concentrate on aspects of fashion:

> The subjects we shall treat of are those that may tend to render your minds not less amiable than your persons. But as external appearance is the first inlet to the treasures of the heart, and the advantages of dress, though they cannot communicate beauty, may at least make it more conspicuous, it is intended to present the Sex with most elegant patterns for the tambour, embroidery, or every kind of needlework.[55]

Women were increasingly regarded as prisoners of the home, with a considerable amount of leisure time which could be occupied in genteel pursuits. Choosing new fabrics for a sofa, deciding on the appropriate pattern of the curtains, arranging the ornaments of a mantelpiece were beginning to be seen as appropriately feminine forms of accomplishment, like playing the piano or painting watercolours.

A second sphere of activity in which there was beginning to be a clearer demarcation of domestic role was in the planning of interiors. The literature of planning indicates that there were some areas which were regarded as specifically male, notably the dining room, where the decoration was expected to be sombre; and other areas over which women were expected to preside, such as the kitchen and the drawing room. As the use of rooms grew increasingly specialized during the course of the eighteenth century, so there was a tendency to focus on a division in territory of members of a household. Where women presided it began to be acknowledged that there might be a different style of decoration, and that women might have a taste distinct from that of men: many of the stereotypes of a feminine style of decoration, the idea of lighter colours, of less robust forms of furniture, and of fussiness in ornament begin to appear in the literature after 1760.

The Hon. John Byng, who began to record his comments as he

travelled round the countryside in the 1780s, is always apoplectic when he senses female influence in any of the inns or houses in which he stays. When he arrives at the house of an old military friend of his in Monmouth, he makes the following comment:

> The parlour was (ill) furnish'd in the modern taste, with French chairs, festoon'd curtains, and puff'd bell ropes; this and his keeping in bed informed me that the gentleman was not master of his own house.[56]

At Weymouth, he stays in lodgings where he is likewise annoyed:

> My chief trouble arises from living in the midst of powder, perfumes, caps, hats, gloves, gauze and petticoats; of which cost and profusion, no batchelor can, or shou'd have, the smallest idea; (I mean for the sake of matrimony and the ladies;) for were he to be let into these mysteries, he would bless his stars that he continued single, in the command of quiet cleanliness, and management; (to all which we are utter strangers,); and I am so overcome of the smell of the marechale, and the quantities thrown about, that I have named our lodgings, Richards's Powder-Mills.[57]

Byng's comments were not simply the cantankerous comments of a misogynist, but of someone who was able to appeal to well established gender stereotypes, confident that his masculine readers would know exactly what he meant about the problems of feminine domination, and would sympathize with him. Since this type of comment is not evident in travel writing in the first half of the century, it suggests once again that it was in the years between 1760 and 1780 that these stereotypes began to be established.

These comments on gender division in the home do not amount to more than a series of hints and suggestions about the origins of the domestic ideology which was current in the nineteenth century. The evidence is elusive. But it does seem that the history of interior decoration should be interpreted in the light of ideas about polite accomplishments, and that distinctions of gender are much more marked in the second half of the century than the first.

The Taste for Gothic

No survey of the nature and character of interiors in the third quarter of the eighteenth century, and of attitudes to them, would be complete without a discussion of that strange but significant sport in the development of eighteenth-century taste: Horace Walpole's villa called Strawberry Hill, at Twickenham.[58] Set among the grand, ostentatious and stately interiors of the nobility, Walpole's little riverside villa was built in conscious opposition to the trends of the time. It attempted to provide surroundings which were in every way idiosyncratic; Walpole strove to make them appear the result of the long process of history and, indeed, the house grew out of a comparatively long gestation involving the ideas and recommendations of a number of artists, architects and friends. It was important not just as an oddity, much visited and admired, but because it was a presage of the way interiors would be used in the future, as a conscious instrument of personal expression, exploiting history to evoke a particular mood: the house was to become a private castle, an escape from time, a place of retreat.

In building Strawberry Hill Horace Walpole became progressively more obsessional about what he was doing. What had begun as a whim, born out of a desire to irritate other people's expectations, gradually became a serious exercise in archaeology, recreating different periods of architecture from room to room. And although Walpole has suffered from his tendency to be frivolous about whatever he was doing, he did use Strawberry Hill as an experimental laboratory for different styles of building. Instead of the house facing outwards to its public, he enticed visitors into a Gothic labyrinth, which was planned as a monument to the complexity of Walpole's own imagination.

The history of Strawberry Hill began in 1747, when Horace Walpole decided that he would like a house outside London, but within easy reach of it. He selected one that had first been built in 1698 and had then had a succession of different tenants. He liked the location in Twickenham, because of its associations with Alexander Pope and the proximity of nice old dowagers. He was also pleased by the nature of the landscape, and that it conformed to pictorial ideas of how a landscape should look, which was hardly surprising since the banks of the Thames around Richmond and Twickenham were a favourite scene for painters of the time. He wrote on 8 June 1747:

> It is a little play-thing-house that I got out of Mrs Chenevix's shop, and is the prettiest bauble you ever saw. It is set in enamelled meadows with filigree hedges:
>   A small Euphrates through the piece is roll'd
>   And little finches wave their wings in gold . . .
> Dowagers as plenty as flounders inhabit all around, and Pope's ghost is just now skimming under my window by a most poetical moonlight.[59]

In 1748 he began to make tentative alterations to the fabric of the house, and paid £105 8s 0d 'for the new Kitchen, Alterations to the Cottage & Work to the New Room'.[60] From the beginning Walpole decided that additions to the house should be in the Gothic style, in which he had developed an interest partly as a result of his admiration for the architecture of the chapel of King's College, Cambridge, where he had been an undergraduate, and partly owing to a streak of natural perversity. But initially these changes to the fabric of the house were simple, designed by an obscure member of the Board of Works, William Robinson.

The next major development to Strawberry Hill was in 1753, when he decided that he would like a library and a dining room. His friend Richard Bentley, the son of the Master of Trinity College, Cambridge, supplied a drawing for the library, which is an interesting contrast to the view of Pepys's library; but Walpole did not approve of it and wrote to Bentley that his design 'cannot have the Strawberry imprimatur: the double arches and double pinnacles are most ungraceful; and the doors below the book-cases in Mr Chute's design had a conventual look, which yours totally wants.'[61] These comments show that Walpole's sense of what was appropriate for the house was already highly developed. In 1756 he paid a Swiss artist, John Henry Müntz, for a portrait of himself in the newly completed library, which demonstrates how the work was executed in a much more substantial way than Bentley had envisaged.

The next major alteration to Strawberry Hill was the so-called Holbein Chamber, begun in 1758. On 18 September 1759 the poet Thomas Gray described the appearance of the room in a letter to his friend Thomas Wharton:

Mr W: has lately made a new Bed-chamber, wch as it is in the best tast of any thing he has yet done, & in your own Gothic way, I must describe a little. you enter by a peaked door at one corner of the room (out of a narrow winding passage, you may be sure) into an Alcove, in wch the bed is to stand, formed by a screen of pierced work opening by one large arch in the middle to the rest of the chamber, wch is lighted at the other end by a bow-window of three bays, whose tops are of rich painted glass in mosaic. the cieling is coved & fretted in star & quatrefoil compartments with roses at the intersections, all in papier-mâché. the chimney on your left is the high-altar in the Cathedral of Rouen (from whence the Screen also is taken) consisting of a low surbased Arch between two octagon Towers, whose pinnacles almost reach the Cieling, all of Nichwork. the chairs & dressing-table are real carved Ebony, pick'd up at auctions.[62]

Horace Walpole's friends were intensely interested in every stage of Strawberry Hill's development. The interiors of the house had become a palimpsest of different periods of history, some of it consisting of reproductions of medieval tombs derived from engravings, some of it an invention of Walpole's friends, and some of the furniture being old pieces bought at auction. The result was a weird mixture of fantasy and archaeological reconstruction.

By 1760 Walpole may have thought that his improvements to Strawberry Hill were complete; but he was someone who liked continually to plan alterations and who could never rest content with his surroundings. On 6 May 1762 he paid £1241 8s 0d 'for the building of the gallery, cloyster, Oratory, Servant's hall, cellar, larder, staircase by the Kitchen, privy, Screen to the little garden, & finishing Kitchen, Larder, Scullery & Ser[van]ts hall'.[63] The gallery was the most substantial new room added to the house, described as

Fifty-six feet long, seventeen high, and thirteen wide without the five recesses. The cieling is taken from one of the side isles of Henry 7th's. chapel. In the windows, painted by Peckitt, are all the quarterings of the family. The great door is copied from the north door of saint Albans, and the two smaller are parts of the same design. The side with recesses, which are finished with a gold network over looking-glass, is taken from the tomb of archbishop Bourchier at Canterbury. The chimney-piece was designed by Mr. John Chute, and Mr. Thomas Pitt of Boconnoch. The room is hung with crimson Norwich damask: the chairs, settees, and long stools are of the same, mounted on black and gold frames. The carpet made at Moorfields.[64]

As is clear from this description, Walpole was not averse to combining modern domestic comforts, such as a carpet from the Moorfields factory, with his attempts to provide an atmosphere of history. His approach was always eclectic. A further improvement to the fabric of the house was a new bedchamber which was added at the north end of the house by 1772; then, finally in 1777, James Essex, an architect from Cambridge, was employed to build the so-called Beauclerc Tower, planned to contain drawings by Lady Diana Beauclerc for Walpole's play *The Mysterious Mother*.

At least as important as the changes which were made to Strawberry Hill after 1760 was the fact that during these years the house became a tourist attraction. Horace Walpole began to complain about the constant visitors after the completion of his gallery. On 3 September 1763 he wrote to George Montagu, an old friend from his schooldays at Eton:

> My house is full of people and has been so from the instant I breakfasted, and more are coming – in short, I keep an inn; the sign, 'the Gothic Castle' – since my gallery was finished I have not been in it a quarter of an hour together; my whole time is passed in giving tickets for seeing it, and hiding myself while it is seen – take my advice, never build a charming house for yourself between London and Hampton-court, everybody will live in it but you.[65]

It is clear that Walpole was ambiguous about the influx of visitors. On the one hand, he was irritated by their number; on the other, they pandered to his narcissism and his sense of having established a personal cult.

Certainly, Walpole's profound desire for privacy did not prevent him publishing in 1774 (admittedly in an edition of only 100 copies), and again in 1784 (a further edition of 200 copies), *A description of the Villa of Mr. Horace Walpole, Youngest Son of Sir Robert Walpole Earl of Orford, at Strawberry-Hill near Twickenham, Middlesex. With an inventory of the furniture, Pictures, Curiosities, &c.*

In preparing the second edition of the *Description*, Walpole commissioned a number of topographical artists to make views of the interiors. He wrote on 16 June 1781 to the Revd William Cole:

> I am now setting about the completion of my *Aedes Strawberria-nae*. A painter is to come hither on Monday to make a drawing of the Tribune and finish T. Sandby's fine view of the Gallery, to which I could never get him to put the last hand. They will then be engraved with a few of the chimneypieces, which will complete the plates.[66]

Unfortunately the engraving of the illustrations did not do justice to the originals and their appearance in the second edition is murky; but many of the originals were bound into Walpole's own copy of the *Description*, which survives in the Lewis Walpole library at Farmington, Connecticut. In addition, a collector of portraits, Richard Bull, commissioned John Carter to make a set of drawings of the interiors for his own extra-illustrated copy of the 1784 *Description*. Carter was an accomplished draughtsman, as well as being a Fellow of the Society of Antiquaries, and his drawings of the Library, Holbein Chamber, Cabinet and Great Parlour are the best evidence of the original appearance of Strawberry Hill.

The 1784 edition not only illustrated many of the rooms, but also contained substantial lists of the contents. The character of the house was established not only by the nature of the architectural decoration – the fragments of medieval glass and the fan vaulting – but at least equally by the massive accumulation of Horace Walpole's collection. Every room was stuffed full of objects, some of great historical interest, some medieval, some modern. Like the architecture, the contents were intended to evoke a sense of history, so that the house was a vehicle of historical and personal reminiscence.

Strawberry Hill is not just the monument of a highly idiosyncratic individual. It allowed visitors to explore the house as a projection of Walpole's mind and to interpret the furnishings of a room as a form of masquerade. It is not coincidental that the house was put together at more or less the same time that Robert Adam was exercising a despotic control over every aspect of an interior from the doorcases to the carpets. Horace Walpole was reacting against the uniformity of contemporary interiors. He believed that rooms should provide a more private experience.

1780–1800

Architectural Drawings

The principal development in architectural drawing during the 1780s and 1790s was the fully realized, three-dimensional view of an interior, showing exactly what a room would look like and how people would appear within it, and conveying the physical atmosphere, the light and shadow, as well as the colour and dimensions. The flattened model of rooms, which was the favoured convention employed by architects in the middle of the eighteenth century, was replaced by a representation in which the whole interior space is imagined precisely as it would appear to a visitor or a spectator with a privileged view through the missing fourth wall.

One reason for this development was the changing status of the architect as an independent professional. In the early seventeenth century it was not thought necessary to predict the physical form of a building in advance of its construction, since the details of the interior were worked out by the craftsmen. By the end of the seventeenth century it was realized that the province of the architect might extend into the form and disposition of the rooms inside; but the amount of calculation involved was still limited. Many architects were essentially amateurs with an educated interest in drawing, but they had nothing that could be described as professional training, beyond the purchase of appropriate manuals.

In the early eighteenth century the architects who experimented with the decoration of interiors were trained as painters, most strikingly so in the cases of Thornhill and Kent, both of whom had served conventional apprenticeships, with Kent, in addition, attending the classes at the Academy of St Luke in Rome. Neither of them would have described himself as an architect. Colen Campbell, the other person who was influential in the establishment of Palladianism in England, was a Scottish lawyer, who was supposed to have received 'a liberal education' and only turned to the practice of architecture late in his life. And the Earl of Burlington saw architecture as a liberal art, which he was able to practise by virtue of intellect and a knowledge of classical buildings.[1]

Yet by the second half of the eighteenth century it is clear that architecture was believed to be a separate and independent profession, requiring a particular set of skills. This development is evident in the way Robert Adam embarked upon a careful course of instruction, first working in his father's firm and then acquiring the requisite knowledge of Continental architecture through travel. Indeed, by the late eighteenth century a period spent in Rome had become a necessary qualification for any status in the practice of architecture.

This change in architecture and its recognition as an independent art was reinforced by the establishment of the Royal Academy in 1768.[2] The Academy did three things for architecture. It provided an appropriate form of peer group recognition to architects throughout their professional career, so that they could climb through the ranks as Associates, then as full Academicians, hoping even to reach the pinnacle as President. Sir William Chambers was one of the people who, along with Reynolds, had been most instrumental in setting up the Academy, of which he became Treasurer. A second important influence of the Royal Academy on the practice of architecture was that, soon after it was established, it instituted a programme of academic training in architecture, which included attending lectures given by Thomas Sandby, the Professor of Architecture, and life drawing in the studios. Students were expected to compete for prizes which were awarded on Foundation Day, when Sir Joshua Reynolds, as President, would deliver a discourse on the practice of art. The winners of the gold medal were then able to compete for the award of a three-year travelling scholarship to Rome. So, from being a haphazard practice, which covered a whole range of activity from the musings of idle members of the nobility to the slavish copying of pattern books by provincial builders, architecture acquired the trappings of a profession, which could be learned and whose performance could be assessed at a competitive examination.

A third consequence of the foundation of the Royal Academy was that architects were expected to exhibit drawings at the annual exhibitions alongside the work of painters. Inevitably this gave to the preparation of drawings a different importance from that accorded to preparing sketches for the use of builders and craftsmen. Architecture was to be looked at as an art, to be hung on the wall, as well as an academic practice intended to produce a building. The need to prepare drawings which would attract the attention of the public, and which could also be entered for competitions, gave rise to much greater elaboration in colour, style and technique.

These developments are illustrated by the training of Sir John Soane, who was not well born, but became an architect by working in the offices of George Dance and Henry Holland, and then entering the schools of the Royal Academy in October 1771.[3] In 1776 he was awarded a gold medal for his design *A Triumphal Bridge with the Plan Elevation and Section*, a monumental drawing which had exactly the right degree of unreality to win an architectural competition. In 1778 he was awarded the three-year travelling scholarship in Rome.

While Soane was in Rome he prepared drawings for a dining room for Frederick Hervey, Bishop of Derry and subsequently Earl of Bristol. It was modelled on a villa they had visited together at Terracina, south of Rome, which was thought to have belonged to Lucullus, described by Plutarch not only as a lover of literature and the arts, but also as a gastronome. Soane and the Bishop of Derry 'banqueted within the ruins on mullet fresh from the ancient reservoirs'.[4] The drawing shows both the very earnest way that Soane approached the reconstruction of the antique and his beautiful, while highly academic, drawing style, conveying the features of ornament with intellectually fastidious care.

In 1783 Soane prepared designs for Henry Greswolde Lewis, another client he had met in Rome. They included a proposal for a bathroom in the basement of the house, with a small swimming pool in the middle of the room and a bath like a sarcophagus. The following year he prepared designs for a bath house for Taverham Hall in Norfolk. At this early stage of his career Soane was working on his own, and the drawings are in the nature of sketches in which he thought out ideas about the appearance of an interior.

As Soane's professional commitments increased it became necessary for him to establish an architectural office, which included staff who specialized in the drafting of preparatory drawings. It is not always clear whether drawings for a Soane interior of the 1790s were produced by Soane himself. On the other hand, he certainly used the process of drawing as a way of projecting the experience of interiors. It was a significant part of the process of composition, and suggested to a client how an interior would look. For example, in the early 1790s he produced a sketch of a proposed staircase at Buckingham House, which shows him using the medium of a watercolour sketch to think out the complex elliptical geometry of the stairways and dome.

In the mid-1790s he was responsible for an even more atmospheric view of the entrance hall of Tyringham Hall in Buckinghamshire. This was one of his most significant commissions of the 1790s, designed for William Mackworth Praed, a Fleet Street banker; and the drawing is presented as a finished work of art, depicting an atmosphere of penumbral gloom.

Of the assistants employed by Soane, the most important was Joseph Michael Gandy, whose early career followed a similar trajectory to his own, beginning in James Wyatt's office and proceeding to the Royal Academy School, where he was awarded a gold medal in 1790.[5] Gandy spent seven years in Rome, where he developed a brilliantly accomplished style of architectural sketching, which would no doubt have enabled him to set up in independent practice, had it not been for his introverted personality and the fact that there were fewer architectural commissions in England during the Napoleonic wars. He returned to London in June 1797 and described in an autobiographical fragment how

> he found himself alone in the greatest metropolis in the world; the ideal castles, palaces, and mansions he had fostered in his mind, and in which he had dwelt with so much pleasure on the Continent, and fondly hoped to rear in England were vanished. The kingdom he perceived was not great enough to build, and his means too small to recommend them or him.[6]

In the absence of architectural commissions, Gandy worked as an assistant to Soane and was responsible for many of the imaginative visions of the way his projects would look, done for prospective clients or as a record of a particular commission for the annual Royal Academy exhibitions. Gandy was a brilliant draughtsman, capable of projecting in his mind exactly what a building would look like, and, more especially, what it would feel like to be in.

His work more than any other demonstrates the power of architecture as an independent art form.

A good example of Gandy's work is provided by his view of the breakfast room at 12 Lincoln's Inn Fields. Soane had bought the house in 1792, and the illustration of the breakfast room is likely to date from between 1797, when Gandy began to work as a draughtsman in Soane's office, and 1801, when he left to set up a practice as an independent architect. It is a complete image of domestic life, with Soane sitting at his breakfast, engrossed in his newspaper, while his wife pours out the tea; there is no need to use imagination in reconstructing the scene.

With the work of Gandy, it is evident how far the concept of architectural drawing had changed from its tentative origins in the early seventeenth century. Instead of merely providing a primitive notation of the dimensions of a room or a projection of the appearance of a single wall, architectural drawings allowed the viewer to stand inside a room, to feel the relationship between the architecture and the furniture, to look out of the window into the garden outside. In this long development, the changes in architectural drawings register the different attitudes to the idea of interiors and how they had become a medium for architectural experiment. The experience of living in buildings was as important as their appearance from outside.

Yet even at the beginning of the nineteenth century not everyone welcomed the extent to which architecture had become an art form. In 1807 J.M.W. Turner was elected Professor of Architecture at the Royal Academy, and the notes for his lectures provide an exposition of architectural drawing. He advocated that architects should cultivate a sensitivity to the effects of light and atmosphere, at the same time warning of that 'far greater fatality for Designs in Architecture which are but Splendid drawings destitute of Practicability by an over indulgence of fanciful combinations'.[7] In his Royal Academy lecture of 1813 Soane returned to the theme of the problems of developing an interest in architectural composition for its own sake:

A superior manner of Drawing is absolutely necessary, indeed it is impossible not to admire the beauties and almost magical effects in the architectural drawings of a Clerisseau, a Gandy, or a Turner. Few architects, however, can hope to reach the excellency of those artists without devoting to Drawing too much of that time which they ought to employ in the attainment of the higher and more essential qualifications of an Architect.[8]

During the eighteenth century tensions had developed between the practice of architecture as an art form and the complex requirements of planning, the organization of an architectural office, and the logistics of building. The design of rooms indicated the extent to which architects viewed architecture as a stimulus to aesthetic experience or in terms of its need to fulfil the requirements of function.

Pattern Books

In the seventeenth century the number of pattern books which were available to assist the artisan and craftsman in the composition of details of the interior was limited; but during the eighteenth century there was a proliferation in both their number and their contents.

At the top end of the market for printed books about architecture were the lavish folio volumes prepared by individual architects, illustrating their work. The most elaborate example of this genre was *The Works in Architecture of Robert and James Adam*, first published in parts during the course of the 1770s and put together as a complete publication in two volumes, which appeared in 1778 and 1779. It included an introduction which described the philosophy of the Adams' architectural practice, with special attention paid to the principles of planning, but also plates of some of their best work. There were perspective views of the long gallery at Syon and of the drawing room at Derby House to supplement the more conventional flat engravings of ceilings, walls and chimneypieces.[9]

Soane followed the example of the Adam brothers in publishing specimens of his designs. His first book, *Designs in Architecture*, appeared in 1778, soon after he had left the Royal Academy schools and before he had gone to Rome.[10] It was intended to include samples of interior decoration; but, in the event, it was limited to a variety of garden buildings, including temples, an obelisk and a mausoleum. Ten years later he published a more substantial work, *Plans, Elevations and Sections of Buildings*, which contained his completed work up to that date. In it he gave a brief introduction to his architectural ideas, including a passage on the role of ornament which was probably deliberately intended as a counterblast to the ideas of the Adams. He wrote:

> Ornaments are to be cautiously introduced; those ought only to be used that are simple, applicable and characteristic of their situations: they must be designed with regularity and be perfectly distinct in their outlines; the Doric members must not be mixed with the Ionic, nor the Ionic with the Corinthian, but such ornaments only should be used, as tend to shew the destination of the edifice, as assist in determining its character, and for the choice of which the architect can assign satisfactory reasons.[11]

He illustrated the application of these principles with a cutaway engraving of the so-called Great Room, or saloon, at Chillington in Staffordshire. Soane's third publication was his *Sketches in Architecture, containing Plans and Elevations of Cottages, Villas and other useful buildings*, which appeared in 1793. This illustrated the trend away from the design of grand country houses to an interest in smaller domestic dwellings, including villas, and rustic cottages with thatched roofs. By using aquatint for the engravings, Soane produced a different visual effect from that of the starkly linear engraving which had been the standard mode in eighteenth-century architectural publications. Instead of concentrating the eye on the architectural qualities and characteristics of a building, its outline and the way it was composed, the emphasis is shifted to the scenic attributes of the surroundings. The buildings begin to melt into the landscape.

Alongside these major publications by individual architects, advertising either their achievements or proposals with which to attract clients, there was also a wealth of more ephemeral publications, which offered information about the design and planning of every type of house from the grandest mansion to the smallest worker's dwelling, from urban villas to country cottages, from the details of individual pieces of furniture to the workings of a stove.[12] Many of the books of architecture were devoted to the exterior appearance of houses in a landscape setting, capitalizing on the interest in scenery which was such a striking feature of the Picturesque movement; but they were supplemented by more specialized publications on furniture.

The most important work on furniture published in the 1780s – probably the most important publication of its kind since Chippendale's *Director* – was Alice Hepplewhite's *The Cabinet-Maker and Upholsterer's Guide; or repository of designs for every article of household furniture, in the newest and most approved taste*, which first appeared in 1788, with the engravings dated 1787. The drawings are apparently by the widow of a cabinetmaker, George Hepplewhite, who had died at 48 Redcross Street, Cripplegate, in 1786. As its title page indicated, it was intended to demonstrate not only the diversity of available styles, from the plainest to the most enriched, but also plans of rooms, 'shewing the proper distribution of the furniture'. *The Cabinet-Maker and Upholsterer's Guide* has generally had a bad press from later historians, on the grounds that it does not provide a clear statement of a particular style of furniture; but this is to misunderstand the role of pattern books, which were not intended to change people's ideas of furniture design, but to demonstrate the available range of types of furniture.

In 1791 Thomas Sheraton's *The Cabinet-Maker and Upholsterer's Drawing-Book* began to appear. It was obtainable fortnightly by subscription. Sheraton was the son of a schoolmaster in Stockton-on-Tees, who had come south to London in order to work as a designer of furniture.[13] His trade card, issued sometime in the second half of the 1790s, shows a set of chairs lined up in a row and states that he 'Teaches Perspective, Architecture and Ornaments, makes Designs for Cabinet-makers and sells all kinds of Drawing Books &c.'[14] Later in his life he fell on hard times, and there is a dismal description of him in the *Memoirs* of the publisher Adam Black, as living 'in an obscure street, his house half shop, half dwelling-house, and looked himself like a worn-out Methodist minister';[15] but his *Drawing-Book* was an impressive production, including a number of new furniture types, engraved in a lighter and less linear style than previous comparable publications. It was obviously intended to establish his reputation as a designer and to gain him commissions; and it included engravings of the interiors of Carlton House, much the most fashionable example of interior decoration of the 1780s, suggesting Sheraton's interest in a new and more French style of interior.

Apart from these manuals of furniture types, other pattern books were issued by manufacturers. These illustrated commodities for sale. In some cases pattern books were used within a particular factory to provide models of different wares. For example, Wedgwood produced a 'First Pattern Book' in 1770, which appears never to have left his factory at Etruria. But, by 1774, he had produced a creamware pattern book which was described as 'A Catalogue of the different Articles of *Queen's Ware*, which may be had either plain, gilt, or embellished with Enamel Paintings, manufactured by Josiah Wedgwood, Potter to her Majesty'. This practice of issuing catalogues to advertise the availability of goods became more common in the last two decades of the century. In 1783 the Leeds pottery produced a pattern book with the accompanying inscription:

> Designs of Sundry Articles of Queen's or Cream Colour'd Earthenware manufactured by Hartley, Greens & Co., at Leeds Pottery with a great variety of other Articles. The same Enamell'd, Printed or Ornamented with gold to any pattern; also with Coats of Arms. Cyphers, Landscapes, etc. etc. Leeds 1783.[16]

Whereas at the beginning of the eighteenth century any form of publication illustrating aspects of interior decoration was extremely rare, by the end of the century readers were saturated with different forms of printed image. Both designers and customers could look through a range of publications which gave recommendations on aspects of design or the availability of particular commodities. They could think and predict how an interior might look, and how much it might cost. They could furnish a room in their mind.

This brought about a transformation in individuals' attitudes to their surroundings. Clients were no longer dependent on the workmanship of craftsmen, who produced rooms according to strict rules and established precedents: they could order motifs in any of a number of styles. One room could be Egyptian, another Moorish; spaces could be manipulated to have a different character. The colours of rooms could be co-ordinated, and rooms furnished differently according to their function. The medium of print made interior decoration into an activity which was open to alternative forms. The domestic interior had become a vehicle which could be moulded according to the tastes of the individual owner. It was an expression of personality.

The Transformation into Genre

One of the features of artistic practice in the last two decades of the eighteenth century was the way in which the conversation piece fell from popularity. Although different types and styles of art became available, including the use of new media such as watercolour, paintings of individuals surrounded by an imagined domestic space disappear from view. Patrons were no longer content to commission a simple and intellectually undemanding form of domestic narrative. They wanted to be idealized and aggrandized, shown in the guise of a classical god or strolling out into the landscape. The conventions of art were sufficiently well understood in society for individuals to want an image which was consciously artistic, not one which strove towards narrative realism. The idea of the conversation piece, with its emphasis on an illusion of reality, was replaced by an interest in genre painting whereby, instead of depicting known individuals in an ostensibly identifiable location, painters would produce pictures in which there was a strong degree of sentimentalization of the life of the poor.

One of the first practitioners of genre painting was Henry Walton, the son of a Norfolk farmer. In 1770 he applied to become a student at the Academy of Drawing in Maiden Lane, and during the early 1770s he exhibited a number of conversation pictures at the Society of Artists. It seems that he then spent time in Paris, where he became familiar with the works of Chardin and Greuze. Greuze, in particular, had made his reputation at the Salon by producing pictures which attempted to distil a complex story into a single effective composition, in order to arouse a strong emotion in the spectator. His work was tremendously

187

successful, much admired by critics and collected by the most prominent Parisian collectors.[17] As Diderot wrote of his *L'Accordée de Village*, which was exhibited at the Salon of 1761, 'Le choix de ses sujets marque de la sensibilité et de bonnes moeurs'.[18] Inspired by Greuze, Walton began to produce comparable pictures, in which the desire for a moral idealization of human nature is a more powerful factor than the demands of truth. It was a style of painting which was ideally suited to public exhibition, since it did not require any knowledge of the identity of the sitter and could be seen to participate in the idea of public improvement, the ostensible inspiration for late eighteenth-century exhibitions of art. Moreover, genre paintings translated very effectively into prints, thereby allowing artists a larger audience for their work.

Walton failed to be elected to the Royal Academy and became more interested in dealing in works of art than painting them, so that he effectively abandoned this style of painting around 1770; but the idea of genre pictures was developed in the 1780s by Francis Wheatley. Wheatley was born in Covent Garden in 1747, the son of a tailor.[19] In 1762, aged fifteen, he was awarded a premium by the Royal Society of Arts for a 'Drawing of a human Figure after a Print or Drawing' and in 1763 he is said to have been abroad, possibly in Paris where, like Walton, he could have seen and admired the works of Greuze. On his return Wheatley specialized in painting landscapes in the style of Gainsborough and conversation pictures, which invariably showed the sitters out-doors, occupied in some appropriate activity such as sketching, flying a kite, or fishing.

After a period spent in Ireland between 1779 and 1783 to escape his creditors, Wheatley returned to England. According to his obituary,

On Mr. W's return to England he endeavoured to alter his manner, by copying Greuze, the French artist of much notoriety in domestic scenes; and in this sort of pursuit he has continued ever since. He appears to have imbibed the prejudices of Mr. Greuze so far as to give his low subjects the air of French peasantry. It is but bare justice to observe that Mr. W has infinitely more nature, as Greuze is hard and stony.[20]

Because Wheatley's pictures are so clearly the product of art, with the subject matter taken from literature and the compositions from other artists, they do not have much value as documents of the appearance of actual interiors of the time. What they reveal is the sentimentalizing of rural life. As urbanization gathered pace and labourers left the countryside for higher wages in the towns, there was a counter-movement in literary sensibility to commemorate the supposed values of rusticity. In *The Schoolmistress*, which Wheatley exhibited in 1791, he depicts his subject sitting on an ancient chair, with a glimmer of light coming through the window, while she provides appropriate instruction to a group of children. In *Night*, painted in 1798, he shows an idealized view of rustic life as a child is put to bed in a wicker cot. Both are the product of a sententious desire for lost innocence and an attempt to provide a palliative to social change.

The other notable artist of the last two decades of the eighteenth century who specialized in genre painting was George Morland. Morland was born on 16 May 1762; his father was an artist and his mother was described at the time of her marriage as 'a most agreeable young lady and a handsome fortune'.[21] He was something of a prodigy and was already exhibiting at the Royal Academy in 1773 at the age of eleven. Like Wheatley, Morland saw a market for improving pictures of the rural poor, which enabled him to work independently of direct patronage. As with Wheatley, his compositions are at least as effective in the form of mezzotints, and many were done as much for the booming print industry as for public exhibition; Morland's brother-in-law was the engraver William Ward, and he did a good deal of work directly for John Raphael Smith, a successful print dealer and

mezzotint engraver. Again as with Wheatley, the atmosphere of
Morland's work suggests that it was a purely invented form
of narrative, without any semblance of realism. A good example of
this atmosphere is provided by *A Visit to the Child at Nurse* painted
around 1788, which shows a lady coming to take her child back
from the nurse: the emphasis is entirely upon the emotions
inspired by the event; but the scene provides a certain amount of
incidental information about a cottage interior, such as the crudely
made wooden stool and the much more elaborate wooden toy.
The Comforts of Industry, painted in 1790, shows the ideal image of
the cottager returning to his wife: they are well dressed and there
is china over the fireplace; but, because the moral aspect of the tale
is pre-eminent, it must be treated with the utmost suspicion as
evidence of the life of the poor.

The reasons for the transformation of the conversation piece
into the genre picture in the 1780s are presumably as complex as
those for the origin of the conversation piece in the 1720s. They
must be sought partly in artistic conventions: in the contemporary
admiration for the works of Greuze on the grounds that they
showed the simplicity and goodness of human nature independent
of the corruption of luxury; in the importation at that time of
prints after his work; and in the opportunities which the public
exhibitions of the Royal Academy and the Society of Artists
provided for the exploration of new artistic ideas. But the
transformation into genre must also be seen as an index of a
further change in attitudes towards the interior.

At the beginning of the eighteenth century it was rare to find a
portrait which showed any indication of the setting. Under the
influence of both Dutch and French paintings it became common
in the 1730s to paint aristocratic sitters at home in their country
houses; but it was a relatively short-lived convention, rapidly
usurped by provincial artists and superseded by a more ambitious
view of the role of art. Portraits ceased to be icons of domestic life
and instead were inclined to glamorize an individual's social
identity. Aristocratic sitters were shown in an ideal landscape

sitting or walking out into their gardens, suggesting their control of sensibility at least as much as their possession of material goods. Portraiture therefore is an indication of the desire for a more subtle characterization of personality, in which a heroic air was in greater demand than the more mundane aspects of pictorial realism. In the middle of the eighteenth century the setting of a portrait was a useful way of indicating rank and social status, but by the end of the eighteenth century this was felt to be unsophisticated and the more specifically artistic qualities of style provided the criteria of judgement for the portrait as a work of art. The enjoyment of leisure and the appreciation of the countryside were a more subtle statement of rank than gilded chairs and silver teapots. Art increasingly occupied a dimension of its own, independent of its use as a system of record.

In place of depicting the nobility and gentry at ease in their homes, it became a convention to show the rural poor hanging out their washing or saying grace before a meal. During the course of the eighteenth century the depiction of interiors had slid gradually, but progressively, down the social scale. But these pictures were certainly not intended to provide a precise record of interiors. Instead they provided moral uplift to their owners, who could survey the conditions of the poor without the prick of conscience.

The Role of Satire

If one is looking for a more realistic depiction of interiors at the end of the eighteenth century than is offered by the anodyne images of the genre painters, this can be found in satirical prints. Of course, such prints obey their own conventions in distorting the setting of the events they depict for the purposes of sharpening the characterization; but a satirical print is probably a less distorting medium of representation than the deliberate fiction of the genre painting.

In the years since Hogarth had first experimented with licentious images of current events, stimulated by hostility to Sir Robert Walpole's regime, the market for satirical prints had burgeoned. Matthias Darly, whom we have come across several times already, as a designer, as the publisher of *A New Book of Designs* in 1754, and as an associate of Chippendale, also exploited the market for satire, which his wife Mary thought would 'keep those that practise it out of the hipps or Vapours'.[22] He included prints by the amateur caricaturist George Townshend in his *A Political and Satyrical History*, published in 1756, and in the same year began to issue small political prints pasted on to cards which could be sent through the post.[23]

During the 1770s Matthias Darly switched the subject matter of his prints from political satire directed against prominent individuals, especially Lord Bute, to a more general form of social satire, beginning with a series lampooning the so-called Macaronies, who deliberately dressed outrageously in order to offend an older generation's concern for sobriety of manners.[24] He advertised his wares as

Drol Prints, consisting of Heads, Figures, Conversations and Satires upon the follies of the Age Design'd by several Ladies, Gentlemen and the most Humorous Artists &c. Pubd. by M Darly Engraver at No.39 near York Buildings Strand, London.[25]

The rival firm of Carington Bowles in St Paul's Churchyard also specialized in humorous mezzotints, which satirized the foibles of the clergy and the professional classes. A third important printseller of the time was Robert Sayer, who described his 'sets of fine prints' as

proper to collect in the cabinets of the curious, and also make furniture elegant and genteel when framed and glazed, or may be fitted up in a cheaper manner, to ornament rooms, staircases &c. with curious borders representing frames, a fashion much in use, and produces a very agreeable effect.[26]

These prints contain much incidental information about the appearance of eighteenth-century interiors. They have the additional advantage of being precisely dated, according to the requirements of the Copyright Act passed by Parliament in 1735. A print entitled *Love and Opportunity*, published by Robert Sayer in 1768, shows all the accoutrements of a standard parlour of this period, including a table, on which are placed a pipe and port bottle, and a mantelpiece, on which are specimens of imported china.

By the 1780s there was a very substantial market for all sorts of prints, especially caricatures, and they were being exported to France, thereby reversing the traditional direction of this trade. It was said of the print dealer John Raphael Smith that:

He inundated France with English coloured prints; and, it has been said, that he who first opened the market there – closed it too; for not confining himself to the traffic of money, he sent cargo upon cargo, of prints of all descriptions, and took part of the amount in merchandise – and among other commodities, received vast imports of claret, champagne, and other wines.[27]

In London the print shops became increasingly commercial, devising different ways of pleasing their customers, including offering bound sets of caricatures, lending them out for the evening, and holding exhibitions.[28] Samuel Fores and William Holland, two of the most prominent specialists in caricature during the 1780s, held regular exhibitions with an entrance charge of a shilling. F. A. Wendeborn commented in his *A View of England towards the Close of the Eighteenth Century*:

I remember when I first came to London, that the print and picture-shops puzzled me, when I saw numbers of fine prints, many of them elegantly framed and glazed, hung up, and exhibited at the windows, and from time to time new ones on different subjects. I saw numbers of people staring at them, on passing the streets, but I hardly ever observed any body going in to buy. It seemed incomprehensible to me, how such shops, at so vast an expence, could maintain themselves without any visible customers, till I got acquainted with an eminent print-seller, who, as I was informed, had acquired, within a few years, a great fortune by his business. He explained the matter to me, and cleared up what appeared to be mysterious, by telling me that he sold great quantities of goods in the country; that he sent them to Scotland, to Ireland, to the East and West-Indies, to America, and to other parts of the world; disposing on an average, weekly, five hundred pounds worth.[29]

A further stimulus to the market for satirical prints, besides the entrepreneurial activites of individual printsellers, was the change in the available techniques of printmaking. Whereas the process of line engraving with a burin required precision of hand and produced a precisely formed outline, etching with a needle produced a more fluid image. The idea of a caricature would have been killed off if it had always had to be laboriously translated into an engraving, but the combination of new techniques, including etching, stipple engraving and aquatint, allowed the artist to translate ideas rapidly on to a plate and to experiment with a complex surface effect. The caricatures of the 1780s depend for their impact not on some laborious written explanation, but on their immediacy of visual expression.

Indeed, it was in the 1780s that Rowlandson and Gillray, two of the great masters of caricature, began to work. Rowlandson had been brought up in Soho, which was the centre of a lively artistic community and of the print trade. He had entered the Royal

Academy School in November 1772.[30] In the late 1770s he began to work as a portrait painter, but he must have realized that his talents lay in the sketch more than in the finished painting. From the early 1780s onwards he produced a tremendous range of work, including watercolours, drawings, prints and book illustrations, some of which were deliberately comic – but the comedy was of the most genial kind.

Rowlandson could draw with ease and was a perceptive observer not just of human foibles, but also of the individuality of place, sketching the scene wherever he went. He kept records when he went on trips into the country, to Greenwich and the south coast, and would often work up his sketches into finished watercolours when he came home. His drawings were done as narratives of a particular moment, slightly exaggerated in order to bring out the humorous and comic elements, but done with a sense of pleasure in visual documentation. His work makes it possible to visualize in great detail many of the characteristics of everyday life at the end of the eighteenth century: the bump of the coach as it moved through the countryside, the atmosphere of an inn.

Gillray was much more deliberately sardonic. Like Rowlandson, he was trained at the Academy schools, after an upbringing in the Moravian community in Chelsea and a period working as a hack engraver in Harry Ashby's print shop on Holborn Hill. Like Rowlandson, he initially wanted to be a portrait painter, issuing a trade card:

> Gillray
> Portrait Painter
> No. 7 Little Newport Street
> Leicester Fields

Yet by the end of the 1780s, like Rowlandson, he had realized that his talents lay in producing prints for a market which was hungry for political satire.

Gillray was a brilliant technician. His plates were very elaborately etched and there is a feeling about all his work that it deliberately incorporated the process of composition, that his characters grew ever more hideous and distended and the incidental details more grotesque as he was working. In a print entitled *This is a Sorry Sight*, of around 1786, every aspect of the scene is invested with a ghastly visual significance. The carpet is of a disgustingly evil texture; the perspective of the left-hand wall is bent in order to create a sense of dislocation in the viewer; there is a water closet in the right-hand corner of the room. Every item in the scene is malevolently recorded. In another print of the same year, *The Miser's Feast*, the same process is at work. Every detail of the furniture and decoration contributes to the bite of the pictorial narrative. It is not just the bodies which have exaggerated proportions, but even the size of the door in relation to the rest of the room. The sense of caricature in physiognomy has been extended to the shape of the teapot, the chamber pot and the chair.

The profusion of graphic work which poured out of the print shops in the course of the 1780s and 1790s makes it possible to obtain a much more detailed picture of all levels of social life than can be done for the beginning of the century. Instead of relying on an image constructed from surviving pieces of furniture, one can place furniture in the mind's eye. One can now observe the diversity of different types of interior and the fact that they were not necessarily unified in the way the furniture was assembled, but might consist of an old chair and table with more modern ornaments on the mantelpiece. An Adam-style mantelpiece might co-exist with a French *torchère*. Furniture was not necessarily acquired in order to provide a visual unity, but was scattered informally around the room. Style in interiors was highly various. Many interiors did not obey its dictates at all.

There is an immense significance in the range of graphic work produced in the 1780s and 1790s because it is evidence of an intensely visual culture, in which the meaning of objects could be read at a glance from their appearance. The meaning of things is nowadays thought to be conveyed principally by words, as if verbal description is the most effective form of communication. But how much more powerful is the organ of sight, which is able to apprehend, to comprehend, and to classify with a speed and immediacy which does not necessarily involve the intervention of words. During the eighteenth century the observation of a setting for the information it might contain was developed through the medium of the print.

The Map of Culture

When one examines the nature of interiors at the beginning of the eighteenth century, the number of available images is small; at this time the idea of design applied to interior decoration scarcely existed. The only people who thought that it was legitimate to consider the interrelationship of the different parts of a room, the style of the furnishing and its visual effect, were a small group among the nobility and a few architects who were aware of developments in interiors on the Continent. Even a well born traveller such as Celia Fiennes tended to look at the interiors of the houses she visited on the basis of individual items of furniture and their cost, without any awareness of messages that the arrangement of an interior might convey.

In London and a few provincial towns, the merchant élite had acquired the trappings of sophisticated living, including imported furniture and, especially, china. It is possible that they were aware that these could be displayed in such a way as to indicate personal character, that there was a degree of personal choice in the acquisition of goods, as a means of making a statement of individuality as well as of social status. But again, any evidence of a real ability to visualize the nature of an interior domestic environment is slight: individual items of furniture might have a private history, but there is no suggestion that they were arranged systematically, or that the relationship between items of furniture was thought to be significant. There is no visual record of a late seventeenth-century parlour and, even if there were, the likelihood is that it would show pictures, tables and chairs organised in a random fashion.

At other levels of society at the beginning of the eighteenth century, furniture and fittings were acquired on the basis of what was available in a particular locality, sold at the local market town or by a travelling chapman. There was no idea of a conscious visualization of the domestic environment as a place for the projection of personality. Indeed, the legacy of Puritanism would have meant that such an idea was offensive. It was only with the beginnings of periodical journalism in Addison and Steele's *Spectator* that advice was offered about appropriate attitudes towards personal belongings, and the ownership of goods was regarded as an aspect of an individual's personality.

By the end of the eighteenth century these attitudes had changed. At the top end of society there was an awareness of the precise meanings which might be attached to the arrangement of interiors. Patrons were aware that they were making a statement of taste in the choice of an architect; and the architect was expected to orchestrate all the different elements of furniture and decoration, including the colour of the wall surfaces and the choice of fabric, to ensure that they were in the latest fashion. Furniture would be purchased from one of the leading London suppliers. Everyone knew that it was possible to acquire different types and styles. The elements of an interior were coordinated to ensure that they created an appropriate atmosphere. Instead of there being one appropriate style for an interior, different styles could be used according to the function of the room, the whim of the decorator, or the taste of the owner.

The most important trend in decoration in the upper echelons of society was a fascination with French forms of decoration, stimulated by a period of close trading contact following the Treaty of Versailles of 1783 and later by the influx of French refugees who had lost their traditional sources of patronage in the French Revolution. This appetite for things French, both in the style of architecture and of furniture, is particularly evident in the changes which were made to Carlton House for the Prince of Wales.[31] When the Prince reached his majority on 12 August 1783 the House of Commons voted him £60,000 for the refurbishment of Carlton House, which had previously belonged to his grandmother Augusta, dowager Princess of Wales (the widow of Prince Frederick). After consulting Sir William Chambers, as Surveyor-General, he turned to Henry Holland, presumably impressed by the elegant interiors Holland had produced for the upstairs rooms at Brooks's Club in St James's Street. That the Prince of Wales and Holland were determined that Carlton House should be a monument to Francophile taste is evident in their choice of a Frenchman, Guillaume Gaubert, as Clerk of Works. Gaubert was responsible not only for the choice of furniture, but also, according to one of his bills, 'inventing and designing the several Ornaments decorations and Furniture and Attending the execution of the same'.[32] A number of French decorators were employed. An entry in an estimate of debts dated 27 October 1784 for 'Fitting and Furnishing the Inside with Furniture for Two Seasons' refers to the practice, common in France, of having two completely different sets of coverings, a *meuble d'été* and a *meuble d'hiver*.

The decoration of Carlton House made an immense impact on contemporaries. Horace Walpole went to a ball there in March 1784 and was overwhelmingly impressed by its magnificence, refinement and elegance. In the dining room, 'the cornice, freize, and pediments, are of white and gold to correspond with the panels and doors, which, when closed, are so contrived that they have not the appearance of doors. The hangings of this apartment are crimson damask.'[33] Of the ballroom he wrote that 'this apartment exhibits a pleasing contrast to the state-room, and is, from the style in which it is laid out, admitted to be as nouvelle as it is beautiful. The panels are of a beautiful white, framed with a light moulding, which appears to be entwined with foliage and flowers after nature.' Most impressive of all was the saloon: 'This apartment may be styled the chef d'oeuvre, and in every ornament discovers great invention. It is hung with a figured lemon sattin.' From Walpole's description, it is evident that every room had a different character. He visited Carlton House again in 1785 and wrote:

We went to see the Prince's new palace in Pall Mall; and were charmed. It will be the most perfect in Europe. There is an August simplicity that astonished me. You cannot call it magnificent; it is the taste and propriety that strike. Every ornament is at a proper distance, and not one too large, but all delicate and new, with more freedom and variety than Greek ornaments; and, though probably borrowed from the Hotel de Condé and other new Palaces, not one that is not rather classic than French.[34]

Horace Walpole was an unusually alert judge of taste, able to deploy a precisely attuned aesthetic vocabulary to assess the resonances of an interior, including its relationship to contemporary French buildings which may have served as models. Design is operating in such a way that judgements of both intention and execution could be descriptively exact.

Following a period in the mid-1780s when work on Carlton House was stopped owing to the Prince of Wales's debts, Dominique Daguerre, the well known French *marchand-mercier*, was called in to supply the furniture. In November 1789, Henry Holland drew up

> An account of the Furniture and Decoration including a new Throne and State Bed, silk damask hangings and furniture trimmed with rich gold lace, gilt bronze chandeliers, girandoles, tables and other articles necessary for furnishing the State Apartments in a suitable manner and to replace many of the articles designed to be used at the time of the Application to Parliament in 1787 and to finish other State Rooms not then Projected.[35]

For the Chinese Drawing Room, it included the following items:

> Ormoulu ornaments to one chimney-piece
> Two enriched pier tables
> Eight enriched and gilt girandoles
> Three enriched and gilt lanthorns
> One clock with an enriched and gilt case
> Four large looking glasses with their frames
> The room furnished with silk made in Spitalfields
> The chairs and sophas covered with the same
> The walls and ceiling richly painted and gilt with Chinese
>   subjects and ornaments
> A Moorfields carpet to a pattern
> A handsome stove grate[36]

From the vocabulary that was used to describe these pieces one can get an idea of the opulence of the fittings of Carlton House, of the amount of money which was lavished on it, and of the degree of consciousness involved in the style of decoration. Some of the rooms were unified by the choice of colour, including the Yellow Bow Room, the Blue Bow Room, and the Flesh-Coloured Room; some were united by a single motif which ran through the furniture of the room, such as the Music Room, which had chairs carved with musical trophies; and some by the choice of theme, such as the Roman Room and the Chinese Drawing Room. Deliberate eclecticism was a virtue.

Henry Holland was also called in to advise on the decoration of new interiors for the second Earl Spencer at Althorp in Northamptonshire.[37] As at Carlton House, he recommended the employment of French decorators, among them T.H. Pernotin, who painted arabesque panels in Lady Spencer's dressing room, including '4 Pannels over Doors and glass' for which he was paid £25, and '6 Pilasters' costing £126.[38] As at Carlton House, the furniture was supplied by Dominique Daguerre. An estimate dated Michaelmas 1790 includes 'Articles of Furniture in hand under Mr Dagures estimate consisting of the Japan c'modes fitting up for the drawing room, the commodes chairs &c. for Lady Spencer's dressing room, £300'; and a subsequent bill lists goods supplied to 'Milord Spencer par daguerre et compagnie de Paris', including 'une grande commode en laque', 'deux secrétaires', and 'un paire de girandole a enfans de coleur antique bronze'.[39]

The magnificence of the interiors at Carlton House and Althorp, and their style of deliberately restrained opulence, was matched by the interiors which Holland designed for the younger Samuel Whitbread, who in 1796 inherited his father's recently acquired house at Southill in Bedfordshire, as well as the family brewery.[40] At Southill, the most obviously French room was Mrs Whitbread's boudoir. Its walls were white with painted decoration by Louis-André Delabrière, who had also worked at Carlton House and before that had been 'Architecte à Mgr. le Comte d'Artois' at the Bagatelle, the pavilion of the Comte d'Artois in the Bois de Boulogne in Paris. Some of the furniture was also painted by Delabrière, including 'Round Seat Chairs with painted Tablet backs'. The hangings were 'rich green & white damask Curtains & Drapery, lined with silk & decorated with gold fringe'. According to the Revd Samuel Johnes, who visited the house in 1800, it looked like 'a small Temple where has been deposited all the rich offerings of every country'.

While members of the nobility indulged in a dream of Francophile refinement, members of the prosperous professional classes were more concerned with solidity and comfort. If what was important at the uppermost level of interior decoration at the end of the eighteenth century was the self-consciousness employed in the selection of an appropriate style, then what is at least as significant is the extent to which this awareness of style in interior decoration had filtered through into the professional classes. In a more substantial segment of society than at the beginning of the century there was a powerful degree of pride in the comforts of the home. Instead of the household consisting of a collection of ill-differentiated rooms, some of which might be used for purposes of business and which might combine the activities of everyday life, eating, sleeping, cooking and receiving visitors, by the end of the century, the home was a well organized machine, in which all these activities were carefully differentiated.

The qualities and characteristics of English pride in the arrangement of their houses was constantly commented upon by foreign visitors. Part of what impressed them was the sheer amount of money which was spent on interior furnishings. When François de la Rochefoucauld visited Euston in Suffolk, he remarked on the way that the use of mahogany indicated a willingness to spend a disproportionate amount of personal income on a particularly expensive form of wood:

It is indeed remarkable that the English are so much given to the use of mahogany; not only are their tables generally made of it, but also their doors and seats and handrails of their staircases. Yet it is just as dear in England as in France. It is a matter which I do not pretend to understand, but I am inclined to think that the English must be richer than we are; certainly I have myself observed not only that everything costs twice as much here as in France, but that the English seize every opportunity to use things which are expensive in themselves.[41]

This opulence in all aspects of domestic furnishings is confirmed by W. de Archenholtz in his *A Picture of England containing a description of the laws, customs, and manners of England*, published in 1797:

No part of Europe exhibits such luxury and magnificence as the English display within the walls of their dwelling house. The staircase, which is covered with the richest carpets, is supported by a balustrade of the finest Indian wood, curiously constructed, and lighted by lamps containing crystal vases. The landing-places are adorned with busts, pictures and medallions; the wainscot and ceilings of the apartments are covered with the finest varnish, and enriched with gold, bass-reliefs, and the most happy attempts in painting and sculpture. The chimneys are of Italian marble, on which flowers and figures, cut in the most exquisite stile, form the chief ornaments; the locks of doors and of steel damasked with gold. Carpets which often cost three hundred pounds a piece, and which one scruples to touch with his foot, cover all the rooms; the richest stuffs from the looms of Asia are employed as window curtains; and the clocks and watches with which the apartments are furnished, astonish by their magnificence, and the ingenious complication of their mechanism.[42]

As Robert Southey commented in his fictitious *Letters from England by Don Manuel Alvarez Espriella*, 'An Englishman delights to show his wealth; every thing in his house, therefore, is expensive.'[43]

Yet the degree of pride which was shown in the furnishings of the home was not simply a matter of the amount of money spent. It was also revealed by the attention paid to the vagaries of fashion, the constant desire to keep up to date and to acquire new furniture as changes in taste dictated. Again Southey is a perceptive commentator on this aspect of domestic furnishings:

> Our breakfast table is oval, large enough for eight or nine persons, yet supported upon one claw in the centre. This is the newest fashion, and fashions change so often in these things, as well as in every thing else, that it is easy to know how long it is since a house has been fitted up, by the shape of the furniture.[44]

A third feature of the pride which was shown in the nature of the home was revealed by the attention which was paid to cleanliness. Brass was well polished; the doorstep was kept clean; carpets were swept; the kitchen was shining. There were manuals which gave instructions on how best to clean household furnishings, such as Susanna Whatman's *Housekeeping Book* of 1776, which gave instructions to the housemaid on scrubbing the floorboards with fuller's earth and fine sand and dusting the furniture with a paintbrush, and how to wash the floorcloths with 'a soft linen and some fresh milk and water'.[45] La Rochefoucauld remarked:

> The cleanliness which pervades everything is a perpetual source of satisfaction. Houses are constantly washed inside and out, generally on Saturdays. People take the greatest possible pains to maintain the standard of cleanliness: you come upon mats and carpets everywhere; there is always a strip of drugget on the stairs, and not a speck of dust anywhere. At first I was quite astonished at all this and did all that I could to make sure whether this cleanliness was natural to the English and so pervaded all their activities, or whether it was a superficial refinement. I was led to see quite clearly that it was only external: everything that you are supposed to see partakes of this

most desirable quality, but the English contrive to neglect it in what you are not supposed to see.[46]

By the end of the eighteenth century the bourgeois home had come into existence, solid, opulent, well cared for and comfortable. Whereas at the beginning of the century there was little idea of people regarding their home life as the most important part of their social identity, by the end of it there was a set of highly developed reflexes which enabled people to look at, judge and assess the contents of a domestic interior and to make judgements about the nature, personality and taste of its owner. Southey wrote in his *Letters from England* that there were two words which were dearest to the English: 'comfort' and 'home'.

In their social intercourse and their modes of life they have enjoyments which we never dream of. Saints and philosophers teach us that they who have the fewest wants are the wisest and the happiest; but neither philosophers nor saints are in fashion in England. It is recorded of some old Eastern tyrant, that he offered a reward for the discovery of a new pleasure; – in like manner this nation offers a perpetual reward to those who will discover new wants for them, in the readiness wherewith they purchase any thing, if the seller will but assure them that it is exceedingly convenient.[47]

How far this sense of comfort and domestic prosperity extended into other ranks of society is not clear. This is not the place to go into the lengthy question of the standard of living of the working classes under the process of industrialization; yet even in the lower ranks of society, it is clear that foreigners were impressed by the amount of care and attention which was lavished on furniture and decoration. According to a German visitor in 1783,

In regard to the arrangement and decoration of the rooms,

English women rival those of every other nation. The commonest handicraftsman has in addition to his work-room at least one room in which he receives strangers and in which nothing is to be seen that suggests his trade.[48]

La Rochefoucauld was at least as impressed by the comforts of small domestic interiors on his travels as he was by grander London houses. He wrote on his arrival at Dover:

I remarked from the first that atmosphere of comfort which characterises the country into which I was entering; I observed that all classes of people – peasants from the neighbouring country, servants even – were well clad and remarkably clean; that the furniture in their houses was all of mahogany, even in our inn; that they had plenty of those tables which are so dear in France.[49]

What is impressive, therefore, in examining the nature of interiors at most levels of society at the end of the eighteenth century, apart from those of the labouring classes, is the degree of pride in their arrangement, the consciousness that the interior was a theatre for the display of personality, as well as for the accumulation of possessions. If one is to judge a society by the quantity of goods possessed by its more prosperous members, by the degree of determination with which those goods were acquired, and by the importance of property to individual self-esteem, there is no doubt that there had been a significant change in the map of culture during the course of the eighteenth century. Taste motivated desire; desire propelled the acquisition of goods; the need for different types of consumer goods stimulated changes in the ways that they were made. As F.A. Wendeborn wrote in his *View of England towards the Close of the Eighteenth Century:*

Those frequent changes of fashion, in regard to dress and

furniture, are a great support of British manufactures; they promote trade, and keep all sorts of tradesmen employed; they increase the pride, the wants, and the cares of families, and procure employment for others; they are beneficial to government by imposts and taxes; they are the principal links in those golden chains of folly, by which men, without knowing it suffer themselves to be bound, and to renounce, insensibly their natural liberty and independence.[50]

Conclusion

For much of the twentieth century paintings have been studied either as if they occupy an aesthetic domain completely separate from their social surroundings, as if the imagined world of the artists bears no direct relationship to the contemporary environment; or instead, as if they are passive illustrations of their world. They have tended to be interpreted either by art historians as a commentary on works by other artists, or by social historians as if they present unproblematic images of their time and place.

In this study I have used visual source material to interpret changes in pictorial convention: not just as passive reflectors of aspects of eighteenth-century society, which might be known at least as well, and probably much better, from other sources; but instead as part of the way people in the eighteenth century viewed and interpreted their surroundings. Images are neither flat, dead representations of what they depict, nor are they unrelated to their surrounding environment. They negotiate the relationship between eye and scene, mind and reality, conscious formulation and unconscious expression. If pictures are to be treated as relics from the past, fragments of individual lives and evidence of past social relations, it is essential that they are interpreted with the same care and sensitivity as more conventional documentary sources.

A second conclusion of this book concerns the dynamics of style in the eighteenth century. In the secondary literature about the applied arts, there remains a view that every feature of an artefact was subordinated to a set of standard stylistic characteristics, whether baroque, Palladian, rococo or neoclassical. Yet this stylistic vocabulary is a later invention, bearing no necessary relationship to the way people thought about the visual characteristics of objects at the time. By largely avoiding the standard stylistic vocabulary, I hope that I have been able to provide a more complete understanding of the origins of objects and interiors. The domestic interior is the product of systems of thought and of political and economic circumstances. It involves technology, aesthetics and social behaviour. By tracing the image of the domestic interior in eighteenth-century England, it has been possible to follow a chain of different influences which transformed attitudes towards domestic life.

A third, and final, conclusion of this book concerns the relationship between fashion and social history. In recent accounts of eighteenth-century history it has become commonplace to emphasize the elements of continuity, the lack of radical change in the essential features of eighteenth-century life. By concentrating attention on the changing features of the domestic interior, certain gradual changes have been discovered in the way that individuals thought about their surroundings.

At the beginning of the eighteenth century only a few members of the court élite were aware of the way that an interior could be arranged to convey messages about individual character and social status. The language of artefacts, as a means of extending communication into the surroundings, was restricted. During the eighteenth century a much larger section of society began to have access to objects which could convey meaning as signs of consumer choice. As tastes changed and more people wanted to own goods that exhibited a degree of individual taste, manufacturers responded by producing a more sophisticated range of products. To take the simplest view, the changes in methods of production which are regarded as such an important feature of eighteenth-century history were fuelled as much by the changing desires of consumers as they were by advances in technology and entrepreneurial initiative.

By the end of the eighteenth century new fashions extended to the breakfast tables of artisans and shopkeepers in small provincial towns. A sense of personality and of one's place in the world derived as much from exterior attributes and material possessions as it did from private morality and individual conscience. Architects had begun to think about ways of organizing the appearance of an interior; artists had learned how to portray individuals in terms of their surroundings; satirists had seized on material goods as a way of communicating messages about character. Men and women were judged by what they owned.

Notes

Abbreviations

BL	British Library.
Colvin	Howard Colvin, *A Biographical Dictionary of British Architects 1600–1840*, London 1978.
DEFM	Geoffrey Beard and Christopher Gilbert (eds), *Dictionary of English Furniture Makers 1660–1840*, Leeds 1986.
DNB	*Dictionary of National Biography.*
HMC	Historical Manuscripts Commission.
Horace Walpole's Correspondence	*The Yale Edition of Horace Walpole's Correspondence*, ed. W.S. Lewis *et al.*, 48 vols., New Haven 1937–1983.
PRO	Public Record Office.
SRO	Scottish Record Office, Register House, Edinburgh.
V&A	Victoria and Albert Museum.
VCH	*Victoria County History.*
Walpole Society	*The Annual Volumes of the Walpole Society*, I–LIV, 1912–1991 (including Vertue Notebooks I–VI, 1930–1955).
Wren Society	*The Volumes of the Wren Society*, I–XX, 1924–1943.

PRE-1700

1 There is an excellent account of the processes of building in Malcolm Airs, *The Making of the English Country House, 1500–1640*, London 1975, especially pp.21–45. For the origins of the architectural profession, see Howard Colvin, 'The architectural profession' in *A Biographical Dictionary of British Architects 1600–1840*, London 1978, pp.26–41; and John Wilton-Ely, 'The rise of the professional architect in England', in Spiro Kostof (ed.), *The Architect: chapters in the history of the profession*, Oxford 1977, pp.180–208.

2 Airs, *Making of the English Country House*, p.35.

3 R.T. Gunther (ed.), *The Architecture of Sir Roger Pratt*, Oxford 1928, p.60.

4 W.D. Caröe, 'Tom Tower', *Christ Church, Oxford: some letters of Sir Christopher Wren to John Fell, Bishop of*

Oxford, Oxford 1923, p.23.

5 Joseph Moxon, *Mechanick Exercises: Or, the Doctrine of Handy-Works*, London 1694, p.162.

6 For this drawing see Mark Girouard, 'The Smythson Collection of the Royal Institute of British Architects', *Architectural History*, 5, 1962, p.48; Margaret Richardson (ed.), *Catalogue of the Drawings Collection of the Royal Institute of British Architects*, 14, Farnborough 1976, p.97; and Laura Jacobus, 'On "Whether a man could see before him and behind him both at once": The role of drawing in the design of interior space in England *c*.1600–1800', *Architectural History*, 31, 1988, p.151.

7 The most recent and authoritative study of Inigo Jones's drawings is John Harris and Gordon Higgott, *Inigo Jones: Complete Architectural Drawings*, New York 1989. See also John Harris, 'Inigo Jones and his French sources', *Bulletin of the Metropolitan Museum of Art*, May 1961, pp.253–64; and John Harris, *Catalogue of the Drawings Collection of the Royal Institute of British Architects: Inigo Jones and John Webb*, Farnborough 1972.

8 John Harris and A.A. Tait, *Catalogue of the Drawings by Inigo Jones, John Webb and Isaac de Caus at Worcester College, Oxford*, Oxford 1979, p.35.

9 H.M. Colvin *et al.*, *The History of the King's Works*, v, 1660–1782, London 1976, p.149.

10 For the life and work of John Webb see the excellent biography by John Bold, *John Webb: architectural theory and practice in the seventeenth century*, Oxford 1989. For his drawings see Harris, *Catalogue of the RIBA Drawing Collection: Jones and Webb*. For the palm as an emblem, see David Watkin, 'The migration of the palm: a case-study of architectural ornament as a vehicle of meaning', *Apollo*, February 1990, pp.78–84.

11 For Roger North see Howard Colvin and John Newman (eds), *Of Building: Roger North's writings on architecture*, Oxford, 1981, and Laura Jacobus, 'On "Whether a man could see before him . . .', p.152.

12 Colvin and Newman, *Of Building*, p.xiii.

13 Colvin and Newman, *Of Building*, p.34.

14 *Wren Society*, IV, plates 27–46; Colvin, *King's Works*, v, p.163.

15 John Harris, 'The Hampton Court Trianon designs of William and John Talman', *Journal of the Warburg and Courtauld Institutes*, XXIII, 1960, pp.139–49; Colvin, *King's Works*, v, p.167; and John Harris, *William Talman, Maverick Architect*, London 1982, p.37.

16 The principal reference book for the study of pattern books is Simon Jervis's invaluable *The Penguin Dictionary of Design and Designers*, Harmondsworth 1984. For the use of pattern books by Elizabethan architects, see Mark Girouard, *Robert Smythson and the Elizabethan Country House*, New Haven and London 1983, pp.14–16; and Alice T. Friedman, *House and Household in Elizabethan England: Wollaton Hall and the Willoughby family*, Chicago and London 1989, pp.76–81.

17 For Serlio see William Bell Dinsmoor, 'The literary remains of Sebastiano Serlio', *Art Bulletin*, 1942, pp.55–91; and Eileen Harris and Nicholas Savage, *British Architectural Books and Writers 1556–1785*, Cambridge and New York 1990, pp.414–17.

18 [Sebastiano Serlio], *the first Booke of Architecture, made by Sebastian Serly*, London 1611. For Robert Peake's career see Leona Rostenberg, *English Publishers in the Graphic Arts 1599–1700*, New York 1963, p.20.

19 Airs, *Making of the English Country House*, p.26; for architectural sources in late sixteenth and early seventeenth-century private libraries see Lucy Gent, *Picture and Poetry 1560–1620, relations between literature and the visual arts in the English Renaissance*,

Leamington Spa 1981, pp.78–86.

20 This literature is authoritatively surveyed in Simon Jervis, *Printed Furniture Designs before 1650*, Furniture History Society, London 1974 and Harris and Savage, *British Architectural Books and Writers*. See also Gervase Jackson-Stops, 'French ideas for English houses. The influence of pattern books 1660–1700', *Country Life*, CXLVII, 1970, pp.261–6.

21 Walter Gedde, *A Book of Sundry Draughtes, Principaly Serving for Glasiers. And not Impertinent for Plasterers, and Gardiners, besides sundry other professions*, London 1615, p.A2.

22 G.B. Parks, 'John Evelyn and the art of travel', *Huntington Library Quarterly*, XI, 1947, pp.251–76.

23 John Evelyn, *Memoirs*, ed. W. Bray, London 1827, II, p.225.

24 C.E. Kenney, 'William Leybourn, 1626–1716', *The Library*, 5:3, December 1950, pp.159–71.

25 H. C. Levis, *A Descriptive Bibliography of the Most Important Books in the English Language Relating to the Art and History of Engraving and the Collecting of Prints*, London 1912, II, p.489; Rostenberg, *English Publishers in the Graphic Arts*, pp.44–50.

26 Rostenberg, *English Publishers in the Graphic Arts*, p.57; Harris and Savage, *British Architectural Books and Writers*, p.379.

27 For Hollar see Graham Parry, *Hollar's England, a mid-seventeenth-century view*, Wilton 1980.

28 For late seventeenth-century prints and book illustrations see Edward Hodnett, *Francis Barlow, first master of English book illustration*, London 1978; and, for English drawings in the late seventeenth century, Lindsay Stainton and Christopher White, *Drawing in England from Hilliard to Hogarth*, London 1987.

29 For Pepys as a book collector see Robert Latham, 'The Pepys Library', *Times Literary Supplement*, 26 July 1974, p.815; Orest Ranum, 'Inventing

private space. Samuel and Mrs Pepys at home, 1660–1669', *Wissenschaftskolleg zu Berlin, Jahrbuch* 1982/3, pp.259–76; R. Chartier (ed.), *A History of Private Life*, vol. III, *Passions of the Renaissance*, Cambridge, Mass. 1989, pp.138–9. For Pepys's activities as a print collector see Jan de Waals, 'The print collection of Samuel Pepys', *Print Quarterly*, 1:4, December 1984, pp.236–57.

30 R.C. Latham and W. Matthews (eds), *The Diary of Samuel Pepys*, I, 1660, London 1971, p.265.

31 Latham and Matthews (eds), *Diary of Pepys*, IV, 1663, p.410.

32 Latham and Matthews (eds), *Diary of Pepys*, IV, 1663, pp.14–15.

33 Latham and Matthews (eds), *Diary of Pepys*, IV, 1663, pp.31–2.

34 Latham and Matthews (eds), *Diary of Pepys*, IV, 1663, p.214.

35 Peter Thornton, *Seventeenth-Century Interior Decoration in England, France and Holland*, New Haven and London 1978, p.306.

36 For this information I am indebted to Dr Richard Luckett, the Pepys Librarian at Magdalene College, and to his assistant Mrs E.M. Coleman.

37 For this aspect of Pepys's life, see Marjorie Hope Nicolson, *Pepys's Diary and the New Science*, Charlottesville, Va. 1965.

38 The most recent discussion of this drawing is in Stainton and White, *Drawing in England*, p.226.

39 E. F. Robinson, *The Early History of Coffee Houses in England*, London 1893, p.46. Further information about coffee houses is given in Aytoun Ellis, *The Penny Universities: a history of coffee-houses*, London 1956.

40 Henri Misson, *Memoirs and Observations in his Travels over England*, London 1719, pp.39–40.

41 Thornton, *Seventeenth-Century Interior Decoration*, p.7. The classic account of changes in French manners in the early seventeenth century is M. Magendie, *La Politesse mondaine et les théories de*

l'honnêteté, au XVII siècle, 2 vols., Paris 1925; for a more recent treatment of the idea of politeness in French literature, see Peter France, *Politeness and its Discontents: problems in French classical culture*, Cambridge 1992.

42 Harold Nicolson, *Good Behaviour, being a study of certain types of civility*, London 1955, p.163.

43 Jean-Michel Tuchscherer, 'The art of silk', in Marianne Carlano and Larry Salmon (eds), *French Textiles From the Middle Ages through the Second Empire*, Hartford, Conn. 1985, p.90.

44 The principal modern source for the Marquise de Rambouillet is Jean-Pierre Babelon, *Demeures parisiennes sous Henri IV et Louis XIII*, Paris 1965.

45 For the origins of the idea of *civilité*, see Roger Chartier, 'From texts to manners. A concept and its books: *civilité* between aristocratic distinction and popular appropriation', in Roger Chartier, *The Cultural Uses of Print in Early Modern France*, Princeton NJ 1987, pp.71–109.

46 Anthony Blunt, 'The précieux and French art', in D.J. Gordon (ed.), *Fritz Saxl 1890–1948. A volume of Memorial Essays from his friends in England*, London, 1957, pp.326–38.

47 There is an extremely clear and stimulating introduction to French ideas of planning in Michael Dennis, *Court and Garden: from the French hôtel to the city of modern architecture*, Cambridge, Mass. 1986. The period is also surveyed in Witold Rybczynski, *Home: a short history of an idea*, London 1988, pp.42–4.

48 For Paris during this period see Orest Ranum, *Paris in the Age of Absolutism: an essay*, New York 1968.

49 For the work of Abraham Bosse see A. Blum, *L'Oeuvre gravé d'Abraham Bosse*, Paris 1924 and A. Blum, *Abraham Bosse et la societé française au dix-septième siècle*, Paris 1924.

50 For Colbert's reforms the standard work remains C. W. Cole, *Colbert and a Century of French Mercantilism*, 2 vols.,

New York 1939. However, his work has been subjected to substantial revision. For an account of Louis XIV's reign see Roger Mettam, *Power and Faction in Louis XIV's France*, Oxford 1988; for a discussion of Louis XIV's manipulation of visual media, Peter Burke, *The Fabrication of Louis*, New Haven and London 1992; and for French industries, P. Deyon, 'Manufacturing industries in seventeenth-century France' in R. Hatton (ed.), *Louis XIV and Absolutism*, London 1976, pp.226–42.

51 The best general account of the arts under Louis XIV is Roger-Armand Weigert, *L'époque Louis XIV*, Paris 1962. See also Norbert Elias, *The Court Society*, trans. Edmund Jephcott, Oxford 1983. For those who find Elias turgid, there is a useful introduction to his ideas in Stephen Mennell, *Norbert Elias: civilization and the human self-image*, Oxford 1989; and for a study of some of the historical antecedents to social behaviour at the court of Louis XIV see Orest Ranum, 'Courtesy, absolutism, and the rise of the French state, 1630–1660', *Journal of Modern History*, 52, September 1980, pp.426–51.

52 For seventeenth-century English visitors to France, see John Lough, *France Observed by British Travellers*, Stocksfield 1984.

53 John Evelyn, *The State of France, as it stood in the IXth yeer of this present Monarch, Lewis XIIII*, London 1652, p.78.

54 B.L. Sloane, MS 1868.

55 *Letters and the Second Diary of Samuel Pepys*, ed. R.G. Howarth, London 1932, pp.51–2.

56 Alexander Globe, *Peter Stent circa 1642–1665*, Vancouver 1985, pp.122–3.

57 There was a substantial amount of research on the impact of the Huguenots at the time of the tercentenary celebrations of 1985. See Tessa Murdoch (ed.), *The Quiet Conquest: The Huguenots 1685 to 1985*,

London 1985; R. Gwynn, *Huguenot Heritage: The history and contribution of the Huguenots in Britain*, London 1985; and Irene Scouloudi (ed.), *Huguenots in Britain and their French Background 1550–1800*, London 1987. The following paragraphs are adapted from Charles Saumarez Smith, 'Decorative arts', in R.P. Maccubbin and M. Hamilton-Phillips (eds), *The Age of William III and Mary II: power, politics and patronage 1688–1702*, exhibition catalogue, Williamsburg, Va. 1989, pp.293–300.

58 *DEFM*, p.528.

59 *DEFM*, p.377.

60 For information on Harache and Willaume, see Arthur G. Grimwade, *London Goldsmiths 1697–1837: their marks and lives*, London 1990. For Huguenot silver generally, there is John Hayward, *Huguenot Silver in England 1688–1727*, London 1959 and Hugh Tait, 'London Huguenot silver' in Scouloudi, *Huguenots in Britain*, pp.89–112.

61 The work of Marot is discussed in Gervase Jackson-Stops, 'Daniel Marot and the 1st Duke of Montagu', *Nederlands kunsthistorisch Jaarboek*, 31, 1980, pp.244–62; Gervase Jackson-Stops, 'Daniel Marot', *Macmillan Encyclopedia of Architects*, ed. Adolph Placzek, New York 1982, pp.108–11, and Gervase Jackson-Stops, 'Huguenot upholsterers and cabinet-makers in the circle of Daniel Marot' in Scouloudi, *Huguenots in Britain*, pp.113–24.

62 For discussion of the critical language employed in seventeenth-century architectural description see Kerry Downes, 'John Evelyn and architecture' in *Concerning Architecture: essays on architectural writers and writing presented to Nikolaus Pevsner*, ed. J. Summerson, London 1968, pp.28–39.

63 The standard history of Hampton Court is provided by Colvin, *King's Works*, v, pp.155–170. Ernest Law, *The History of Hampton Court*, III, London 1891, pp.1–169 remains a useful narrative. For details of the furniture see F.J. Rutherford, 'The furnishings of Hampton Court Palace for William III, 1699–1701', *Old Furniture*, II, October 1927, pp.15–33. Documents concerning the building and furnishing of Hampton Court were published in 'Hampton Court Palace 1689–1702', *Wren Society*, IV, 1927.

64 Christopher Morris (ed.), *The Journeys of Celia Fiennes*, London 1947, pp.59–60. This edition is more complete than the more recent, illustrated one, as is pointed out by John Bold in his review in *Oxford Art Journal*, 7:1, 1984, pp.67–9.

65 D. Defoe, *A Tour through the Whole Island of Great Britain*, ed. P. N. Furbank and W. R. Owens, New Haven and London 1991, p.72.

66 For Queen Mary's porcelain collection see Arthur Lane, 'Queen Mary II's porcelain collection at Hampton Court', *Transactions of the Oriental Ceramic Society*, vol. 25, 1949–50, pp.21–31.

67 Colvin, *King's Works*, v, pp.163–4.

68 MS L. 464–1905, National Art Library, V & A.

69 *Journeys of Celia Fiennes*, pp.354–5.

70 Colvin, *King's Works*, v, pp.183–81; see also R. W. Symonds, 'The making of Kensington Palace', *Country Life Annual*, 1955, pp.129–133 and T. H. Lunsingh Scheurleer, 'Documents on the furnishing of Kensington House', *Walpole Society*, XXXVIII, 1960–1962, pp.15–58.

71 *Wren Society*, VII, p.136.

72 Lunsingh Scheurleer, 'Furnishing of Kensington House', p.19.

73 For the interior furnishings of Chatsworth see Francis Thompson, *A History of Chatsworth*, London 1949.

74 Chatsworth MSS. Transcripts of the furniture accounts are available in the Furniture and Woodwork Information Section, V&A.

75 Charles Leigh, *The Natural History of Lancashire, Cheshire, and the Peak, in*

Notes

Derbyshire: with an Account of the British, Phoenician, Armenian, Greek and Roman Antiquities in those Parts, London 1700, pp.44–5.

76 Carlisle RO, D/LONS/L. Information about the building of Lowther is contained in Howard Colvin *et al., Architectural Drawings from Lowther Castle, Westmorland*, London 1980.

77 *Journeys of Celia Fiennes*, p.200.

78 *Journeys of Celia Fiennes*, p.200.

79 *Journeys of Celia Fiennes*, p.153.

80 *Journeys of Celia Fiennes*, p.153.

81 *Journeys of Celia Fiennes*, pp.153–4.

82 *Journeys of Celia Fiennes*, p.154.

1700–1720

1 John Harris, 'John Talman's design for his Wunderkammern', *Furniture History*, XXI, 1985, pp.211–13.

2 Laurence Whistler, *The Imagination of Vanbrugh and his Fellow Artists*, London 1954, p.101, fig.38.

3 There is another elevation of the hall in the Minet Library, Surrey Collection (MSS 2522 and 2531). See Kerry Downes, *Hawksmoor*, London 1979, p.77; and Robert R. Wark, *Early British Drawings in the Huntington Collection*, San Marino, Cal. 1969, p.29.

4 Whistler, *The Imagination of Vanbrugh*, p.102.

5 G. Webb (ed.), *The Complete Works of Sir John Vanbrugh*, vol.4, *The Letters*, London 1928, pp.33–4.

6 Nikolaus Pevsner, 'Jean Bodt in England', *Architectural Review*, CXXX, July 1961, pp.29–34; John Harris, 'Bodt and Stainborough', *Architectural Review*, CXXX, July 1961, pp.34–5; and Tessa Murdoch (ed.), *The Quiet Conquest: The Huguenots 1685–1985*, exhibition catalogue, London 1985, pp.190–91

7 J. J. Cartwright (ed.), *The Wentworth Papers, 1705–1739*, London 1883, p.79.

8 The best sources for the life of Thornhill are W. R. Osmun, 'A study of the works of Sir James Thornhill', Ph.D. dissertation, University of London, 1950; and Edward Croft-

Murray, *Decorative Painting in England 1537–1837*, vol I, *Early Tudor to Sir James Thornhill*, London 1962, pp.69–78. See also *English Baroque Sketches: the painted interior in the age of Thornhill*, Marble Hill House, London 1974.

9 British Museum, Department of Prints and Drawings, 1884–7–26–40.

10 Edgar de N. Mayhew, *Sketches by Thornhill in the Victoria and Albert Museum*, London 1967, pp.5–6.

11 Whistler, *The Imagination of Vanbrugh*, p.104.

12 Webb, *Vanbrugh Letters*, p.70.

13 T. P. Hudson, 'Moor Park, Leoni and Sir James Thornhill', *Burlington Magazine*, CXIII, November 1971, pp.657–61.

14 Hudson, 'Moor Park, Leoni and Sir James Thornhill', p.657.

15 Lorna Weatherill, *Consumer Behaviour and Material Culture in Britain 1660–1760*, London 1988, Table 2.2, p.27.

16 Antony Griffiths, 'A checklist of catalogues of British print publishers, c. 1650–1830', *Print Quarterly*, I:I, March 1984, p.8 There is an excellent exploration of popular reading habits in Margaret Spufford, *Small Books and Pleasant Histories: popular fiction and its readership in seventeenth–century England*, London 1981.

17 British Library 94.e.21; F. G. Stephens, *Catalogue of Prints and Drawings in the British Museum, Division 1: Political and personal satires*, vol. 2, London 1873, pp.290–92; John Brewer, *The Common People and Politics 1750–1790s*, Cambridge 1986, pl.6.

18 Stephens, *Political and personal satires*, 2, p.344.

19 For Elisha Kirkall's life, see Edward Hodnett, 'Elisha Kirkall c.1682–1742. Master of white-line engraving in relief and illustrator of Croxall's Aesop', *Book Collector*, Summer 1976, pp.195–209.

20 *Walpole Society*, XII, 1933–4, Vertue, III, p.6.

21 *An Enquiry into the Origins of Printing in Europe*, London, 1752, pp.25–6; reference to this passage is made in Jacob Kainen, *John Baptist Jackson: 18th-century master of the color woodcut*, Washington, DC 1962, p.15.

22 British Library 12271a; Stephens, *Political and personal satires*, 2, pp.146–8.

23 There is a useful volume of essays on overseas trade edited by W. Minchinton, *The Growth of Overseas Trade in the Seventeenth and Eighteenth Centuries*, London 1969, and an excellent summary of developments in Ralph Davis, *English Overseas Trade 1500–1700*, London 1973. The basis for a more favourable assessment of trade in the first two decades of the eighteenth century is provided by D. W. Jones, *War and Economy in the Age of William III and Marlborough*, Oxford 1988, especially pp.43–9.

24 Henri Misson, *Memoirs and Observations in his Travels over England*, London 1719, p.190.

25 For these developments, see P.G.M. Dickson, *The Financial Revolution in England: a study in the development of public credit 1688–1756*, London 1967.

26 Jones, *War and Economy*, pp.182–193.

27 For inland trade, see T. S. Willan, *The English Coasting Trade 1600–1750*, 2nd edn, Manchester 1967 and J.A. Chartres, *Internal Trade in England 1500–1700*, London 1977.

28 Chartres, *Internal Trade*, p.10.

29 A. H. John, 'The course of agricultural change 1660–1760', in L.S. Pressnell (ed.), *Studies in the Industrial Revolution*, London 1960, pp.125–55; E. L. Jones (ed.), *Agriculture and Economic Growth in England 1660–1815*, London 1967.

30 John Irwin and Katherine B. Brett, *Origins of Chintz*, London 1970.

31 Latham and Matthews (eds), *Diary of Pepys*, IV, 1663, p.299.

32 [Daniel Defoe], *A Review of the State of the British Nation*, January 29, 1708, p.602.

33 I have been unable to trace the source of this quotation.

34 Peter Earle, *The Making of the English Middle Class: business, society and family life in London, 1660–1730*, London 1989, p.295. For the display of ceramics in the households of the nobility, see Anna Somers Cocks, 'The nonfunctional use of ceramics in the English country house during the eighteenth century' in Gervase Jackson-Stops *et al.* (eds), *The Fashioning and Functioning of the British Country House*, National Gallery of Art, Washington, Studies in the History of Art, no. 25, Hanover and London 1989, pp.195–215.

35 *The Case of the Joyners Company, against the Importance of Manufactured Cabinet-Work from the East Indies* (BL 816 m 13 (2)). See also E. T. Joy, 'The overseas trade in furniture in the eighteenth century', *Furniture History*, I, 1965, pp.I–II.

36 The standard account of specialist china dealers remains A. J. Toppin, 'The china trade and some London chinamen', *Transactions of the English Ceramic Circle*, 1935, pp.37–56.

37 For the silk industry during this period, see N.K.A. Rothstein, 'The silk industry in England 1702–1766', MA dissertation, University of London, 1961; and Peter Thornton, *Baroque and Rococo Silks*, London 1965.

38 *The State of the Silk and Woollen Manufacture, Considered: In Relation to a French Trade*, London 1713, p.5.

39 On 23 February 1706 William Nicolson, Bishop of Carlisle, described how he went to visit 'Mr. Dandridge, a Drawer of Patterns for the Silk-Weavers in Moor-fields' (Clyve Jones and Geoffrey Holmes (eds), *The London Diaries of William Nicolson Bishop of Carlisle 1702–1718*, Oxford 1985, p.384).

40 W. H. Quarrell and Margaret Mare, *London in 1710 from the Travels of Zacharias Conrad von Uffenbach*, London 1934, p.86.

41 For details of the expansion in Midlands industries see W.H. Court,

The Rise of the Midland Industries, Oxford 1938; and M.B. Rowlands, *Masters and Men in the West Midland Metalware Trades before the Industrial Revolution*, Manchester 1975.

42 Rowlands, *Masters and Men*, pp.148–9.

43 *A Brief Essay on the Copper and Brass Manufactures of England, Only Relative to the Present Debate in the House of Commons*, London 1712, p.9.

44 *DEFM*, p.205.

45 *DEFM*, pp.464, 662.

46 According to the dated entries in Sir Ambrose Heal, *The London Furniture Makers from the Restoration to the Victorian Era 1660–1840*, London 1953, the following were all based in this area: John Abraham, a frame carver and gilder worked on Long Acre; Jacob Arbunot, a cabinetmaker and looking-glass manufacturer had premises on the south side of Long Acre before moving to a new shop called the Royal Cabinet off the Strand; Thomas Arne worked at the Two Crowns and Cushion in King Street, Covent Garden; Edward Bartlett was a cane maker in Russell Street, Drury Lane; Henry Berrow, an upholsterer, moved in 1714 from the George and Mitre in King Street to the Crown in Bow Street; Abraham Bomer was a looking-glass maker in Bedfordbury, Covent Garden; James Bradford was a japanner and cabinetmaker at the Angel at the corner of Poppins Alley off Fleet Street; William Bramant was an upholsterer in the Strand; Arthur Calcott was an upholsterer at the sign of the Black-Moor Head upon the Pavement in St Martin's Lane; William Clarke was an upholsterer at the Lyon and Lamb in James Street, Covent Garden; John Cox was an upholsterer at the Iron Balcony in Drury Lane next door to the Lord Craven's; William Dale was an upholsterer near Mr Button's coffee house, over the corner of the Piazza in Covent Garden; Thomas Daniel was a cabinetmaker in Long Acre; J. Davis was an upholsterer next door but one to the Golden Sugar Loaf on the Terrace in St Martin's Lane, 'where Gentlemen may be furnished with Tents and Field-beds to their satisfaction, and at very reasonable Prices, likewise Bells and Cases, for Colours and Drums'; Joseph Devenish was an 'upholder' at St Paul's, Covent Garden; Nathaniel Fauset was an upholsterer in the Strand; Nicholas Felliot was a cabinetmaker on Long Acre; Thomas Ferrers was an upholsterer at the Sun in Fleet Street; in 1710 Thomas Gablin, an 'upholder', 'removed from *The Blackamoor's Head* in Shandos Street to *Blackamoor's Head* in Bedford Court, Covent Garden'; John Gilboa was a cabinetmaker in Long Acre; Henry Heasman was an upholsterer in the Piazza in Covent Garden; Thomas Howcraft was a cabinetmaker at the sign of the India Cabinet in Long Acre; James Knight was another cabinetmaker in Long Acre; Philip Maram was an upholsterer in Church Lane off the Strand; Luke Matthews was an 'upholder' in St Martin's Lane; Edmond Norton was an upholsterer in Drury Lane; Francis Peirce was a cabinetmaker in Long Acre; Christopher Pembroke was an 'upholder' at the sign of the Bull near Half Moon Street in the Strand; Thomas Phill was an 'upholder' at the Three Golden Chairs in the Strand; William Pyke was an upholsterer in St Martin's Lane; Augustinus Quino was a cabinetmaker in Long Acre; Hambden Reeve was an upholsterer in the Strand who supplied 'a large fine Dimity Bed tick and Bolster covered with White Satin and filled with Seasoned Swans Downe containing ninety pounds of Downe in them' to Kensington Palace; Thomas Shipley was a cane chair maker at Knuckles Alley, off Drury Lane; there was a looking-glass maker called Mr Stephen between the White Bear and the

Golden Sugar Loaf in Long Acre;
Edward Vernon was a cabinetmaker in
Long Acre; Robert Webb was an
upholsterer at the Queen's Head and
Three Tents in Bedford Street,
Covent Garden; Stephen West was an
upholsterer at the corner of Blackmoor
Street, Drury Lane.

47 Weatherill, *Consumer Behaviour and
Material Culture*, p.40.

48 [Defoe], *Review*, 1713.

49 There is a full, but uneven biography
by Robert Voitle, *The Third Earl of
Shaftesbury 1671–1713*, Baton Rouge
and London 1984; a useful account of
his moral ideas in Lawrence Klein,
'The Third Earl of Shaftesbury and the
progress of politeness', *Eighteenth-
Century Studies*, 18:2, Winter 1984–5,
pp.186–214; and a revisionist account
of his ideas in Robert Markley,
'Sentimentality as performance:
Shaftesbury, Sterne, and the theatrics
of virtue', in Felicity Nussbaum and
Laura Brown (eds), *The New Eighteenth
Century*, London 1987, pp.210–30.
Lawrence Klein has published a
revised version of 'The rise of
"politeness" in England, 1660–1715',
Ph.D. dissertation, Johns Hopkins
University, 1984 under the title
*Shaftesbury and the Culture of Politeness:
moral discourse and cultural politics in early
eighteenth-century England*, Cambridge
1994.

50 Peter Kivy, *A Study of Francis
Hutcheson's Aesthetics and its Influence in
Eighteenth Century Britain*, New York
1976, p.9.

51 Anthony Ashley Cooper, 3rd Earl of
Shaftesbury, *An Inquiry concerning
Virtue, or Merit*, ed. D. Walford,
Manchester 1977, p.83.

52 For the origins of the idea of taste, see
David Summers, *The Judgment of Sense:
Renaissance naturalism and the rise of
aesthetics*, Cambridge 1987; and
Giorgio Tonelli, 'Taste in the history
of aesthetics from the Renaissance to
1770', *Dictionary of the History of Ideas*,
New York 1973, IV, pp.353–7.

53 Anthony Ashley Cooper,
*Characteristicks of Men, Manners,
Opinions, Times*, London 1711, III,
p.161.

54 For Shaftesbury's views on art see J. E.
Sweetman, 'Shaftesbury and art
theory', Ph.D. dissertation, University
of London, 1955.

55 Anthony Ashley Cooper,
*Characteristicks of Men, Manners,
Opinions, Times*, ed. J.M. Robertson,
London 1900, I, p.179.

56 Cooper, *Characteristicks*, ed.
Robertson, I, p.245.

57 PRO 30/24/27/15/9.

58 For recent commentary on Addison
and Steele see Edward A. and Lilian D.
Bloom, *Joseph Addison's Sociable
Animal*, Providence, Rhode Is. 1971;
and Michael Ketcham, *Transparent
Designs: reading, performance and form in
the Spectator Papers*, Athens, Georgia
1985.

59 *The Tatler* ed. G.A. Aitken, London
1898, I, p.9.

60 *The Spectator*, ed. D.F. Bond, Oxford
1965, III p.69.

61 *The Spectator*, ed. Bond, III, p.245.

62 Mandeville has attracted a good deal of
recent commentary, no doubt because
he was an exponent of ideas which
were current in the 1980s. Hector
Monro, *The Ambivalence of Bernard
Mandeville*, Oxford 1975, explores the
possibility that Mandeville was more
of a moralist than contemporaries
thought; Irwin Primer (ed.), *Mandeville
Studies. New explorations in the art and
thought of Dr Bernard Mandeville*, The
Hague 1975, is a useful collection of
essays; Thomas A. Horne, *The Social
Thought of Bernard Mandeville: virtue and
commerce in early eighteenth-century
England*, London 1978, is a
straightforward account of his ideas; a
more subtle exposition is contained in
M.M. Goldsmith, *Private Vices, Public
Benefits: Bernard Mandeville's social and
political thought*, Cambridge 1985.

63 Nicholas Barbon, *A Discourse of Trade*,
London 1690, p.65.

64 Bernard Mandeville, *The Fable of the Bees*, ed. Philip Harth, Harmondsworth 1970, pp.138–9.

65 Mandeville, *Fable of the Bees*, p.144

1720–1740

1 For the circumstances surrounding the publication of *Vitruvius Britannicus*, see P. Breman and D. Addis, *Guide to Vitruvius Britannicus*, New York, 1972; T.P. Connor, 'A study of Colen Campbell's *Vitruvius, Britannicus*, Ph D. dissertation, University of Oxford, 1977; T.P. Connor, 'The making of *Vitruvius Britannicus*', *Architectural History*, vol. 20, 1977, pp.14–30; Eileen Harris, '*Vitruvius Britannicus* before Colen Campbell', *Burlington Magazine*, CXVIII, May 1986, pp.340–46; and Harris and Savage, *British Architectural Books and Writers*, pp.142–3.

2 John Harris and Gervase Jackson-Stops (eds), *Britannia Illustrata*, Bungay 1984.

3 For Campbell's work as an architect, see H. E. Stutchbury, *The Architecture of Colen Campbell*, Manchester 1967, and Charles Saumarez Smith, 'Colen Campbell', *Macmillan Encyclopedia of Architects*, ed. Adolph Placzek, New York 1982, I, pp.368–70.

4 Sarah Markham, *John Loveday of Caversham 1711–1789, the life and tours of an eighteenth-century onlooker*, Wilton 1984, p.72

5 The first biography of Kent was by Margaret Jourdain, *The Work of William Kent, artist, painter, designer and landscape gardener*, London 1948; this has been superseded by Michael I. Wilson, *William Kent*, London 1984.

6 For the early career of Kent see Edward Croft-Murray, *Decorative Painting in England 1537–1837*, vol. 2, *The Eighteenth and Early Nineteenth Centuries*, Feltham 1970, pp.229–30.

7 G. Beard, 'William Kent and the cabinet-makers', *Burlington Magazine*, CXVII, December 1975, p.868.

8 G.S.H. Fox-Strangways, Earl of Ilchester, *Lord Hervey and his Friends 1726–1738*, London 1950, pp.71–72.

9 Sir John Clerk, cited by John Fleming, *Robert Adam and his Circle in Edinburgh and Rome*, London 1962, p.26

10 Sir John Evelyn, Diary, Christ Church Library MS, entry for 30 May 1728.

11 For the layout of the interiors of Chiswick, see Treve Rosoman, 'The decoration and use of the principal apartments of Chiswick House, 1727–70', *Burlington Magazine*, CXXVII, October 1985, pp.663–77; and Richard Hewlings, *Chiswick House and Gardens*, London 1989.

12 Henry E. Huntington Library, MS HA 8042, cited in Beard, 'William Kent and the cabinet-makers', p.867.

13 Jourdain, *Work of William Kent*, p.65.

14 For the conventions of portraiture in the first two decades of the eighteenth century, see J. D. Stewart and Herman W. Liebert, *English Portraits of the Seventeenth and Eighteenth Centuries*, Clark Library, Los Angeles 1974; and J. D. Stewart, *Sir Godfrey Kneller and the English Baroque Portrait*, Oxford 1983.

15 R.P. Maccubbin and M. Hamilton-Phillips (eds), *The Age of William III and Mary II: power, politics, and patronage 1688–1702*, exhibition catalogue, Williamsburg, Va. 1989, p.xxiii.

16 Elizabeth Einberg (ed.), *Manners and Morals: Hogarth and British painting 1700–1760*, exhibition catalogue, London 1987, p.55.

17 For the work of Tillemans, see Robert Raines, 'Peter Tillemans, life and work, with a list of representative paintings', *Walpole Society*, XLVII, 1980, pp.21–59.

18 Roger de Piles, *The Art of Painting*, London 1706, p.444.

19 Laroon's career is fully documented in Robert Raines, *Marcellus Laroon*, London 1966.

20 *Walpole Society*, XII, 1933–4, Vertue, III, p.65.

21 Ralph Edwards, 'The conversation pictures of Joseph van Aken', *Apollo*, XXIII, February 1936, pp.79–85.

22 *Walpole Society*, XII, 1933–4, Vertue,

III, p.80.

23 Horace Walpole, *Anecdotes of Painting in England*, ed. Revd J. Dallaway, London 1827, IV, p.117.

24 Ellen G. D'Oench, *The Conversation Piece: Arthur Devis and his contemporaries*, exhibition catalogue, New Haven 1980, p.69.

25 *Walpole Society*, XII, 1933–4, Vertue, III, p.40.

26 John Macky, *A Journey through England in Familiar Letters from a Gentleman Here to his Friend Abroad*, London 1724, p.22.

27 The most complete account of this painting appears in Richard Dorment, *British Painting in the Philadelphia Museum of Art: from the seventeenth through the nineteenth century*, Philadelphia 1986, pp.157–62.

28 *Walpole Society*, XII, 1933–4, Vertue, III, p.46.

29 *Memoirs of Viscountess Sundon, Mistress of the Robes to Queen Caroline*, ed. Mrs Thomson, London 1847, II, p.112.

30 *Walpole Society*, XII, 1933–4, Vertue, III, p.38.

31 *Walpole Society*, XII, 1933–4, Vertue, III, p.81.

32 John Ingamells and Robert Raines, 'A catalogue of the paintings, drawings and etchings of Philip Mercier', *Walpole Society*, XLVI, 1978. pp.1–70.

33 Ralph Edwards, *Early Conversation Pictures from the Middle Ages to about 1730*, London 1954.

34 *The Autobiography and Correspondence of Mary Granville, Mrs Delany*, ed. Lady Llanover, London 1861, I, p.283.

35 John Summerson, *The Unromantic Castle and other essays*, London 1990, p.82.

36 For the development of London during these years, see John Summerson, *Georgian London*, rev. edn, London 1970, pp.100–111.

37 Daniel Defoe, *A Tour through the Whole Island of Great Britain*, ed. Pat Rogers, Harmondsworth 1971, p.300.

38 This development can be traced in anthologies of eighteenth-century buildings; for example, Horace Field and Michael Bunney, *English Domestic Architecture of the XVII and XVIII Centuries*, London 1905; and Colin Amery (ed.), *Period Houses and their Details*, London 1974.

39 I owe this account of room use to Earle, *The Making of the English Middle Class* pp.209–10.

40 César de Saussure, *A Foreign View of England in the Reigns of George I and George II*, ed. M. van Muyden, London 1902, pp.68–9.

41 Peter Borsay, 'The English urban renaissance: the development of provincial urban culture c.1680–c.1760', *Social History*, 5, 1977, pp.581–603; Peter Borsay, *The English Urban Renaissance: culture and society in the provincial town 1660–1770*, Oxford, 1989; and Peter Borsay (ed.), *Eighteenth Century Town, 1688–1820*, London 1990.

42 Richard Neve, *The City and Country Purchaser, and Builder's Dictionary: Or, the Compleat Builders Guide*, 2nd edn, London, 1726, p.xi.

43 Among the many building manuals published between 1720 and 1740 are the following: William Halfpenny, *The Art of Sound Building*, London 1725; Batty Langley, *Practical geometry applied to the useful arts of building*, London 1726; Batty Langley, *A sure guide to builders, or the principles and practice of architecture made easy for the use of workmen*, London 1726; Batty Langley, *The Builder's Chest Book, or a Compleat Key to the Five Orders of Columns in Architecture*, London 1727; Batty Langley, *The Young Builder's Rudiments*, London 1730; William Salmon, *Palladio Londinensis, or the London Art of Building*, London 1734; *The Builder's Dictionary: Or, Gentleman and Architect's Companion*, 2 vols, London 1734; Edward Hoppus, *Andrea Palladio's Architecture in Four Books*, London 1735; Edward Hoppus, *The Gentleman and Builder's Repository: Or, Architecture Display'd*, London,

1737; William Jones, *Gentlemen's or Builder's Companion*, London 1739; and Batty and Thomas Langley, *City and Country Builder's and Workmen's Treasury of Designs*, London 1739. For comprehensive bibliographical guides to these publications, see John Archer, *The Literature of British Domestic Architecture 1715–1842*, Cambridge, Mass. 1985 and Harris and Savage, *British Architectural Writers*.

44 Batty Langley, *The City and Country Builder's and Workman's Treasury of Designs*, London 1745, introduction.

45 John Wood, *A Description of Bath*, London 1765, preface.

46 Ian Watt, *The Rise of the Novel: studies in Defoe, Richardson and Fielding*, Reading 1981, pp.28–9.

47 Daniel Defoe, *Roxana, or the fortunate mistress*, ed. David Blewett, Harmondsworth 1982, p.214.

48 Defoe, *Roxana*, pp.218–19.

49 Defoe, *Roxana*, pp.265–7.

50 The most convenient modern edition is D. Defoe, *A Tour through the Whole Island of Great Britain*, ed. P.N. Furbank and W.R. Owens, New Haven and London 1991, although it should be noted that, as with the modern illustrated edition of Celia Fiennes's *Journeys*, this omits passages of the original text. The full text is given in *A Tour through the Whole Island of Great Britain*, ed. Pat Rogers, Harmondsworth 1971. There is an essay on the *Tour* by G.D.H. Cole, reprinted in his *Persons and Periods*, London 1938; and a recent discussion by Peter Borsay, 'Urban development in the age of Defoe', *in Britain in the First Age of Party 1680–1750: essays presented to Geoffrey Holmes*, ed. C. Jones, London 1987, pp.195–219.

51 Defoe, *Tour*, ed. Rogers, p.115.

52 Defoe, *Tour*, ed. Rogers, pp.169–170.

53 For the nature of topographical description during the 1720s, see Esther Moir, *The Discovery of Britain*, London 1964 and Adrian Tinniswood, *A History of Country House Visiting: five centuries of tourism and taste*, Oxford 1989.

54 BL Add. 47030, Letter Books of the first Lord Egmont.

55 There is an extremely full account of this in Joseph M. Levine, *The Battle of the Books: history and literature in the Augustan age*, Ithaca and London 1991.

56 Charles Boyle, *Dr. Bentley's Dissertations on the Epistles of Phalaris and the Fables of Aesop*, London 1698, p.188.

57 Levine, *Battle of the Books*, p.72.

58 Ralph Thoresby, *Diary*, ed. Revd J. Hunter, London 1830, I, p.340. There is a learned account of Woodward in Joseph M. Levine, *Dr Woodward's Shield: history, science, and satire in Augustan England*, Berkeley, Cal. 1977.

59 For William Nicolson, see Joseph M. Levine, 'Nicolson as a virtuoso', in Clyve Jones and Geoffrey Holmes (eds.), *The London Diaries of William Nicolson 1702–1718*, Oxford 1985, pp.11–17.

60 Joan Evans, *A History of the Society of Antiquaries*, London 1956, p.51.

61 For the life of William Stukeley, see Stuart Piggott, *William Stukeley: an eighteenth-century antiquary*, rev. edn, London 1985. For the decline of antiquarian scholarship, see D.C. Douglas, *English Scholars 1660–1730*, rev. edn, London 1951; and B.J. Enright, 'Richard Rawlinson, 1690–1755, and eighteenth-century book collecting', *The Book Collector*, 39:1, Spring 1990, pp.27–54.

62 There are conflicting accounts of attitudes to the reign of Augustus in the early eighteenth century in Howard D. Weinbrot, *Augustus Caesar in 'Augustan' England*, Princeton 1978; and Howard Erskine-Hill, *The Augustan Idea in English Literature*, London 1983.

63 For a study of the Grand Tour, see Jeremy Black, *The British Abroad: the Grand Tour in the eighteenth century*, London 1992.

64 For the life of Lord Burlington, James

Lees-Milne, *Earls of Creation: five great patrons of eighteenth-century art*, London 1962, pp.85–151, remains the most vivid, as well as the best written, account. It should be supplemented by Jacques Carré, 'Lord Burlington (1694–1753), Le connoisseur, le mécène, l'architecte', Ph.D. dissertation, Dijon 1980.

65 George Sherburn, *The Correspondence of Alexander Pope*, i, 1704–1718, Oxford 1956, p.347.

66 For accounts of Holkham, see Leo Schmidt, Holkham Hall I and II', *Country Life*, CCXVII, 1980, pp.214–17, 299–301; and John Kenworthy-Browne, 'Matthew Brettingham's Rome Account Book 1747–1754', *Walpole Society*, 49, 1983, pp.37–132.

67 Matthew Brettingham, *The Plans, Elevations and Sections, of Holkham in Norfolk, The Seat of the late Earl of Leicester*, London 1773, p.vi.

68 Lees-Milne, *Earls of Creation*, pp.41–82.

69 *Horace Walpole's Correspondence*, 20, p.142.

70 Philip Dormer Stanhope, Earl of Chesterfield, *Letters*, ed. Lord Mahon, London and Philadelphia 1892, III, p.31.

71 G.S. Thomson, *Letters of a Grandmother 1732–1735*, London 1943, p.21.

72 Jones and Holmes, *London Diaries of William Nicolson*, p.219; *The Diary of Ralph Thoresby FRS*, ed. Revd J. Hunter, London 1830, II, p.29.

73 Campbell, *Vitruvius Britannicus*, III, p.11.

74 Fox-Strangways, *Lord Hervey and his Friends*, p.74.

75 HMC *Portland*, VI, p.164.

1740–1760

1 The major study of Hayman's career is Brian Allen, *Francis Hayman*, New Haven and London 1987.

2 The pioneering study of this group of artists was Mark Girouard, 'Coffee at Slaughter's. English art and the rococo – I', *Country Life*, CXXXIX, 13 January 1966, pp.58–61; 'Hogarth and his friends. English art and the rococo – II', *Country Life*, CXXXIX, 27 January 1966, pp.188–90; and 'The two worlds of St Martin's Lane. English art and the rococo – III', *Country Life*, CXXXIX, 3 February 1966, pp.224–7. These articles have since been reprinted in Mark Girouard, *Town and Country*, London and New Haven 1992, pp.15–34.

3 For the work of Gravelot, see Hanns Hammelmann, *Book Illustrators in Eighteenth-Century England*, London 1975, p.38; Robert Halsband, 'The rococo in England: book illustrators, mainly Gravelot and Bentley', *Burlington Magazine*, CXXVII, December 1985, pp.870–80.

4 Elizabeth Johnston, 'Joseph Highmore's Paris journal, 1734', *Walpole Society*, XLII, 1970, pp.61–105.

5 Allen, *Hayman*, p.51.

6 For the painting of Tyers, see John Ruch, 'A Hayman portrait of Jonathan Tyers's family', *Burlington Magazine*, CXII, August 1970, pp.495–7.

7 Allen, *Hayman*, p.131.

8 For these paintings, see Brian Allen, 'Francis Hayman and the supper box paintings for Vauxhall Gardens', in *The Rococo in England: a symposium*, ed. Charles Hind, London 1987, pp.113–33.

9 Samuel Richardson, *Pamela or, virtue rewarded*, ed. P. Sabor, Harmondsworth 1980, p.44.

10 Richardson, *Pamela*, pp.50–51.

11 For the illustrations of *Pamela*, see T. C. Duncan Eaves, 'Graphic illustrations of the novels of Samuel Richardson, 1740–1810', *Huntington Library Quarterly*, 14, 1950–1, pp.349–83; and Elizabeth Einberg and Judy Egerton, *The Age of Hogarth: British painters born 1675–1709*, London 1988, pp.50–51.

12 Samuel Richardson, *Correspondence*, ed. Anna Laetitia Barbauld, London 1804, I, p.56.

13 *Walpole Society*, XII, 1933–4, Vertue, III, p.29.

14 Eaves, 'Graphic illustrations of the

Notes

novels of Samuel Richardson',
pp.358–9.

15 Richardson to Lady Bradshaigh, cited
in T.C. Duncan Eaves and Ben D.
Kimpel, *Samuel Richardson: a biography*,
Oxford 1971, p.189.

16 There have been two recent
exhibition catalogues on Devis: Ellen
D'Oench, *The Conversation Piece:
Arthur Devis and his contemporaries*,
New Haven 1980; and S. Sartin (ed.),
*Polite Society by Arthur Devis
1712–1787: portraits of the English
country gentleman and his family*, Preston
1983. In addition there is a brief but
suggestive, discussion of Devis's work
in Ann Bermingham, *Landscape and
Ideology: the English rustic tradition,
1740–1860*, London 1987, pp.26–8.

17 Pierre Rosenberg, *Chardin 1699–1779*.
Cleveland, Ohio 1979, p.231.

18 *The Builder's Dictionary: or, Architect's
Companion*, London 1734, II, entry on
'Wainscot'.

19 T. Skaife, *A Key to Civil Architecture; or
The Universal British Builder*, London
1774. p.183.

20 There was a pioneering monograph on
plasterwork by Laurence Turner,
Decorative Plasterwork in Great Britain,
London 1927. The major recent work
is Geoffrey Beard, *Decorative
Plasterwork in Great Britain*, London
1975; also, Alastair Laing, 'Foreign
decorators and plasterers in England',
in *The Rococo in England: a symposium*,
pp.21–45.

21 The most recent texts on wallpaper in
England are C.C. Oman and J.
Hamilton, *Wallpaper. A history of
illustrated catalogue of the collection of the
Victoria and Albert Museum*, London
1982; J. Hamilton, *An Introduction to
Wallpaper*, London 1983; A. Wells-
Cole, *Historic Paper Hangings from
Temple Newsam and other English
Houses*, Temple Newsam Country
House Studies no. I, Leeds 1983; and
Treve Rosoman, *London Wallpapers,
their manufacture and use, 1690–1840*,
London 1992. There is an

authoritative discussion of American
wallpapers in C. Lynn, *Wallpaper in
America from the Seventeenth Century to
World War I*, New York 1980.

22 *Correspondence between Frances, Countess
of Hartford and Henrietta Louisa,
Countess of Pomfret between the Years
1738 and 1741*, 2nd. edn, London
1806, II pp.253–4.

23 Joseph Collyer, *The Parent's and
Guardian's Directory, and the Youth's
Guide, in the Choice of a Profession or
Trade*, London 1761, p.207.

24 T. Mortimer, *The Universal Director: or
the Nobleman and Gentleman's True
Guide to the Masters and Professors of the
Liberal and Polite Arts and Sciences*,
London 1763, p.54.

25 *Letters written by the late Right
Honourable Lady Luxborough, to William
Shenstone, Esq.*, London 1775, p.22.

26 *Correspondence of Thomas Gray*, ed.
Paget Toynbee and Leonard Whibley,
Oxford 1935, II, p.640.

27 The great expert on the history of
eighteenth century paint is Ian
Bristow, who has published
*Architectural Colour in British Interiors
1615–1840* and *Interior House-painting
Colours and Technology*, New Haven
and London 1996. See also Ian
Bristow, 'Ready-mixed paint in the
eighteenth century', *Architectural
Review*, 161, 1977, pp.246–8; and Ian
Bristow, 'Interior house-painting from
the Restoration to the Regency', 2
vols., D. Phil. dissertation, University
of York, 1983.

28 William Salmon. *Palladio Londinensis:
Or, The London Art of Building*, London
1752, p.63.

29 R. Campbell, *The London Tradesman.
Being a Compendious View of All the
Trades, Professions, Arts, both Liberal and
Mechanic, now practised in the Cities of
London and Westminster*, London 1747,
p.103.

30 Peter Kalm, *Travels into North America*,
2nd. edn, London 1772, I, p.195.

31 'Contract for painting the interior of
Timothy Orne's house', *Essex Institute*

Historical Collections, LXII, October 1926, p.296.

32 This colour range is derived from T. Skaife, *A Key to Civil Architecture; or The Universal British Builder,* London 1776, p.139.

33 The most comprehensive discussion of the structure of the eighteenth-century furniture trade is Pat Kirkham, 'The London furniture trade 1700–1850', *Furniture History,* xxiv, 1988. See also E.T. Joy, 'Some aspects of the London furniture industry', MA dissertation, University of London, 1966.

34 Campbell, *London Tradesman,* pp.169–70.

35 *DEFM,* pp.388–9.

36 *DEFM,* p.926.

37 The definitive biography of Chippendale is Christopher Gilbert, *The Life and Work of Thomas Chippendale,* 2 vols., London 1978.

38 For the work of Darly, see H.H. Atherton, *Political Prints in the Age of Hogarth: a study of the ideographic representation of politics,* Oxford 1974, pp.18–19.

39 Gilbert, *Thomas Chippendale,* I, p.26.

40 The Linnells are the subject of a comprehensive monograph by Helena Hayward and Pat Kirkham, *William and John Linnell: eighteenth-century London furniture makers,* 2 vols., London 1980.

41 *DEFM,* p.739.

42 G. Eland (ed.), *Purefoy Letters, 1735–1753,* 2 vols, London 1931.

43 Eland, *Purefoy Letters,* I, p.110.

44 Eland, *Purefoy Letters,* I, pp.107–8.

45 Eland, *Purefoy Letters,* I. p.111.

46 For the history of eighteenth-century shopping, see Dorothy Davis, *A History of Shopping,* London 1966; and H.-C. Mui and Lorna H. Mui, *Shops and Shopkeeping in Eighteenth-Century England,* London 1989.

47 Daniel Defoe, *The Complete English Tradesman,* London 1745, I, pp.205–6.

48 A. Rouquet, *The Present State of the Arts in England,* ed. R.W. Lightdown, London 1970, pp.119–21.

49 *The World,* no. 38, 1753, pp.229–30.

50 This section is adapted from a lecture first delivered at the Victoria and Albert Museum and partly published as 'Leaves from an eighteenth-century Filofax: design practice in the 1750s', *Designer,* March 1987, pp.19-21.

51 G. Berkeley, Bishop of Cloyne, *Works,* ed. A.A. Luce and T.E. Jessop, London 1953, VI, p.110.

52 E. Chambers, *Cyclopedia: Or, An Universal Dictionary of the Arts and Sciences,* London 1728, D. p.192.

53 *Gentleman's Magazine,* October 1731.

54 *Daily Post,* July 1733.

55 R. Campbell, *The London Tradesman. Being a Compendious View of All the Trades, Professions, Arts both Liberal and Mechanic, now practised in the Cities of London and Westminster,* London 1747, p.171.

56 Campbell, *London Tradesman,* p.115.

57 Campbell, *London Tradesman,* p.99.

58 J. Gwynn, *An Essay on Design. Including Proposals for Erecting a Public Academy To be Supported by a Voluntary Subscription,* London 1749, p.43.

59 Gwynn, *Essay on Design,* p.70.

60 Gwynn, *Essay on Design,* p.70.

61 Gwynn, *Essay on Design,* pp.70–71.

62 M. Postlethwayt, *The Universal Dictionary of Trade and Commerce,* London 1751, I, p.xi.

63 *Reflections on Various Subjects Relating to Arts and Commerce: Particularly, The Consequences of admitting Foreign Artists on easier Terms,* London 1752, pp.19–20.

64 Postlethwayt, *Universal Dictionary,* II, p.778.

65 *Gentleman's Magazine,* February 1756, pp.61–2.

66 Berkeley, *Works,* VI, p.110.

67 R. Dossie, *The Handmaid to the Arts,* London 1758, preface.

68 T. Mortimer, *The Universal Director: or the Nobleman and Gentleman's True Guide to the Masters and Professors of the Liberal and Polite Arts and Sciences; and of the Mechanic Arts, Manufactures and Trades, Established in London and*

Westminster, and their Environs, London 1763. p.4.

69 Mortimer, *Universal Director*, p.17.

70 J. Gee, *The Trade and Navigation of Great-Britain Considered*, London 1729, p.13.

71 Jervis, *Dictionary of Design and Designers*, pp.137–8.

72 C. Gilbert, 'The early furniture designs of Matthias Darly', *Furniture History*, XI, 1975, p.33.

73 M. Darly, *The Ornamental Architect, or Young Artists Instructor*, London 1771, preface.

74 My interpretation of the economic history of the period has been principally drawn from the following works: E. W. Gilboy, 'Demand as a factor in the Industrial Revolution', *Facts and Factors in Economic History: articles by former students of E. F. Gay*, Cambridge, Mass. 1932, pp.620–39; C. Wilson, *England's Apprenticeship 1603–1763*, London 1965; E.L. Jones (ed.), *Agriculture and Economic Growth in England 1660–1815*, London 1967; D. E.C. Eversley, 'The home market and economic growth 1750–1780', *Land, Labour and Population in the Industrial Revolution: essays presented to J.D. Chambers*, ed. E.L. Jones and G.E. Mingay, London 1967, pp.206–59; E. L. Jones, 'The fashion manipulators: consumer tastes and British Industries 1660–1800', *Business Enterprise and Economic Change: essays in honour of H.F. Williamson*, Kent State, 1973; A.J. Little, *Deceleration in the Eighteenth-Century British Economy*, London 1976; D.C. Coleman, *The Economy of England 1450–1750*, Oxford 1977; R. Floud and D. McCloskey, *The Economic History of Britain since 1700*, Cambridge 1981; Neil McKendrick, John Brewer and John Plumb, *The birth of a consumer society: the commercialization of eighteenth-century England*, London 1982; D.A. Baugh, 'Poverty, Protestantism, and political economy: English attitudes towards the poor, 1600–1800', *England's Rise*

to Greatness 1660–1763, ed. S. Baxter, Berkeley, Cal. 1983, pp.63–107; J. Black (ed.), *Britain in the Age of Walpole*, London 1984; M. Berg, *The Age of Manufactures 1700–1820*, London 1985.

75 J.B. Le Blanc, *Letters on the English and French Nations*, Dublin 1747.

76 J. Tucker, *Instructions for Travellers*, 1757, p.26.

77 Le Blanc, *Letters*, p.202.

78 *The Letters of Mrs. Elizabeth Montagu, with some of the Letters of her Correspondents*, 3rd. edn, London 1813, III, p.130.

79 For information about Kirtlington, see *Country Life*, 13 April 1912, pp.544–5; Preston Remington, 'A Mid-Georgian Interior from Kirtlington Park', *Bulletin of the Metropolitan Museum of Art*, Summer 1955, pp.155–69; and Ingrid Roscoe, 'The decoration and furnishing of Kirtlington Park', *Apollo*, CXI, January 1980, pp.22–9.

80 For the work of Sir Robert Taylor, see Marcus Binney, *Sir Robert Taylor: From Rococo to Neoclassicism*, London 1984.

81 See, for example, William Halfpenny, *A New and Compleat System of Architecture Delineated*, London 1749; William and John Halfpenny, *Rural Architecture in the Chinese Taste*, London 1752; William and John Halfpenny, *Rural Architecture in the Gothick Taste*, London 1752; E. Edwards and Matthew Darly, *A New Book of Chinese Designs*, London 1754; William and John Halfpenny, *The Modern Builder's Assistant*, London 1757 [printed in error on the frontispiece MDCCVLII]; Abraham Swan, *A collection of designs in architecture*, London 1757. Many of Abraham Swan's designs were reproduced in Arthur Stratton, *Some XVIIIth Century Designs for Interior Decoration*, London 1923. These publications are discussed in Dora Weibenson, 'Documents of social change: publications about the small house', in Ralph Cohen (ed.), *Studies*

in British Art and Aesthetics, Berkeley, Cal. 1985, pp.82–106.

82 This is on the authority of J. T. Smith, Nollekens and his Times, new edn, London 1986, p.15. For the life of James Stuart, see the long and excellent entry by Howard Colvin in his Biographical Dictionary of British Architects 1660–1840, London 1978, pp.793–7; and David Watkin, Athenian Stuart: pioneer of the Greek revival, London 1982.

83 These 'Proposals' were published in James Stuart and Nicholas Revett, The Antiquities of Athens, London 1762, I, pp.v–vi.

84 These drawings are discussed by John Harris in 'Newly acquired designs by James Stuart in the British Architectural Library, drawings collection', Architectural History, vol. 22, 1979, pp.74–5; and Damie Stillman, English Neo-Classical Architecture, London 1988, I, pp.126–7.

85 Paget Toynbee (ed.), 'Horace Walpole's journal of visits to country seats', Walpole Society, XVI, 1928, p.15.

86 Romney Sedgwick, The House of Commons 1715–1754, London 1970, I, p.599.

87 John Fowler and John Cornforth, English Decoration in the 18th Century, London 1974, pp.26–7; Watkin, Athenian Stuart, pp.33–4; Stillman, English Neo-Classical Architecture, I, pp.112–15; Leslie Harris (ed.), Robert Adam and Kedleston: the making of a neoclassical masterpiece, London 1987.

88 This commission is discussed by John Harris, Sir William Chambers, Knight of the Polar Star, London 1970, pp.63 and 225.

1760–1780

1 Scottish Record Office GD 18/4981, cited in John Fleming, Robert Adam and his Circle, London 1962, p.7; and Howard Colvin, Biographical Dictionary of British Architects 1660–1840, London 1978, p.56. See also John Gifford, William Adam 1689–1748: a life and times of Scotland's universal architect, Edinburgh 1989.

2 Fleming, Robert Adam, pp.76–7.

3 Fleming, Robert Adam, pp.139–40.

4 Fleming, Robert Adam, pp.135.

5 Fleming, Robert Adam, p.152.

6 Fleming, Robert Adam, p.165. For the relationship between Adam and Piranesi, see Damie Stillman, 'Robert Adam and Piranesi', Essays in the History of Architecture presented to Rudolf Wittkower, ed. D. Fraser el al., London 1967, pp.197–206.

7 Fleming, Robert Adam, pp.246–7.

8 Cecil Aspinall-Oglander, Admiral's Wife. Being the life and letters of the Hon. Mrs Edward Boscawen from 1719 to 1761, London 1940, pp.65–6.

9 Aspinall-Oglander, Admiral's Wife, pp.72–3.

10 Aspinall-Oglander, Admiral's Wife, p.129.

11 Adam's work at Kedleston is discussed in Leslie Harris (ed.), Robert Adam and Kedleston: the making of a neoclassical masterpiece, London 1987.

12 The literature on the Adam brothers is, of course, substantial. See, for example, Julius Bryant, Robert Adam: architect of genius, London 1992; and Steven Parissien, Adam Style, London 1992; but the best studies of his work on interiors remain Damie Stillman, The Decorative Work of Robert Adam, London 1966; and Eileen Harris, The Furniture of Robert Adam, London 1973.

13 For the Duchess, see James Grieg (ed.), The Diaries of a Duchess. Extracts from the diaries of the first Duchess of Northumberland (1716–1776), London 1926.

14 Horace Walpole's Correspondence, 20, p.341.

15 The Works in Architecture of Robert and James Adam, Esquires, London 1778, I, p.9.

16 Horace Walpole's Correspondence, 32, p.126.

17 John Summerson, Kenwood: a short account of its history and architecture,

London 1975.

18 *The Works in Architecture of Robert and James Adam, Esquires*, London 1778, I, pp.5–6.

19 *Works in Architecture*, I, pp.10–11

20 HMC *Marquis of Bath*, I, p.345

21 The most authoritative introduction to the work of Zoffany is Mary Webster, *Johan Zoffany 1733–1810*, London 1976. There is a chapter on Zoffany in Ronald Paulson, *Emblem and Expression: meaning of English art of the eighteenth century*, London 1975, pp.138–58; and an article by Gervase Jackson-Stops, 'Johan Zoffany and the eighteenth-century interior', *Antiques*, June 1987, pp.1264–75.

22 For Zoffany's relations with Garrick, see William T. Whitley, *Artists and their Friends in England 1700–1799*, London 1928, II, pp.249–53.

23 For this picture, see Webster, *Zoffany*, p.34; and Oliver Millar, *The Later Georgian Pictures in the Collection of Her Majesty the Queen*, London 1969, I, p.149.

24 Christopher Gilbert, *The Life and Work of Thomas Chippendale*, London 1978, I, p.155.

25 For this painting, see Mary Webster, 'Zoffany's painting of Charles Towneley's library in Park Street', *Burlington Magazine*, CVI, 1964, pp.316–23; *The Age of Neo-Classicism*, London 1972, pp.182–3; Brian Cook, 'The Towneley marbles in Westminster and Bloomsbury', *British Museum Yearbook*, 2, 1977, pp.34–78; and Dan Cruickshank, 'Queen Anne's Gate', *The Georgian Group Journal*, 1992, pp.61–2.

26 J.T. Smith, *Nollekens and his Time*, new edn, London 1986, p.168.

27 Smith, *Nollekens and his Time*, p.164.

28 For the history of carpets, see Bertram Jacobs, *The Story of British Carpets*, London 1968; and Christopher Gilbert (ed.), *Country House Floors 1660–1850*, Temple Newsam Country House Studies no. 3, Leeds 1987. There are useful discussions of British carpets

imported into America in Nina Fletcher Little, *Floor Coverings in New England before 1850*, Sturbridge, Mass. 1967; Rodris Roth, *Floorcoverings in 18th-Century America*, Washington DC 1967; and Mildred B. Lanier, *English and Oriental Carpets at Williamsburg*, Charlottesville, Va. 1975.

29 *The Daily Courant*, 29 November 1711.

30 Nathan Bailey, *Dictionarium Britannicum: or a Compleat Universal Etymological English Dictionary*, London 1730, under 'Carpet'.

31 For information about the manufacture of carpets at Kidderminster, see Barrie Trinder and Jeff Cox, *Yeomen and Colliers in Telford*, Chichester 1980, p.93; for the carpet factory at Wilton, see Victoria County History, *Wiltshire*, IV, pp.181–2.

32 Joseph Collyer, *The Parent's and Guardian's Directory, and the Youth's Guide, in the Choice of a Profession or Trade*, London 1761, p.94.

33 *The Minutes of the Society*, April 7, 1757. I am grateful for this reference to Susan Bennett.

34 For the life of Bramah, see Ian McNeil, *Joseph Bramah: a century of invention, 1749–1851*, Newton Abbot 1968.

35 For the early history of stoves, see Josephine H. Peirce, *Fire on the Hearth: the evolution and romance of the heating stove*, Springfield, Mass. 1951; Samuel Y. Edgerton, 'Heat and style: eighteenth century house-warming by stoves', *Journal of the Society of Architectural Historians*, 20:1, March 1961, pp.20–26; and Lawrence Wright, *Home Fires Burning: a history of domestic heating and cooking*, London 1964.

36 *An Autobiography of Benjamin Franklin*, ed. L. Larabee *et al.*, New Haven 1964.

37 The most substantial biography of Boulton remains H.W. Dickinson, *Matthew Boulton*, Cambridge 1937. See also E. Robinson, 'Matthew Boulton,

patron of the arts', *Annals of Science*, 9, 1953, pp.368–76; E. Robinson, 'Eighteenth-century commerce and fashion: Matthew Boulton's marketing techniques', *Economic History Review*, 1963, pp.39–60, and there is an authoritative examination of his work in ormolu in Nicholas Goodison, *Ormolu: the work of Matthew Boulton*, London 1974.

38 Robinson, 'Eighteenth-Century Commerce and Fashion', p.43.

39 Dickinson, *Boulton*, p.55.

40 Goodison, *Ormolu*, p.47.

41 The principal authority on this aspect of Wedgwood's career is Neil McKendrick. See in particular, N. McKendrick, 'Josiah Wedgwood: an eighteenth-century entrepreneur in salesmanship and marketing techniques', *Economic History Review*, XII, 1959–60, pp.408–33; and N. McKendrick, 'Josiah Wedgwood and the commercialization of the potteries', in N. McKendrick *et al.*, *The Birth of a Consumer Society: the commercialization of eighteenth-century England*, London 1982, pp.100–145.

42 *Letters of Josiah Wedgwood 1772–1780*, ed. Lady Farrar, London 1903, II, p.382.

43 This is a difficult subject. There is now a substantial literature on aspects of gender in the eighteenth century, but it is concentrated on literature and, for good reasons, does not appear to have investigated in detail the origins of domestic ideology. The works which I have found to be most suggestive for understanding this subject have been Ruth H. Bloch, 'Untangling the roots of modern sex roles: a survey of four centuries of change', *Signs: journal of women in culture and society*, 4:2, Winter 1978, pp.237–52; Ruth Perry, *Women, Letters and the Novel*, New York 1980; Janet Todd, *Sensibility: an introduction*, London 1986; and Jane Spencer, *The Rise of the Woman Novelist from Aphra Behn to Jane Austen*, Oxford 1986.

44 The clearest indication of her views on interiors appears in G.S. Thomson (ed.), *Letters of a Grandmother 1732–1735*, London 1943.

45 *Letters written by the late right honourable Lady Luxborough to William Shenstone Esq.*, London 1775.

46 J. Grieg (ed.), *The Diaries of a Duchess. Extracts from the diaries of the first Duchess of Northumberland (1716–1776)*, London 1926; Gervase Jackson-Stops and Victoria Percy, '"Exquisite taste and tawdry ornament", the travel journals of the 1st Duchess of Northumberland', *Country Life*, 7 February 1974, pp.250–52.

47 Madame du Bocage, *Letters concerning England, Holland and Italy*, London 1770, I, p.7.

48 HMC *Marquis of Bath*, I, p.345.

49 Mrs Montagu to Leonard Smelt, 26 April 1780, cited in David Watkin, *Athenian Stuart: pioneer of the Greek revival*, London 1982, p.46.

50 Dickinson, *Boulton*, p.54.

51 The most substantial life of Mrs Delany is Ruth Hayden, *Mrs Delany: her life and her flowers*, London 1980.

52 For the circle of bluestockings and its relationship to literature, see Chauncey Brewster Tinker, *The Salon and English Letters. Chapters on the interrelationship of literature and society in the age of Johnson*, New York 1915; W.S. Scott, *The Bluestocking Ladies*, London 1947; Irvin Ehrenpreis and Robert Halsband, *The Lady of Letters in the Eighteenth Century*, Los Angeles 1969; the relevant entries in Janet Todd (ed.), *A Dictionary of British and American Women Writers 1660–1800*, London 1984: and Sylvia Harcstark Myers, *The Bluestocking Circle: women, friendship, and the life of the mind in eighteenth-century England*, Oxford 1990.

53 For women's magazines of this period, see Alison Adburgham, *Women in Print: writing women and women's magazines from the Restoration to the accession of Victoria*, London 1972.

54 Adburgham, *Women in Print*, p.128.
55 Adburgham, *Women in Print*, pp.128–9.
56 *The Torrington Diaries containing the tours through England and Wales of the Hon. John Byng (later fifth Viscount Torrington) between the years 1781 and 1794*, London 1934, I, p.23.
57 *Torrington Diaries*, I, pp.91–2.
58 The pioneering history of Strawberry Hill was W.S. Lewis, 'The genesis of Strawberry Hill', *Metropolitan Museum Studies*, 1934, V, pp.57–92. Its development can also be studied in Paget Toynbee (ed.), *Strawberry Hill Accounts*, Oxford 1927. More recently contributions to the history of Strawberry Hill have included J.M. Crook, 'Strawberry Hill revisited', *Country Life*, 7, 14, and 21 June 1973, pp.1598–1602, 1726–30, and 1794–7; and Clive Wainwright, *The Romantic Interior: the British collector at home 1750–1850*, New Haven and London 1989, pp.71–107.
59 *Horace Walpole's Correspondence*, 37, pp.269–70.
60 Toynbee, *Strawberry Hill Accounts*, p.1.
61 *Horace Walpole's Correspondence*, 35, p.157.
62 *Correspondence of Thomas Gray*, ed. Paget Toynbee and Leonard Whibley, Oxford 1935, II, p.641.
63 Toynbee, *Strawberry Hill Accounts*, p.9.
64 *A description of the Villa of Mr. Horace Walpole, Youngest Son of Sir Robert Walpole Earl of Orford, at Strawberry-Hill near Twickenham, Middlesex. With an inventory of the furniture, Pictures, Curiosities, &c.*, Twickenham 1774, p.47.
65 *Horace Walpole's Correspondence*, 10, p.98.
66 *Horace Walpole's Correspondence*, 2, p.274.

1780–1800

1 For a discussion of the status of architects in the early eighteenth century, see Geoffrey Holmes, *Augustan England: professions, state and society, 1680–1730*, London 1982, pp.21–28. See also John Wilton-Ely, 'The rise of the professional architect in England' in Spiro Kostof (ed.), *The Architect: chapters in the history of the profession*, Oxford 1977, pp.180–208.
2 For the early history of the Royal Academy, see William Sandby, *The History of the Royal Academy*, 2 vols., London 1862; J.E. Hodgson and F.A. Eaton, *The Royal Academy and its Members, 1768–1830*, New York 1905; and Sidney Hutchison, *The History of the Royal Academy, 1768–1968*, London 1968.
3 For the early life of Soane, the major source of reference is Pierre de la Ruffinière du Prey, *John Soane: the making of an architect*, Chicago 1982. This is based on his Ph.D. thesis, which has also been published as *John Soane's Architectural Education, 1753–80*, New York 1977.
4 Sir John Soane, *Memoirs of the Professional Life of an Architect between the Years 1768 and 1835*, London 1835, p.15.
5 For Gandy, see John Summerson, 'The Vision of J.M. Gandy', *Heavenly Mansions and other essays on architecture*, London, 1949, pp.111–34; and the catalogue of an exhibition held at the Architectural Association, *Joseph Michael Gandy (1771–1843)*, London 1982.
6 *Gandy Green Book*, p.2, cited in Brian Lukacher, 'Gandy's dream revisited', in *Joseph Michael Gandy (1771–1843)*, London 1982, p.6.
7 BL Add. 46151 K, p.13, cited in Lukacher, *Gandy*, p.8.
8 *Sir John Soane's Lectures on Architecture*, ed. A. Bolton, London 1922, p.134.
9 A.T. Bolton, 'Robert Adam, FRS, FSA., architect to King George III and to Queen Charlotte, as a bibliographer, publisher and designer of libraries', *Transactions of the Bibliographical Society*, XIV, 1915–17, pp.255–8; Harris and Savage, *British Architectural Books and Writers*, pp.83–88.
10 For the circumstances of publication,

see du Prey, *John Soane: the making of an architect*, p.88; and Harris and Savage, *British Architectural Books and Writers*, p.427.

11 John Soane, *Plans, Elevations and Sections of Buildings*, London 1788, p.8.

12 See, for example, George Richardson, *A New Collection of Chimney Pieces, Ornament in the Style of The Etruscan, Greek and Roman Architecture*, London 1781; James Miller, *The Country Gentleman's Architect, in a great variety of New Designs*, London 1787; John Plaw, *Rural Architecture; or Designs from the Simple Cottage, to the Decorated Villa*, London 1790; George Richardson, *New Designs in Architecture, consisting of Plans, Elevations, and Sections for various buildings*, London 1792; Charles Middleton, *Picturesque and Architectural Views for Cottages, Farm Houses, and Country Villas*, London 1793; Robert Morison, *Designs in Perspective for Villas in the Ancient Castle and Grecian Style*, London 1794; John Plaw, *Ferme Ornée; or Rural Improvements. A series of Domestic and Ornamental Designs, suited to Parks, Plantations, Rides, Walks, Rivers, Farms, &c.*, London 1795; James Malton, *An Essay on British Cottage Architecture: being An attempt to perpetuate on Principle, that peculiar mode of Building, which was originally the effect of Chance*, London 1798.

13 *DEFM*, p.808. See also Ralph Fastnedge, *Sheraton Furniture*, London 1962.

14 Ambrose Heal, *The London Furniture Makers from the Restoration to the Victorian Era 1660–1840*, London 1953, p.167.

15 *Memoirs of Adam Black*, ed. A. Nicolson, Edinburgh 1885, pp.31–2.

16 Donald Towner, *Creamware*, London 1978 p.214.

17 For the work of Greuze, see Anita Brookner, *Greuze. The rise and fall of an 18th century phenomenon*, London 1972.

18 Jean Seznec and Jean Adhémar (eds.), *Diderot Salons*, Oxford 1957, i, p.144.

19 The major reference work on Wheatley is Mary Webster, *Francis Wheatley*, London 1970.

20 *Gentleman's Magazine*, 1801, p.857.

21 W.T. Whitley, *Artists and their Friends in England, 1700–1799*, London and Boston 1928, ii, p.143.

22 Richard T. Godfrey, *Printmaking in Britain: a general history from its beginnings to the present day*, Oxford 1978, p.73.

23 M.D. George, *English Political Caricature to 1792: a study of opinion and propaganda*, Oxford 1959, p.115.

24 For the macaronies see Paul Langford, *A Polite and Commercial People: England 1727–1783*, Oxford 1989, pp.576–7.

25 Dorothy George, *Catalogue of Political and Personal Satires*, v, 1771–1783, London 1935, p.xxxiv.

26 Antony Griffiths, 'A checklist of catalogues of British print publishers c.1650–1830', *Print Quarterly*, 1:1, March 1984, p.9.

27 Henry Angelo, *Reminiscences*, ed. Lord Howard de Walden, London 1904, i, p.190.

28 George, *Political Caricature*, p.175; D. Kunzle, *The Early Comic Strip: narrative strips and picture stories in the European broadsheet from c.1450 to 1825*, Los Angeles 1973, p.359.

29 F.A. Wendeborn, *A View of England towards the Close of the Eighteenth Century*, London 1791, i, p.191.

30 For Rowlandson's work, see Robert Wark (ed.), *Rowlandson's Drawings for a Tour in a Post Chaise*, San Marino, Cal. 1963; John Hayes, *Rowlandson Watercolours and Drawings*, London 1972; Robert Wark, *Drawings by Thomas Rowlandson in the Huntington Collection*, San Marino, Cal. 1975; John Riely, *Rowlandson Drawings from the Paul Mellon Collection*, New Haven 1978; and John Barrell, 'The private comedy of Thomas Rowlandson', *Art History*, 6:4, December 1983, pp.423–41.

31 For the history of Carlton House, see Dorothy Stroud, *Henry Holland*, London 1966, pp.61–85; Geoffrey de

Bellaigue, 'The Furnishings of the Chinese Room, Carlton House', *Burlington Magazine*, CIX, September 1967, pp.518–28; Geoffrey de Bellaigue, 'George IV and French furniture', *Connoisseur*, June 1977, pp.116–25; and *Carlton House: the past glories of George IV's palace*, The Queen's Gallery, London 1991.

32 de Bellaigue, 'George IV and French furniture', p.527.

33 Horace Walpole, *Anecdotes of Painting*, ed. F.W. Hilles and P.B. Daghlian, New Haven 1937, v, p.163.

34 Dorothy Stroud, *Henry Holland, his life and architecture*, London 1966, p.67.

35 Stroud, *Henry Holland*, p.80.

36 Stroud, *Henry Holland*, p.81.

37 For Althorp in the later eighteenth century, see Christopher Hussey, *English Country Houses: mid-Georgian 1760–1800*, London 1956, pp.203–13; and Peter Thornton and John Hardy, 'The Spencer furniture at Althorp, III, Lady Spencer's furniture from Spencer House and the furnishings provided for Althorp by Henry Holland', *Apollo*, LXXXVIII, October 1988, pp.266–77.

38 Stroud, *Henry Holland*, p.100.

39 Stroud, *Henry Holland*, p.101.

40 For the history of Southill, see A.E. Richardson *et al.*, *Southhill, a Regency house*, London 1951.

41 François de la Rochefoucauld, *A Frenchman in England 1784*, Cambridge 1933, p.30.

42 W. de Archenholtz, *A Picture of England containing a description of the laws, customs, and manners of England*, London 1791, pp.82–3.

43 [Robert Southey], *Letters from England by Don Manuel Alvarez Espriella*, London 1807, I, p.151.

44 [Southey], *Letters from England*, I, p.154.

45 *The Housekeeping Book of Susanna Whatman 1776–1800*, ed. Thomas Balston, London 1956, p.17–21.

46 la Rochefoucauld, *A Frenchman in England 1784*, pp.42–3.

47 [Southey], *Letters from England*, I, p.182.

48 John Alexander Kelly, *England and the Englishman in German Literature of the Eighteenth Century*, New York 1921, p.69.

49 la Rochefoucauld, *A Frenchman in England 1784*, p.4.

50 Wendeborn, *A View of England*, I, p.225.

Bibliography

Source material

1. Architectural Drawings

The standard source for the study of architectural drawings is the collection of catalogues of the drawings collection of the Royal Institute of British Architects. There are equally substantial holdings of architectural drawings, but as yet less well catalogued, at the Victoria and Albert Museum and Sir John Soane's Museum. John Harris, who was for many years curator of the RIBA drawings collection, has been the major pioneer in their systematic study. His publications on the subject include *The Palladians*, London 1981, and an article on drawings of interiors with Susan R. Stein, 'The architect and the interior: drawings of British country houses', *Antiques*, January 1986, pp.232–9. For American collections of architectural drawings, see John Harris, *A Catalogue of British Drawings for Architecture, Decoration, Sculpture and Landscape Gardening, 1550–1900, in American Collections*, Upper Saddle River, NJ, 1971. For architectural drawings in so far as they relate to furniture, see Jill Lever, *Architects' Designs for Furniture*, London 1982. Studies of the conventions of architectural drawing include Peter Führing, *Design into Art: drawings for architecture and ornament in the Lodewijk Houtakker collection*, London 1989; and E. Blau and E. Kaufman, *Architecture and its Image: four centuries of architectural representation*, Cambridge, Mass. 1990. For studies of individual architects who were influential in establishing conventions for the depiction of interiors, see Michael Wilson, *William Kent: architect, painter, designer, gardener, 1685–1748*, London 1984; David Watkin, *Athenian Stuart, pioneer of the Greek revival*, London 1982; John Fleming, *Robert Adam and his Circle in Edinburgh and Rome*, London 1962; Damie Stillman, *The Decorative Work of Robert Adam*, London 1966; Alistair Rowan (ed.), *Catalogue of Architectural Drawings in the Victoria and Albert Museum: Robert Adam*, London 1988; Pierre de la Ruffinière du Prey, *John Soane: the making of an architect*, Chicago and London 1982; John Summerson *et al.*, *John Soane*, London 1983; Dorothy Stroud, *Sir John Soane Architect*,

Bibliography

London 1984; and Pierre de la Ruffinière du Prey (ed.), *Catalogue of Architectural Drawings in the Victoria and Albert Museum: Sir John Soane*, London 1985.

2. Paintings

The major reference books for the study of eighteenth-century paintings are E.K. Waterhouse, *Painting in Britain 1530–1790*, Harmondsworth 1953, which is now in need of updating; Joseph Burke, *English Art 1714–1800*, Oxford 1976, a rather pedestrian account; and Ellis Waterhouse, *The Dictionary of British 18th Century Painters*, Woodbridge 1981. More recently, the conventions of portraiture have begun to be a subject of systematic study, as, for example, in Richard Wendorf, *The Elements of Life: biography and portrait-painting in Stuart and Georgian England*, Oxford 1990; and Marcia Pointon, *Hanging the Head: portraiture and social formation in eighteenth-century England*, New Haven and London 1993. The serious study of conversation pieces began before the second world war with the publication of G.C. Williamson's *English Conversation Pictures*, London 1931; and Sacheverell Sitwell's *Conversation Pieces: a survey of English domestic portraits and their painters*, London 1936. Later came Ralph Edwards, *Early Conversation Pictures from the Middle Ages to about 1730: a study in origins*, London 1954. But the person who pioneered the study of original illustrations as evidence for understanding the arrangement of domestic interiors was Mario Praz, with his *Illustrated History of Interior Decoration from Pompeii to Art Nouveau*, London 1964, republished 1981; it has become a minor classic. More recently this has been a fashionable subject of study for furniture historians. The definitive text on the subject is Peter Thornton's *Authentic Décor: the domestic interior 1620–1920*, London 1984. There have been two admirable exhibition catalogues devoted to the work of Arthur Devis: Ellen G. D'Oench, *The Conversation Piece: Arthur Devis and his contemporaries*, New Haven 1980; and S. Sartin (ed.), *Polite Society by Arthur Devis 1712–1787: portraits of the English country gentleman and his family*, Harris Museum and Art Gallery, Preston 1983. And there have been two attempts to interpret the meaning of conversation pieces in Ann Bermingham, *Landscape and Ideology: the English rustic tradition, 1740–1830*, London 1987; and Richard Leppert, *Music and Image: domesticity, ideology and socio-cultural formation in eighteenth-century England*, Cambridge 1988.

3. Prints and Drawings

There are a number of catalogues of eighteenth-century British drawings, for example, Robert R. Wark, *Early British Drawings in the Huntington Collection 1600–1750*, San Marino, California 1969; David Blayney Brown, *Ashmolean Museum, Oxford: catalogue of the collection of drawings*, IV, *The earlier British Drawings*, Oxford, 1982; and Lindsay Stainton and Christopher White, *Drawing in England from Hilliard to Hogarth*, London 1987. For the history of prints, the most accessible general survey is Richard Godfrey, *Printmaking in Britain*, Oxford 1978. Much more substantial evidence of the history of eighteenth-century prints is contained in the monumental *Catalogue of Prints and Drawings in the British Museum, Division 1, Political and personal satires*, in 11 volumes, begun by F. G. Stephens in 1874 and completed by Dorothy George in 1954. On the basis of her work on the catalogues, Dorothy George published a narrative history of political imagery, *English Political Caricature to 1792: a study of opinion and propaganda*, 2 vols., Oxford 1959; and a more general study of satire, *Hogarth to Cruikshank: social change in graphic satire*, London 1967. David Kunzle, *The Early Comic Strip: narrative strips and picture stories in the European broadsheet from c.1450 to 1825*, Los Angeles 1973, is a more serious study than its title might suggest. There is a perceptive introduction to the analysis of political prints in John Brewer (ed.), *The Common People and Politics 1750–1790*, Cambridge 1986; and a survey of the secondary literature on popular prints in a review article by Roy Porter, 'Seeing the past', *Past and Present*, 118, 1988, pp.186–205.

4. Printed Books

Any research on eighteenth-century printed books is facilitated by access to the Eighteenth-Century Short Title Catalogue, available for on-line database searches; the British Library holdings can also be consulted on microfiche. The standard bibliographies of architectural books are John Archer, *The Literature of British Domestic Architecture 1715–1842*, Cambridge, Mass. 1985; and Eileen Harris and Nicholas Savage, *British Architectural Books and Writers 1556–1785*, Cambridge and New York 1990. For furniture, there are invaluable publications by Peter Ward-Jackson, *English Furniture Designs of the Eighteenth Century*, London 1958; and Elizabeth White, *Pictorial Dictionary of British 18th Century Furniture Design: the printed sources*, Woodbridge 1990. In addition, there is *A Bibliography of Eighteenth-Century Furniture Studies using the Blaise-Line computer search facility*, which was prepared by Richard de Peyer for the Regional Furniture Society.

5. Topographical Description

As will have been evident to any reader of this book, I have made considerable use of contemporary descriptions of houses not merely in order to reveal what their interiors looked like, but, at least as important, how they were viewed by contemporaries. Esther Moir, *The Discovery of Britain*, London 1964, discusses this genre; G. E. Fussell, *Exploration of England: a select bibliography of travel and topography 1570–1815*, London 1935, is a useful bibliography; and there is an excellent guide to manuscript travels, Robin Gard (ed.), *The Observant Traveller: diaries of travel in England, Wales and Scotland in the County Record Offices of England and Wales*, London 1989. Those which I have found especially useful have been: Guy Miège, *The New State of England under Their Majesties K. William and Q. Mary*, London 1691; Christopher Morris (ed.), *The Journeys of Celia Fiennes*, London 1947; W. H. Quarrell and M. Mare, *London in 1710 from the Travels of Zacharias Conrad von Uffenbach*, London 1934; Henri Misson, *M. Misson's Memoirs and Observations in his Travels over England*, London 1719; Daniel Defoe, *A Tour through the Whole Island of Great Britain*, ed. Pat Rogers, Harmondsworth 1971 and in an abbreviated but illustrated edition ed. P.N. Furbank, W.R. Owens and A. J. Coulson, New Haven and London 1991; C. de Saussure, *A Foreign View of England in the Reigns of George I and George II: the letters of C. de Saussure to his family*, London 1902; Sarah Markham, *John Loveday of Caversham 1711–1789, the life and tours of an eighteenth-century onlooker*, Wilton 1984; Peter Kalm, *Kalm's Account of his*

Bibliography

Visit to England on his way to America in 1748, London 1892; J. J. Cartwright (ed.), 'The travels through England of Dr Richard Pococke during 1750, 1751, and later years', *Camden Society*, XLII, 1888; Battista Angeloni, *Letters on the English Nation: by Battista Angeloni, A Jesuit who resided many years in London*, 2 vols, London 1755; William Toldervy, *England and Wales Described in a Series of Letters*, London 1762; Count Frederick Kielmansegge, *Diary of a Journey to England in the Years 1761–1762*, London 1902; Mrs P. J. Grosley, *A Tour to London; or, New Observations on England and its Inhabitants*, 2 vols, London, 1772; Paget Toynbee (ed.), 'Horace Walpole's journal of visits to country seats', *Walpole Society*, XVI, 1928; *Dr. Campbell's Diary of a Visit to England in 1775*, ed. James Clifford, Cambridge 1947; [Carl Philip Moritz], *Journeys of a German in England in 1782*, ed. R. Nettel, London 1965; François de la Rochefoucauld, *A Frenchman in England 1784*, Cambridge 1933, F. A. Wendeborn, *A View of England towards the close of the Eighteenth Century*, 2 vols, London 1791; and W. de Archenholtz, *A Picture of England*, London 1797. There are accounts of country house visiting in the eighteenth century in Adrian Tinniswood, *A History of Country House Visiting: five centuries of tourism and taste*, Oxford 1989; and Ian Ousby, *The Englishman's England: taste, travel and the rise of tourism*, Cambridge 1990.

6. Diaries and Correspondence

Diaries are seldom as rewarding a source for the study of interiors as one would like: household improvements are often not discussed; and they are generally buried in a wealth of information about health, diet and other everyday activities. Diaries and letters which give some idea of eighteenth-century conditions of living include: W. Matthews (ed.), *The Diary of Dudley Ryder*, London 1939; E. Hobhouse (ed.), *The Diary of a West Country Physician AD 1684–1726*, London 1934; Margaret Blundell (ed.), *Blundell's Diary and Letter Book, 1702–1728*, Liverpool 1952; G. Eland (ed.), *Purefoy Letters, 1735–53*, 2 vols, London 1931; and B. Cozens-Hardy (ed.), *The Diary of Sylas Neville 1767–1788*, Oxford 1950. A bibliography of eighteenth-century diaries is provided by William Matthews, *British Diaries. An annotated bibliography of British diaries written between 1442 and 1942*, Berkeley, Cal. 1950.

7. Aesthetic Ideas

I have found the most coherent introduction to eighteenth-century aesthetics to be Peter Kivy, *The Seventh Sense: a study of Francis Hutcheson's Aesthetics and its influence in eighteenth-century Britain*, New York 1976. David Summers, *The Judgment of Sense: Renaissance naturalism and the rise of aesthetics*, Cambridge 1987, is a wonderful study of the whole range of classical and Renaissance aesthetics, which illuminates the issues which were still current in the eighteenth century. The major reference work for any study of eighteenth-century aesthetics is Johannes Dobai, *Die Kunstliteratur des Klassizismus und der Romantik in England*, 4 vols, Berne 1974–84; and there is a useful anthology of source material in B. Denvir (ed.), *The Eighteenth Century: art, design and society, 1689–1789*, London 1983. In addition, there are a number of books which relate changes in aesthetic theory to the study of literature. Of these, I would especially recommend Martin C. Battestin, *The Providence of Wit, aspects of form in Augustan* literature and the arts, Oxford 1974; Walter Jackson Bate, *From Classic to Romantic. Premises of taste in eighteenth-century England*, Cambridge, Mass. 1946; Martin Price, *To the Palace of Wisdom: studies in order and energy from Dryden to Blake*, New York 1964; and Marilyn Butler, *Romantics, Rebels and Revolutionaries: English literature and its background 1760–1830*, Oxford 1981.

Secondary Studies

1. Architecture

The standard account of eighteenth-century architectural history remains Sir John Summerson's *Architecture in Britain, 1530–1830*, London 1953. Christopher Hussey, *English Country Houses: Early Georgian 1715–1760*, London 1955, and *English Country Houses: Mid Georgian 1760–1800*, London 1956, provide a wealth of information about country houses, as well as suggestive introductions to the period. Damie Stillman, *English Neo-Classical Architecture*, 2 vols, London 1988, is a more recent, comprehensive study of the second half of the century, including excellent chapters on interior decoration. Mark Girouard, *Life in the English Country House*, New Haven 1978, was a pioneering account of the way that country house interiors were organized. There are two useful reference books in which to trace contemporary descriptions of country houses: John Harris (ed.), *A Country House Index*, rev. edn London 1979; and Michael Holmes (ed.), *The Country House Described: an index to the country houses of Great Britain and Ireland*, Winchester 1986. For urban history, Dorothy George's *London Life in the Eighteenth Century*, London 1925, and Sir John Summerson's *Georgian London*, London 1945, are classic studies of their subject. More recent books on the process of urban change in the eighteenth century include: C.W. Chalklin, *The Provincial Towns of Georgian England: a study of the building process, 1740–1820*, London, 1972; Penelope Corfield, *The Impact of English Towns 1700–1800*, Oxford 1982; Peter Clark, *The Transformation of English Towns 1600–1800*, London 1984; Peter Borsay, *The English Urban Renaissance: culture and society in the provincial town, 1660–1770*, Oxford 1989; and Mark Girouard, *The English Town*, New Haven and London 1990. Dan Cruickshank and Neil Burton, *Life in the Georgian City*, London 1990 is a mine of useful information about housing in eighteenth-century London, with a particularly good chapter on heating, lighting and sewerage by Neil Burton.

2. Interior Decoration

The pioneer in the study of English interior decoration was Margaret Jourdain, who worked as a historical advisor to Francis Lenygon, the grandest of interior decorators before the first world war. Her first book was published under his name: *The Decoration and Furniture of English Mansions during the XVII and XVIII*, London 1909. Next she published, again under his name, two folio volumes, *Decoration in England from 1660 to 1770*, London 1914; and *Furniture in England from 1660 to 1770*, London 1914. These books had a long life, being revised and republished through the 1920s.

Bibliography

Her subsequent work included writing Colonel H. H. Mulliner's book, *The Decorative Arts in England 1660–1780*, London 1924 (Mulliner was the head of a coachbuilding firm in Birmingham); *English Interiors in Smaller Houses, from the Restoration to the Regency, 1660–1830*, London 1923; a pioneering book on *The Work of William Kent*, London 1948; and *Georgian Cabinet Makers*, London 1944, rev. edn 1955, in which she collaborated with Ralph Edwards, a former Keeper of the Department of Furniture and Woodwork at the V&A. After the second world war, the most influential figure in the study of eighteenth-century interiors was John Fowler, who collaborated with John Cornforth in writing *English Decoration in the 18th century*, London 1974. John Fowler's personality and influence is discussed in John Cornforth, *The Inspiration of the Past: country house taste in the twentieth century*, London 1985. More recently the key figure in the academic study of interiors has been Peter Thornton in his two major books, *Seventeenth-Century Interior Decoration in England, France and Holland*, New Haven and London 1978; and *Authentic Décor: the domestic interior 1620–1920*, London 1984. For Scottish interiors see Ian Gow, *The Scottish Interior: Georgian and Victorian décor*, Edinburgh 1992. The major studies of American interiors are Harold L. Peterson, *American Interiors From Colonial Times to the Late Victorians*, New York 1971; Edgar de N. Mayhew and Minor Myers, Jr, *A Documentary History of American Interiors from the Colonial Era to 1915*, New York 1980; and E.D. Garrett, *At Home: the American family, 1750–1870*, New York 1990. There is a comprehensive annotated bibliography, *Decorative Arts and Household Furnishings in America 1650–1920*, ed. Kenneth L. Ames and Gerald W.R. Ward, Winterthur 1989, which is useful for bibliographies of British source material as well as American. W. Rybczynski, *The Home: a short history of an idea*, London 1988, is a widely available and challenging study of attitudes to the home.

3. Furniture
The indispensable source for any study of British furniture is Geoffrey Beard and Christopher Gilbert, *Dictionary of English Furniture Makers 1660–1840*, Leeds 1986, a composite work prepared under the auspices of the Furniture History Society. Although it is now regarded as dated, I still find useful the entries in Ralph Edwards, *Dictionary of English Furniture*, London 1924, extensively revised 1954, reissued 1983. For the workings of the furniture industry Pat Kirkham's excellent Ph.D. thesis has been published by the Furniture History Society as *The London Furniture Trade 1700–1870*, London 1988. Christopher Gilbert, *The Life and Work of Thomas Chippendale*, 2 vols, London 1978; and Helena Hayward and Pat Kirkham, *William and John Linnell: eighteenth-century London furniture makers*, 2 vols, London 1980, are the most authoritative studies of individual furniture makers.

4. Material Culture
In the United States, as compared to England, the last thirty years has seen the development of serious academic study of the material remains of the past. The two best introductory works on the interpretation of material evidence are Henry Glassie, *Pattern in the Material Folk Culture of the Eastern United States*, Philadelphia 1968; and

The Rise of Design

James Deetz, *In Small Things Forgotten: the archaeology of early American life*, Garden City, NY, 1977. Thomas J. Schlereth (ed.), *Material Culture Studies in America*, Nashville, Tenn. 1982; and Robert Blair Saint George, *Material Life in America 1600–1860*, Boston 1988, are convenient collections of essays which describe different approaches to material evidence; Thomas J. Schlereth (ed.), *Material Culture: A Research Guide*, Lawrence, Kansas 1985 provides a systematic bibliography to the field.

5. Theory

This book has been informed by accounts of modern society which examine attitudes towards consumer goods and their use as part of an information system. An early pioneer in the study of how the individual interacts with physical surroundings was Erving Goffman in *The Presentation of Self in Everyday Life*, London 1959. More recently Mary Douglas and Baron Isherwood have provided a searching account of modern attitudes towards consumption in *The World of Goods: towards an anthropology of consumption*, London 1979. I much prefer their psychological account of the benefits of consumption to that of Pierre Bourdieu in *Distinction: a social critique of the judgement of taste*, London 1984. Arjun Appadurai, *The Social Life of Things: commodities in cultural perspective*, Cambridge 1986, is a stimulating set of essays by anthropologists about how material possessions have been regarded in a variety of societies, and Daniel Miller, *Material Culture and Mass Consumption*, Oxford 1987, is an account of previous studies of consumption. Issues surrounding consumption have become the subject of lively discussion in the secondary historical literature, as evident in John Brewer and Roy Porter (eds), *Consumption and the World of Goods*, London and New York 1993. There is a comprehensive bibliography to the subject area in John Brewer (ed.), *Consumption and Culture in the Seventeenth and Eighteenth Centuries: a bibliography*, William Andrews Clark Memorial Library, Los Angeles 1991.

6. Recent research

Since the original publication of this book there has been much subsequent work on all aspects of eighteenth-century design history, but particularly on attitudes to consumerism. The most important work of synthesis on eighteenth-century culture is John Brewer, *The Pleasures of the Imagination: English Culture in the Eighteenth Century*, London, 1997. Amanda Vickery has written a spirited account of the experiences of women in eighteenth-century Lancashire in *The Gentleman's Daughter: Women's Lives in Georgian England*, New Haven, 1998, and Marcia Pointon has also explored attitudes of women towards their possessions in *Strategies for Showing: Women, Possessions and Representation in English Visual Culture, 1665–1800*, Oxford, 1997. Diana Donald has discussed issues of caricature in *The Age of Caricature: Satirical Prints in the Age of George III*, New Haven, 1996. There are also two invaluable collections of essays, Ann Bermingham and John Brewer (eds.) *The Consumption of Culture 1600–1800: Image, Object, Text*, London 1995, and Maxine Berg and Helen Clifford (eds.), *Consumers and Luxury: Consumer Culture in Europe 1650–1850*, Manchester, 1999.

Index